MW01633874

World Class Manager

World Class Manager

*Olympic Quality Performance
in the New Global Economy*

GERHARD PLENERT

PRIMA PUBLISHING

Library of Congress Cataloging-in-Publication Data

Plenert, Gerhard Johannes.
    World class manager : Olympic quality performance in the new global economy / Gerhard Plenert.
        p.   cm.
    Includes index.
    ISBN 0-7615-0030-8
    1. Strategic planning.   2. Organizational change.
3. Industrial management.   4. Competition, International.
I. Title.
HD30.28.P57   1995
858.4—dc20   95-3880
                                                        CIP

95 96 97 98 99 AA 9 8 7 6 5 4 3 2 1

Printed in the United States of America

How to Order:

Single copies may be ordered from Prima Publishing, P.O. Box 1260BK, Rocklin, CA 95677; telephone (916) 632-4400. Quantity discounts are also available. On your letterhead, include information concerning the intended use of the books and the number of books you wish to purchase.

To "The Gang,"

the quality circle of my life
    that fills my life with unending changes:

    Heidi Lynette Plenert
    Dawn Janelle Plenert
    Gregory Johannes Plenert
    Gerick Johannes Plenert
    Joshua Johannes Plenert
    Natasha Ida Plenert
    Zackary Johannes Plenert
    Chelsey Jean Plenert

CONTENTS

ABOUT THE AUTHOR

Gerhard Plenert, Ph.D., CPIM, worked in private industry management for fifteen years, traveling throughout the world. Eight years ago, he returned to school to earn a Ph.D. at the Colorado School of Mines. He later spent four years teaching and doing research at California State University, Chico. In 1990 he joined Brigham Young University's Institute of Business Management.

At CSUC, Dr. Plenert was the director of the California Productivity and Quality Center. He is now the director of the Productivity and Quality Research Group at BYU. His research specialty is International Management, and he has published two books: *International Management and Production—Survival Techniques for Corporate America* (Tab Professional and Reference Books, 1990) and *The Plant Operations Handbook* (Business One Irwin, 1993).

Dr. Plenert realizes that the subject matter of this book is fluid and dynamic. He is very interested in your experiences, comments, ideas, and recommendations. They would be extremely helpful to further editions. Please send your comments to him at Brigham Young University, Institute of Business Management, 660 TNRB, Provo, UT 84602.

> *There is nothing permanent except change.*
>
> Heraclitus, Greek philosopher

"Why another management book?" is like asking "Why change?" The only thing in life that is certain is change! And we need to be ready for change by planning for it. A World Class Manager (WCM) is a manager who *makes change happen* rather than one who is just *affected by change*. A World Class Manager:

- Plans for change
- Incorporates systems that will facilitate change
- Empowers employees to make changes
- Rewards successful change programs

A World Class Manager is a manager who realizes that he or she is not able to stay on top of all the changes that are happening within the organization. WCMs realize that in order to successfully utilize changes to their advantage they need business partners (employees) who will freely and openly search for changes that can be exploited to the advantage of the organization. They need employees who can quickly react to change. That is why a WCM is one who openly facilitates the changes that are innovated by his or her employees.

Many areas of change need to be continually addressed in today's competitive environment. Key among these are:

- Global management strategies
- Time-to-market/technology development strategies
- Information/integration strategies

- Teaming/human resource management strategies
- Training/education strategies

A World Class Manager is one who realizes that there is not one correct solution for any situation. Rather, there is a series of alternatives, and one alternative may be more successful in a specific situation than another. Information and training will help employees make advantageous choices from among the alternatives.

A World Class Manager is one who realizes that "copying" will never allow him or her to do any better than catch up. Competitiveness requires "innovation," not a copy-cat attitude. For example, the current focus in the United States on copying Japanese methodologies can never do more than make us equal with the Japanese—and that's just not good enough.

This new book teaches what makes managers World Class. It discusses the various aspects of the WCM, giving explanations and examples of the concepts. It presents alternatives for competitive improvement that are available to the WCM. It also offers the reader sources for further in-depth study of each of the concepts presented.

> You must give up the present
> to have a future.

ACKNOWLEDGMENTS

To give credit where credit is due, I would have to return to the earliest days of my work experience, when I worked in a variety of small- to medium-size plants in Oregon. Later I worked for NCR Corporation and Clark Equipment Company in plants all over the world—as far away as Indonesia, Malaysia, Singapore, Australia, Chile, and Germany, and as close as Canada and Mexico. The resulting exposure to a variety of management challenges has given me the professional background for the concepts described in this book.

I also want to recognize Jennifer Basye Sander, senior acquisitions editor at Prima Publishing, who was my mentor and who helped make *World Class Manager* a reality. In addition, the academic setting at Brigham Young University gave me the resources I needed to write this book. I further want to recognize my family—my wife, Renee Sangray Plenert, and my children—who gave me the time I needed to make the book work.

G. J. P.

INTRODUCTION

Nothing is constant but change!
All existence is a perpetual flux
of "being and becoming."

Ernst Heinrich Haeckel

This book focuses on current and future managers who are trying to improve themselves and their job skills, who want to become "World Class." This is not a strategy book, although strategy is a very important part of World Class Management. Nor is it a book about goal setting, although without a clear vision of their mission and goals, World Class Managers don't have a well-defined target to shoot for. This is a book about *change*—how to prepare for it, how to challenge it, how to take advantage of it, and how to use it to gain competitive advantage. This book offers:

1. A discussion of WCM and change models
2. A discussion of the key strategy areas that a WCM needs to be involved in, for example, global management, information management, and so on
3. A detailed discussion of competitive strategies, such as time-to-market strategies
4. A detailed discussion of the characteristics of a WCM
5. A detailed discussion of how the WCM fits into and motivates the enterprise

6. References for further study of the concepts introduced

This book is a handbook for change that you will want to keep with you as you change and grow within your organization.

The wise man is satisfied with nothing.

William Godwin, English minister, reformer, philosopher

PART ONE

Overview

CHAPTER 1

World Class Management

> *. . . for a conscious being, to exist is to change, to change is to mature, to mature is to go on creating oneself endlessly.*
>
> Henri Bergson, French philosopher

As a farmer was walking through one of his fields one day, he came across a frightened baby eagle clumsily stumbling, trying to run to escape. He felt sorry for the bird. It looked as though its parents had abandoned it, and it was too young to be able to fly. The farmer picked up the little bird, took it back to the farm, and placed it with a flock of baby turkeys that had recently hatched. The eagle grew up eating turkey food, walking like a turkey, talking with turkeys, learning from turkeys, and thinking that being a turkey was the best thing to be.

One day the farmer decided the eagle was old enough to return to the wild on its own, so he took it out to the field to show it that it could fly. He picked up the eagle and threw it up in the air. But the eagle, still thinking like a turkey, fell back to the ground. The farmer tried again, throwing the eagle higher. He reasoned that if the eagle saw that it hurt to hit the ground it might be forced to spread its wings and fly. But again the eagle fell to the ground. The farmer repeated this process over and over again for several days until one day the eagle, frustrated and tired of hitting the ground, spread its wings and realized it wasn't a turkey after all. It could fly. It was an eagle.

Many of us have been raised like managerial turkeys, thinking that the way we were taught to do things is the best way and that we shouldn't question anything. It is time to quit falling to the ground and to realize that we are eagles. We may hit the ground a few times before we realize it, but *we are eagles*, and we can fly. This book will help us fly. The goals of this book are as follows:

- To motivate the reader to find and implement positive changes in a goal-oriented direction
- To turn the reader into a leader who motivates and directs change
- To make the reader world class

World Class Management and flying like an eagle are related. Actually, they are quite similar, but you'll have to read this entire chapter to find out all the ways they are similar. First we must start by establishing a better definition of what a World Class Manager is. To accomplish this, we need to:

1. Figure out where we are (point A)
2. Figure out where we want to be (point B)
3. Develop a strategy (travel plan) to get us from point A to point B
4. Consider the tools that are available to help us reach our destination

These four steps are what this book is all about. The first three chapters help us define point A and point B. Chapters 4 through 10 help us develop a strategy. Chapters 11 through 17 provide the tools. Finally, Chapters 18 and 19 send us on our way.

The process begins! The first step is to look at some of the different types of management styles that exist so we can figure out what type of manager we are.

Now here, you see, it takes all the running you can do, to keep in the same place. If you want to get somewhere else, you must run at least twice as fast as that.

Lewis Carroll, British mathematician, *Through the Looking Glass*

THE TYPES OF MANAGERS

There are several types of managers and numerous ways to categorize them. For example, there is the *sunrise manager*, who has a view toward the future, as opposed to the *sunset manager*, who fights fires in the here and now. We often think of the sunrise manager as the dreamer with the wild ideas that never go anywhere, whereas the sunset manager is the workaholic who is great at getting things done in a hurry. Another way of looking at these managers is to consider the sunrise manager as a progressive, leading-edge, technology-minded manager. This type of manager is brought into an organization when it is looking for growth or change. A sunset manager, on the other hand, is brought in when an organization is trying to stabilize a current situation. For example, trying to revive or sustain existing programs that are starting to falter would be a good reason to hire a sunset manager. Are you a sunrise manager or a sunset manager?

Another way to classify managers is to consider their attitudes toward their subordinates. The two extremes are the *authoritarian manager* and the *participative manager*. Authoritarian managers are typified by being secretive, having a finger in everything that happens, always having the final word, and telling rather than asking. This type of manager is often referred to as a *Theory-X manager*.

Participative managers value employee opinions. They spend more time listening than talking during a meeting. They look for ideas from the bottom, realizing that the employees have the best understanding of day-to-day operations. These managers use bottom-up ideas for top-down management and implementation of the ideas for change. They are concerned about employee job satisfaction and rewards. This type of manager is often referred to as a *Theory-Y manager*.[1]

There is also a second type of participative manager. These managers tend to empower employees to make their own decisions and to implement their own ideas. A manager who uses this form of participative management is referred to as a *Theory-Z manager*.[2] In this management style, we switch from the top-down decision-making process characteristic of the Theory-X or

Theory-Y management style to a bottom-up decision-making process characteristic of the Japanese management style. Theory-Z managers are heavily involved in teaming, such as the quality circles of old, and use the teams to develop, approve, and implement ideas.[3] Managers take on the role of facilitator and are responsible for making sure the approved ideas get implemented in a timely fashion and correctly. These managers are no longer the decision makers and drivers of forward progress. Theory-Z managers keep their teams focused and present them with areas that need consideration and evaluation but let the team make its own improvement decisions. Are you a Theory-X, Theory-Y, or Theory-Z manager?

A third way to classify managers uses the five C's: cash, crisis, conflict, cool, and change managers.

Cash Manager   Cash managers focus on costs and budgets and have probably come through the accounting or finance ranks. This type of manager tends to be risk-averse and looks for stability rather than opportunity. Cash managers find it advisable to patch and repair old technology, as opposed to replacing it with new technology, primarily because the high expense of purchasing the new technology would be too difficult to cost-absorb in one or two fiscal years. This management style is the reason why we still have so many outdated factories in the United States when we know they cannot be competitive in the long run. Because the old factories are still demonstrating some minor profit levels, they are kept and maintained until they are totally unprofitable. Then the plants are transferred overseas, where labor costs are cheaper. The cash manager feels the need to look for short-term profitability rather than long-term competitiveness.

Crisis (or Crash) Manager   Crisis managers believe you shouldn't fix anything that isn't broken. This style of manager, like the cash manager, strives toward stability, looking at problems as disruptions that need to be conquered rather than opportunities for future improvements. These managers attack problems without considering the roots of the problems, thereby fixing only a symptom and not the cause. Often the fix includes the installation of another "system" to monitor the problem and catch it if it comes up again.

Conflict Manager   Conflict managers looks at the work-place as a battlefield of competing players. They always feel the need to take and maintain the upper hand through whatever means necessary. Control is the primary tool of power, and intimidation is the primary motivating force. This type of manager is the reason why unions were formed.

Cool Manager   Cool managers believe the work force is best motivated by giving it whatever it wants. These managers try to bribe their way into the hearts of their children, which is how they view their employees. They want to be everybody's best friend and want everyone to smile at them as they walk by. The cool manager often has a wishy-washy management style that results in more confusion than direction.

Change Manager   Change managers search for challenges in competitiveness. These managers thrive on positive, goal-focused changes, seeing them as opportunities that make work exciting. Changes are viewed as opportunities for growth, and problems are seen as opportunities for change. Rather than trying to fix problems, change managers spend time looking for the roots of a problem and attempt to generate the necessary changes that will make the problem disappear.

Using the five Cs to define a management style requires integration with the other classifications. For example, you could have a manager who is sunrise, cool, and Theory-X. This would be a happy, smiley, bossy dreamer. Have you identified yourself yet? We now add one more classification category before integrating all the management styles.

A final but important method for classifying a manager is to contrast the "boss" with the "leader." A boss directs employee traffic, whereas a leader shows the way by example and by stepping out into the traffic in front of the employees. Bosses manage, but leaders tend to lead out and search for a difference. Bosses see themselves as "king of the hill" and want to keep the hill for themselves, whereas leaders show and help everyone, by example, how to get to the top of the hill themselves. Bosses strive with a "do as I say" philosophy, whereas leaders use the "do as I do" technique. With leaders, employees tend to have a clear definition of what is expected because the example set by the leader has shown them their objective. Simply put, bosses provide stability and governance, while leaders open the door for innovation.[4]

The boss is someone who has to be there for the business to run correctly. Without the boss, the employees lose their decision-making ability. The situation is often one of "while the cat's away, the mice will play." Alternatively, leaders are people who, if they did not show up to work for a few days, would not be missed. All the employees would know how to keep the business functioning, and the leader's absence would hardly be noticed. Good leaders are people who manage themselves into obsolescence.

Insecure managers create complexity.
Real leaders don't need clutter.

John F. Welch, Jr., Chairman and CEO,
General Electric [5]

WHAT TYPE OF MANAGER ARE YOU?

Now it's time for you to classify yourself. You need to combine the different types of management style in order to define your own personal style. What type of manager do you think you are? Are you a Theory-X–sunset–cash manager, which would be a bean-counting, bossy fire-fighter telling everyone what to do, how to do it, and when to do it and insisting that no one does anything until directed? Or are you a Theory-Y–sunrise–cool leader who loves everyone, likes to show rather than tell employees how to do their job, and shares your schemes of grandeur with your employees? Figure out what type of manager you are. Remember:

> Before you can figure out
>   how to get where you're going,
>   you have to know
>   where you're starting from.

Use Figure 1.1 to evaluate yourself. Place an N, O, or Y next to each management type in order to get a clear picture of where you are now. After you have classified yourself, have your peers evaluate you. Use Figure 1.1 as a grading sheet to help them evaluate you. Next have your employees evaluate you, using some form of blind vote. You may be surprised to find out what kind of manager others think you are.

Now you know a little more about yourself. You know what your management style is right now. The next step toward being a World Class Manager is to define your management style *goal*. After that, you need to set a travel plan that will take you from where you are and get you to where you're going. We'll spend the rest of the book doing that, but first let's take a close look at our target.

> The road to World Class leadership
>   is not a journey,
>   it's a race!

THE WORLD CLASS MANAGEMENT STYLE

The chart in Figure 1.2 has been created in an attempt to help you both to classify yourself in your present state and to clearly define your target. With four different methods for classifying management styles, a diagram representing all of the management options would require four dimensions. Unfortunately, a sheet of paper limits us to two dimensions. Even Steven Spielberg (from the movies) has difficulty showing us four dimensions on a two-dimensional surface (the movie screen). Figure 1.2 breaks down the two most complex management style

In front of each management style, indicate whether you (or the person you are evaluating) fit the description:

N—not really one of these

O—occasionally one of these

Y—definitely one of these

___ *Sunrise Manager*—has a view toward the future; a dreamer full of wild ideas; progressive, leading edge, technology-minded

___ *Sunset Manager*—spends time fighting day-to-day fires; workaholic who is great at getting things done

___ *Theory-X Manager*—secretive; has his/her fingers in everything that happens; always has the final word; tells, rather than asks questions

___ *Theory-Y Manager*—values the opinion of the employees; spends more time listening than talking; looks for ideas from the bottom up but makes the final decision

___ *Theory-Z Manager*—tends to empower the employees to make their own decisions and lets them implement their own ideas

Figure 1.1   Find Your Management Style

classifications. In Figure 1.2, we see all sorts of mixes and matches of management styles. These mixtures of styles are detailed in the following list.

- *Theory-X Manager–Cash Manager*—impersonal and quick to fire; bases all decisions on short-term financial reports
- *Theory-X Manager–Crisis Manager*—the "general"; charges his or her troops against the oncoming enemy, which is often a variety of problems, including the biggest problem of all—change
- *Theory-X Manager–Conflict Manager*—the "boss"; expects the respect of the employees and demands immediate response to his or her whims and wishes

— *Cash Manager*—cost and budget obsessive; looks toward stability rather than opportunity; prefers to patch and repair rather than replace because it is cheaper

— *Crisis (or Crash) Manager*—believes that you shouldn't fix anything that isn't broken; looks at problems as disruptions that need to be conquered; attacks problems

— *Conflict Manager*—looks at the workplace as a battlefield of competing players; feels the need to take and maintain the upper hand

— *Cool Manager*—feels the work force is best motivated by giving employees whatever they want; wants to bribe his/her way into the hearts of the employees; wants to be everybody's best friend

— *Change Manager*—searches for challenges in competitiveness; thrives on changes, innovations, improvements, technology

— *Boss*—directs employee traffic; see themselves as "king of the hill" and want to keep the hill for themselves; "do as I say" philosophy

— *Leader*—shows the way by using example and by stepping out into the traffic in front of the employees; not afraid to show everyone how to get to the top of the hill; "do as I do" philosophy

	Theory-X	Theory-Y	Theory-Z
Cash	Totally impersonal, quick to fire	Calculated but sharing	Cost-conscious employees
Crisis	The "general"	Self-directed fire-fighting	Frustrated employees
Conflict	The "boss"	Confusion	WAR
Cool	Decision with confusion	Self-directed confusion	No direction
Change	Enforced improvements	Overriding motivation	On the right track

Figure 1.2   What Type of Manager Are You?

- *Theory-X Manager–Cool Manager*—the manager makes the final decisions, but, in an attempt to keep everyone happy, many of the decisions are political and therefore contradictory and result in more confusion than progress
- *Theory-X Manager–Change Manager*—forces change on employees, leaving them rebellious and resistant
- *Theory-Y Manager–Cash Manager*—wants the employees' ideas, but will make the final decision in all cases based on the short-term financial viability
- *Theory-Y Manager–Crisis Manager*—expects employees to be self-directed fire-fighters, maintaining the status quo
- *Theory-Y Manager–Conflict Manager*—listens to employees just to satisfy their egos and basically sees employees as a necessary evil requiring toleration
- *Theory-Y Manager–Cool Manager*—solicits the employees' ideas and says yes to everyone, leaving employees without any real guidance from the top
- *Theory-Y Manager–Change Manager*—wants employees to search for opportunities for change but reserves the right to override any suggestions, since the manager has the broader insight needed for all decisions made in the enterprise
- *Theory-Z Manager–Cash Manager*—this management style has teams analyzing all changes on a financial basis
- *Theory-Z Manager–Crisis Manager*—teams work on solving problems with a short-term perspective aimed at getting the problem fixed quickly
- *Theory-Z Manager–Conflict Manager*—teams continually find themselves having to defend against a management that considers them ignorant
- *Theory-Z Manager–Cool Manager*—completely employee-oriented, but in the effort to keep everyone happy ends up being an ineffective facilitator, causing frustration and a lack of direction
- *Theory-Z Manager–Change Manager*—facilitates change and motivates employee teams to search for opportunities for change; the teams see themselves as owners of the change

and therefore attempt to implement the change and take pride in the results; fire-fighting is kept to a minimum, and fires are looked at as being caused by some root problem that needs to be identified and changed with a long-term perspective.[6] This is the management style of a World Class Manager.

World Class Management involves being a Theory-Z change manager. It doesn't matter where on Figure 1.2 we find ourselves now; we should strive toward Theory-Z–change manager status. Now let's take a look at the last two remaining classification categories. As a World Class Manager we want to be a sunrise rather than a sunset manager, always looking for alternatives and options for improvement but realizing that many of these options will fail. Also, as a World Class Manager we want to be leaders rather than bosses, motivating and guiding our employees by our hard work and our farsighted example.

We now know what a World Class Manager should look like. A WCM should be a:

- *Sunrise Manager*—having a long-term orientation; looking for the "better way"
- *Theory-Z Manager*—having employees involved with and guiding the business process through participative and empowered team efforts
- *Change Manager*—guiding a dynamic, evolving business organism that capitalizes on change opportunities
- *Leader*—being a character-building, motivational example

The wicked leader is he who the people despise.
The good leader is he who the people revere.
The great leader is he who the people say, "We did it ourselves."

Lao Tsu

Having categorized World Class Managers and determined how to "slot" them, let's now determine why we want to fit into this slot. It's like saying we should be eagles when most of us are quite happy being turkeys and think that a turkey is a good thing to be. A World Class competitive stance will not allow us to be anything but World Class Managers. World Class Managers look to the future—a highly competitive future, a future full of changes. World Class Managers realize that their employees are the key to motivating successful change and that employees are led, not bossed. Turkeys walk into the future, tripping over change as it occurs, but eagles fly over the changes and out into a successful future.

WORLD CLASS MANAGEMENT EXAMPLE

Numerous organizations are attempting to move themselves toward World Class Management status. For example, Tridon-Oakdale placed its management team in a hotel just to remove them from the everyday bustle of fire-fighting. The goal set for these managers was to "work out a new vision for Tridon." The result was a complete turnaround in both management style and output performance. Some of the changes that occurred included the following:

- An organization chart turned upside down, with employee teams on the top
- A new quality standard that far exceeded that of Tridon's competitors
- "Legendary Customer Service"
- Competitive pricing
- Reduced inventory and lead times
- A $6 million turnaround

Some of the keys to success included these efforts:

- A new mission statement with a commitment to change
- An improved focus on building relationships among all employees
- Employee participation—"the goal is to have everyone speak"

- Total Quality Control[7]
- Kanban—Just-in-Time manufacturing[8]
- "Smart Change" management that focused on doing the right things
- Group technology—a focus on technology improvements

Tridon has demonstrated that World Class Management works, but it considers itself to be just getting ready for the next wave of improvements.[9]

Now that we are in a constant state of change, nothing will ever remain the same.

Don Green, Chairman, Tridon

THE MANAGEMENT OF CHANGE

A World Class Manager views the future as an opportunity, and the here and now as adequate for the past but just not good enough for the future. This type of manager views all aspects of the enterprise—systems, production philosophies, and even management styles that were in existence 20 to 30 years ago—as wholly deficient for today and especially inadequate for the future.

By their very nature, World Class Managers are risk takers, since change always involves risk. Additionally, the long-term perspective of World Class Managers often makes them unpopular in the short run. World Class Managers enjoy the excitement of being leading-edge innovators, despite the occasional failures they will suffer on this risky management road.

World Class Management is soaring with the eagles. It's finding the eagle within you and changing your life-style so that you can soar. It's the ability to *change yourself faster than the changes that affect you.* World Class Managers are in control of change rather than letting change control them. They are innovators and an adventurers. WCMs have the ability to listen when listening is wiser than talking, which is almost always.

World Class Management is managing and motivating positive, goal-directed change. It's being in control of change. It's using change to your advantage. But being in control of change is not a simple task. There are many facets to change—it takes this entire book to discuss them. To be effective users of change, we need to consider all these facets, plan for them, strategize their usage, and utilize them to our advantage.

All change is not positive change. Changing simply for the sake of changing is foolish. Thinking through the consequences and effects of changes is as important as implementing the changes. Changes need to make a positive contribution to goal achievement without sacrificing the value system (ethics and integrity) of the enterprise. However, avoiding change for fear of making a mistake is the same as deciding not to be World Class.

To manage change, we need to be innovators and creators. An innovator searches for opportunities to change. An innovator sees opportunity in every problem and looks for ways to take advantage of opportunities. Innovators work with others as team players, because they understand the synergistic ideas created by teamwork. The creator takes newly found opportunities and turns them into defined projects, activities, or programs that will take advantage of the recent discoveries.

The management of change also requires an adventurer and a general. The adventurer is not afraid to take a chance on change and looks for the opportunity to do battle—to take an idea and drive forcefully forward. An adventurer despises the routine and mundane and looks for opportunities to break away, always searching for new areas to discover. Generals know that they can't win the battle alone. Even Michael Jordan (of the Chicago Bulls), probably one of the greatest basketball players of his time, could not have won one basketball game without four other players on the court.

Two basic questions still need to be answered:

1. Why should we go through the process recommended by this book? Change is inevitable and will run you over if you're not ready for it. This book will teach you how to prepare for change.

2. Why is change necessary? There are several reasons for change. The first is competition, whether from domestic or foreign competitors. We need to improve to stay on top of our competitors. Another reason for change is to take advantage of technological advancements, such as automation or computerization. Still another reason for change is the changing habits of our customers. Customer awareness programs, environmental consciousness, resource scarcity, governmental regulations, and economic swings will affect the way customers think and act and force us to change the way we manage.

To live is to change, and to be perfect is to have changed often.

John Henry Newman, English cardinal, writer

At this point, having a somewhat clearer view of the characteristics of a World Class Manager, we are ready to take a look at why change is such an important part of the life-style of this type of manager.

A DISCUSSION OF CHANGE

One day a man was leading his donkey down the street. After a short distance, the donkey decided he didn't want to travel any farther. He stopped in his tracks, put his rump on the ground, and wouldn't budge. The man tugged at the donkey's rope and tried to coax him to get up and walk. The coaxing soon turned to name calling and threats involving glue factories. The donkey didn't move. A neighbor was passing by and stopped to help the frustrated donkey owner.

"The only way you're going to get that donkey to move is by talking nicely to it," the neighbor advised.

Indignantly the donkey owner challenged his neighbor to see if he could do any better with the stubborn critter. The neighbor picked up a two-by-four that was lying by the side of the road and proceeded to give the donkey a swift, hard wallop right between the eyes. Then he pulled on the rope softly and asked the donkey to get up. The donkey immediately stood up and followed the neighbor down the street.

"Didn't you say I should talk nicely to the donkey," the donkey owner protested.

"Of course! And I did," said the neighbor, "but first I had to get his attention."

Sometimes we managers are like donkeys. Sometimes we need to be hit by a two-by-four on the side of the head before we will start paying attention.[10] Often, "change" brings out the donkey in all of us. Remember:

> Change and innovation are stifled not
>   by the way things are
>   but by the way we perceive things.

Change is as old as time, and as leading-edge as the future. Even the rate at which changes occur is changing. But as prevalent as change is, we often want to resist it with all the effort we can muster. Perhaps if we understand change better, we will tend to be more like eagles.

There the two sources of change:

1. The changes that come from us
2. The changes that happen to us

Let's treat the second source of change first. We need to be prepared for changes that will happen to us. We need to watch for these changes and manage them into opportunities. We need to become World Class Managers who watch for and use growth and development opportunities. This brings us to another thought:

> It doesn't matter how far
>   in front of the pack you are;
>   if you're not moving fast enough,
>   you'll get run over.

Change is innovation; it's developing leading-edge competitive strategies and moving forward. Remember (this goes along with the previous thought):

> It doesn't matter how fast you're moving,
> if you're not moving in the right direction,
> you'll never achieve your goal!

The first type of change, change that comes from us, requires us to originate the change. For some managers, this type of change is a little harder to manage because of the effort involved in creating the changes. It suggests that we need to find and generate our own opportunities for change, our own innovations. Also, most organizations tend toward bureaucracy, which suppresses change. Most organizational structures are motivated by measurement systems that stifle and often punish change. We need instead measurement systems that motivate the discovery of change.[11] The search for change opportunities can mean a structural reorganization as well as a mental reorganization of our enterprise.[12]

This book focuses on both types of change. It also discusses why your organization needs change—not only to stay ahead, but also to survive in a competitive environment. The purpose of this book is to help you become a leader who can help your organization manage change. This book aims to motivate you to find and implement positive changes in a goal-oriented direction and to turn you into a leader who motivates and directs change. Finally, the purpose of this book is to help you become a World Class Manager.

To get the most out of this book, carefully read the Preface, the Introduction, and all the chapters. What you're doing is hunting for ideas. Mark those that fit you best and, after reading the book, reread those ideas that impressed you the first time through. Then search for ways to incorporate these ideas into your management style. The last step in the use of this book is to Total Quality Manage (TQM) the review process by repeating this process every six months to one year. As your goals and job function "change," so will the information and tools you need to help you through the change process. Reviewing this book regularly will help you reanalyze your position and put it into perspective, both for you individually and for you in your role within the company as a whole.

> *The single greatest power in the world today is the power to change. . . . The most recklessly irresponsible thing we could do in the future would be to go on exactly as we have in the past ten or twenty years.*
>
> Karl W. Deutsch, Professor of International Peace, Harvard

MODELS FOR CHANGE

Numerous models exist for implementing change, from slow and systematic, such as Total Quality Management (TQM), to the fast and radical, such as Process Reengineering (PR) (both concepts are discussed in Chapter 11). Some models motivate change through their measurement process, and some measurement systems discourage change (see Chapter 8 for more information on the measurement of change). Correctly implemented change models give us an entirely new focus on what change can do for us.

When we manage change rather than letting change manage us, our focus becomes more global, technology-oriented, flexible, and customer-responsive (see Part II). We need to focus on competitive, customer-oriented areas of change (see Chapter 3).

I spent most of my working years dealing with technology transfer to industrial settings all over the world. One of my favorite questions is "How do you deal with change and innovation, such as the implementation of new technology in your environment?" Another question I often ask is "How do you motivate innovation?" Many answers are similar to the following response: "Innovation is great and we like it, as long as it has already been tried somewhere else." The attitude of most people in response to my questions is similar to that expressed in the following quotation:

The innovator makes enemies of all those who prospered under the old order, and only lukewarm support is forthcoming from those who would prosper under the new.

Niccolo Machiavelli[13]

Innovation is seldom rewarded, and only in the case of extreme success is the innovator thanked for his risk taking. The result is a fear of innovation and change, as shown in the following model, in which we see that time causes change to occur, which builds uncertainty, which causes fear.

$$\text{Time} \rightarrow \text{Change} \rightarrow \text{Uncertainty} \rightarrow \text{Fear}$$

We need to conquer the fear by demonstrating that the model can be changed to one in which time causes change that is viewed as an opportunity for innovation.

$$\text{Time} \rightarrow \text{Change} \rightarrow \text{Opportunity} \rightarrow \text{Innovation}$$

Change is forced upon us through problems and errors, but problems and errors are also the seeds of opportunity and innovation. A World Class Manager focuses on the opportunities rather than the problems. Problems and errors bring the opportunities to our attention, but the WCM will resist solving the problem and will prefer to focus on the opportunity for change. Out of context, these statements sound idealistic. However, what they really mean is that problems or errors occur because of some basic need that is not being taken care of properly. The "problem" can be solved by measuring and identifying the root source of the problem effectively. The "opportunity" to fix the root cause offers us the chance to build a better mousetrap that avoids the cause of the problem. One example is the creation of Post-it™ Notes, which started as a problem (attaching notes to a letter, book, or report without destroying it the way staplers or tape do) that was converted into an opportunity (develop a new adhesive that allows for easy removal). The opportunity has now been translated into a major product and market segment.

We need to establish an environment of motivated innovation within our organization by removing the fear of change. We need to *focus* on innovation in our enterprises, and we can achieve this only with properly motivated changes.

Small companies and countries, which are often the companies and countries that are innovative, are outachieving large companies and countries, which tend to be slow to move. For example:

1. If you want process innovation, where do you go? For a long time, Japan has demonstrated its international competitiveness through its ability to reduce production lead times and production costs. The Japanese were considered small at one time.

2. If you want to introduce a new product into the market quickly, where do you go? Taiwan has become the Time-to-Market innovation leader.

3. Minimum-cost and maximum-flexibility steel production has been taken over completely by the small steel companies in the United States, which for a long time have been successful in beating out the big guys, both foreign and domestic, in competition and quality.

The examples are endless.

We have defined World Class Management in terms of the style of management and the role of change. Let's take another look at World Class Management, this time addressing the role of innovation and creativity.

INNOVEERING

A World Class organization is an innovative, creative, goal-oriented organization. A World Class Manager motivates the process I refer to as *innoveering*, which means "creatively innovated changes." Changing just for the sake of changing only creates turmoil. Changing to move positively forward toward a goal without sacrificing the integrity of the organization is World Class.

Recently, the topic of creative thinking has become very popular. Books such as *Breakthrough Thinking* and *A Whack on the Side of the Head* have stressed the importance of imagination in the change process.[14] For example, von Oech stresses the need for creativity in order to discover new solutions to problems and to generate new ideas when old ones become obsolete.[15] Stephen R. Covey, in his book *The Seven Habits of Highly Effective People*, focuses his second habit on creativity.[16] Peters, Waterman, and Austin, in their search for eight common characteristics of excellent companies, focus on employee innovation within the corporate value system.[17]

Innoveering is innovative change engineering. It is change that uses technology (Chapter 7), integration (Chapters 8 and 14), and innovative strategies (Chapters 5 through 10) and focuses on a continuous improvement model (Chapter 11). Again, change in and of itself is not necessarily good. We need positively directed, goal-oriented, innovative, creative change. Then we have innoveering. That's when we become World Class.

One of the best examples of innoveering is the Toyota Just-in-Time production system. Just-in-Time (JIT) is a production planning philosophy developed in Japan that focuses on waste minimization through inventory reductions. JIT didn't exist before being developed by Toyota. JIT wasn't copied—it was innoveered. A brief summary of the story follows.

It was post–World War II and Japan was trying to rebuild its industry. The Japanese tried copying Western (primarily United States) production methodologies, which were considered the best in the world, but they soon encountered four problems:

1. The Japanese lacked the cash flow to finance the large in-process inventory levels required by the U.S. batch-oriented production systems.
2. The Japanese lacked the land space to be able to build large U.S.-style factories.

3. The Japanese didn't have the natural resource accessibility that the United States had.
4. Japan had a labor excess rather than a labor shortage, which meant that labor efficiency systems weren't very valuable.

The Japanese innoveered these problems into opportunities. They realized that their competitive problem was a process problem, not a product problem. They proceeded to copy product technology and worked diligently to innovate *process technology* oriented around materials efficiency rather than labor efficiency. The result was the flow-through JIT production methodology for which Toyota has now become famous. But Toyota would be the first to admit that it wasn't easy. Toyota officials scoff at U.S. attempts to copy JIT after 2 or 3 years of implementation. They will readily state that it took them 30 years to develop JIT. But they got there one innoveering change at a time.

The result of JIT was that the Japanese built smaller factories (about one-third the size of their U.S. counterparts) in which the only materials that were in the factory were those on which work was currently being done.[18] In this way, inventory levels were kept low, investment in in-process inventory was at a minimum, and the investment in purchased natural resources was quickly turned around so that additional materials could be purchased.[19]

But the Toyota innoveering process has not ended. It continues, focusing on changes and improvements both in the product area and in the process area. Toyota continues its innoveering through a continuous improvement process referred to as *waste elimination*. The company views waste as anything that does not add value to the product. Waste can occur in labor, materials, machinery processes, or any other aspect of the company. Toyota's seven key areas of waste elimination follow:

1. Waste of over-production—reduced set-up times, process synchronization, visibility
2. Waste of waiting—balance uneven work loads
3. Waste of transportation
4. Waste of processing—why is the product made?
5. Waste of stocks—inventory reduction

6. Waste of motion—motion for economy and consistency
7. Waste of making defective products[20]

Toyota is determined to continue to improve. Innovative change is constant. Integration involving all levels of employees is critical (as discussed further in Chapters 8 and 14). Toyota is an eagle in the world of innoveering. However, we in the United States are past the point of trying to copy Japan. We need to innoveer beyond what we can copy from anyone else if we are to stay competitive. As long as we are playing copycat, the best we can ever do is catch up, and that's just not good enough![21] The only way we can get ahead is by innoveering. The Japanese will stay ahead only as long as we, by focusing on copying rather than on innoveering, allow them to.

Imagination is more important than knowledge.

Albert Einstein

HOW DO WE MANAGE CHANGE?

The biggest struggle in learning to manage change is identifying where, when, and how to begin. One purpose of this book is to give you the answers to these questions. Where do we begin?—with you, the reader! When do we begin?—*immediately*. How do we begin?—by carefully laying out a plan for innovation and change. This plan is developed by:

1. Deciding on a focus or a vision for our change efforts (Chapter 3)
2. Developing strategies for change that focus on our vision (Chapter 4)
3. Solidifying each of the strategic areas around the vision (here we discuss how the strategies are defined and implemented; Chapters 5–10)
4. Discussing the characteristics, abilities, and traits that a World Class Manager should have to motivate innoveering,

    including a discussion of the specific change tools available to the manager (Chapters 11–17)

5. A wrap-up of whether or not you are working toward becoming World Class (Chapters 18 and 19)

We have already identified and discussed two types of change: changes that come from us and the changes that happen to us. How these changes affect the strategies of the enterprise is discussed in Chapters 2 through 4. Chapters 5 through 10 go into detail on the different areas of World Class Management change strategy. Chapters 11 through 17 discuss the individual and enterprise tools available to the World Class Manager. Chapters 18 and 19 challenge your ability to manage change, that is, your ability to be World Class.

Let's move forward. Let's stop being stubborn donkeys that need two-by-fours to be motivated to change. Let's learn how to be high-flying eagles that soar to the greatest heights and view the "big picture" from their magnificent zenith. Let's learn about *world class management*, which uses goal-oriented, positive-change leadership to motivate and direct the change process. Let's evolve into effective masters of the change process. Let's change, innovate, and improve ourselves, our family environment, our working environment, and our enterprise.

The definition of insanity is continuing to do the same things and expecting different results.

Nadler and Hibino, *Breakthrough Thinking*

CHAPTER 2

We, the People

Give me a place to stand and I will move the world.
Archimedes, Greek mathematician

Anthropologists recently discovered a semicivilized community living on a remote part of the island of Borneo. Their standard of living, dress, and housing was similar to most Western civilizations. However, the anthropologists noticed something odd about these individuals—they didn't wear shoes. The scientists would encounter individuals with severe slashes, bruises, and blisters on their feet because of the rough footpaths. But the Borneo residents simply refused to wear shoes.

The anthropologists discovered a shoe factory right in the center of the town. The shoe factory was empty of equipment, but a sign out in front of the building announced a weekly meeting for all those interested in shoes. These meetings had been going on for ten years. The citizens religiously attended the meetings and discussed the benefits of wearing shoes, for example, how shoes would reduce the pain and make walking more comfortable. But whenever it was suggested that they start making shoes in the factory, no one was interested. So they never started making shoes in the factory.

The anthropologists decided to take a pair of shoes and give them to one of the citizens. They got him to try the shoes on and to use them for a day. But the next day, they found this same individual again walking without shoes. The anthropologists were baffled and questioned the citizen, "Why aren't you wearing the shoes we gave you?"

He replied, "Oh, I understand that they are good for me, and that they would make me more comfortable. But they're just too much trouble and I'm too busy to put them on." And so he walked off, cutting and bruising his feet as he went.

Do we know anyone who refuses to wear shoes? We probably see such people every day, every time we look in the mirror. Where does this stubborn streak come from? *Tradition!* The greatest resistance to change comes from what we already know and from what we already believe. Just look at a small child who is not yet hindered by tradition. The child will learn and believe anything. You need not be gullible, but simply open-minded like the little child. Learn and understand before you rush to condemn.

Change is especially hard for managers. As we've learned from the quotes in Chapter 1, the only thing certain in life is change. But we don't want change to happen to us; instead, we want to utilize and control change to our advantage. A well-known anonymous axiom states:

> People like things to change,
>   but they don't like to be changed.

Stated differently, it means that people like it when changes occur if the changes benefit them. However, people don't like changes imposed upon them.

Federal Express (FedEx), a 1990 Malcolm Baldrige National Quality Award winner, is the brainchild of founder and CEO Frederick W. Smith, who virtually invented the air express industry.[1] The key focus of the FedEx quality program is to achieve 100% customer satisfaction through continuous improvement and change. The continuous improvement process involves the customer in the change process through a Survey-Feedback-Action (SFA) program.[2]

FedEx has based its quality program on three precepts. The first and therefore most important is that *customer satisfaction starts with employee satisfaction.** In order to make this precept effective, FedEx has implemented a program call the Guaranteed Fair Treatment Program (GFTP). The aim of the GFTP process is to maintain a truly fair working environment in which anyone who has a grievance or concern about his or her job or who feels mistreated can have these concerns addressed through the management chain, all the way to Fred Smith if necessary.

FedEx considers its employees to be its most important resource and wanted to provide a fair and equitable process for handling grievances. The GFTP philosophy provides an atmosphere for employees to discuss their complaints with management without fear of retaliation. An employee is given seven days to submit a grievance, after which time management has ten days to respond. If the employee doesn't agree with the manager's decision, the employee has seven days to appeal the decision up the chain of the review process.

A key element of the GFTP program is that managers are evaluated from both directions, from the top down and from the bottom up. The manager's boss evaluates the manager's ability to implement change through innovation and improvements. The manager's subordinates evaluate the manager's responsiveness to the needs of the employees. A manager must receive favorable ratings from both directions in order to receive promotions, raises, or bonuses.[3]

The FedEx quality program exhibits both an emphasis on change (SFA) and an emphasis on the management–employee relationship aspects of how change is implemented (GFTP). FedEx managers have told me that FedEx is the most challenging, while at the same time the most rewarding, company they have worked for because the FedEx program puts the manager into the challenging position of attempting to effect change while at the same time not being allowed to be excessively forceful in

---

*FedEx focuses on a corporate quality philosophy of People–Service–Profit. People (employees) are first; Service (customers) is second; and Profit is third.

implementing the change. The best managers are those who implement change by giving the employees ownership in the change. This reminds me of another quote:

I want workers to go home at night and say, "I built that car."

Pahr G. Gyllenhammar, Chairman, Volvo

THE WORLD CLASS PERSON

At this point, we have identified that change is inevitable and that therefore it is important for change to become a part of our life and the life of our enterprise. We have also learned that change management needs to be participative, not forced. But why is a chapter on people the second chapter in this book? Because, like Steve Young of the San Francisco 49ers football team, you can't complete one touchdown pass without the linemen to protect you and the receivers to catch the ball and run with it. You need the rest of your team. You can't become World Class alone!

What do we as managers need in order to be effective motivators of change? What do we need to do in order to become World Class in people relations? We will investigate the following nine key areas:

1. The circle
2. Goal setting
3. Leadership
4. Values and ethics
5. Adding value to society as an enterprise
6. Continuous learning
7. Innovation and change creation
8. Measuring/rewarding
9. Stake holders

The Circle

> *You can make more friends in two months by becoming interested in other people than you can in two years by trying to get other people interested in you.*
>
> Dale Carnegie

The circle is a term used to refer to a group of cohorts working together to achieve a common purpose. Examples include the quality circle, the management circle, the family circle, and so on. In order to be a World Class Manager, we need to define our circles and make them as effective as possible. The first quality circle in the life of any manager should be the family circle.

> *No other success [in life] can compensate for failure in the home.*
>
> David O. McKay

The family is the first and highest-priority circle in your life. The family is your reward structure, it's the reason for working, and it's what brings quality into your life. A disastrous home life destroys your work life, whereas a disastrous work life doesn't seem so bad if you have a successful home life. It is self-destructive to let your work life become your reason for living, because "change" can destroy that life in minutes.

Another important circle of everyone's life is the society of which they are members. In the United States, success is measured by individual earning power. In most other parts of the world, success is measured by one's ability to contribute to society. Far too many of us are not contributing (adding value) to society but rather are only self-gratifying (trying to fill our own pockets at the expense of others). In reality, your own personal value is increased only by how much you work with and help others.

The third circle of importance in each of our lives is the circle we work in. These circles are often referred to as teams (see Chapter 14). But are we really forming teams, or are we just grouping? A group is a collection of people thrown together in a room for the purpose of making some kind of decision. A team is a collection of individuals who have worked together over a long period of time and have found a creative harmony and synergy. In teams, we find sharing, not domineering as we find in groups.

In all the circles in our lives, we need to establish quality. I am bothered by terms like "quality time," used in referring to time spent with our children, as if this phrase offers some kind of excuse for spending as little time as possible with them. There is no "quality time" if an insufficient amount of time is spent, whether it's with our children, our spouse, or our employees. The biggest challenge of a World Class Manager is to prioritize his or her time in order to achieve "sufficient quality time" to make a difference in the circles that are important in the manager's life.

Goal Setting

If you can't see a target, how can you expect to hit it? Unfortunately, far too many people and companies go through life without targets to shoot at. They let changes affect the road they take in life without ever identifying why they're traveling down the road to begin with. If we're working only for money, then money is all we'll ever get out of our work. However, if we work for some greater purpose in life, such as a successful family and marriage or being the best at whatever it is we do, we'll find that the money comes along as an added benefit, and we'll have a lot more fun earning it.

We need goals at many levels and within many time frames. Just a few areas in which we should have long-range (20+ years), mid-range (5+ years), and short-range goals (1 year) follow:

- Family goals—Sit down with your spouse and children and determine what's important to the family.
- Personal goals—What do you want out of life? What will give your life meaning?

- Career goals—Where do you want your career path to lead, realizing that most people change professions on the average of about four times during their life?
- Corporate goals—What does your company's business plan state as the goals of the company?
- Job function goals—What do you want to accomplish in the job function you are performing? Are you hoping to build better relationships in your circles? Do you want to become World Class? Far too often I have encountered people who, when asked "How do you decide what areas of your job function you want to perform well in?" answer "Whatever it takes to keep my job and get a raise." My reaction is, "I'm glad you don't work for me!"

After you have determined these goals, you need to do two things:

1. Develop an action plan that will work toward the achievement of the goal.
2. Communicate the goal to all involved. For example, in numerous organizations the corporate goals are pretty much kept secret among top management, yet employees are expected to achieve these goals, of which they are unaware. You can never over-communicate your goals.

Your personal success needs to be defined. Even playing the lottery requires the selection of numbers and the purchasing of a ticket. Most other goals, for example, family or work goals, need a more clearly defined game plan. Several good books address the development of life and work goals. I highly recommend the Covey and von Oech books if you haven't already read them.[4]

We have noticed a slight reversal of the goal-setting process in organizations. Previously, the trend was for the vision and mission of the organization to be defined by top management. Recently, however, the trend has been for employees to define the mission of the organization and for a top-management vision statement to be developed from this employee-defined mission statement. For example, Tridon-Oakdale, discussed in Chapter 1, brought a team of managers together and had them establish the mission statement of the corporation. This process gave the managers both an ownership in the goals and an added commitment to achieving the goals of the organization.

Mojonnier has highlighted top management's role in fostering positive organizational change as it relates to four essential elements:

1. Create a detailed vision statement.
2. Assess your current organization's total culture.
3. Develop a strategy for achieving your vision.
4. Establish midpoint goals to motivate your troops.[5]

Goals define success. Without defined goals, you will never know if you have been successful.

Leadership

> *You cannot be friends upon any other terms than upon the terms of equality.*
>
> Woodrow Wilson

The most powerful teaching tool has always been the power of example. Every parent has learned this principle the hard way. Children always seem to "do as I do" rather than "do as I say." And the principle is just as applicable to the workplace as it is to the home. If you are disgruntled about changes that are being passed down to you, don't expect your employees to be motivated by changes you pass to them.

The leader (refer back to the definitions in Chapter 1) runs his or her organization through respect, whereas the manager drives his or her people by intimidation. Just ask yourself what environment you would prefer to work under and show your employees the same level of respect.

A leader positively influences and motivates changes. An effective leader helps position an organization for success.

Values and Ethics

> *The integrity of men is to be measured by their conduct, not by their professions.*
>
> Junius

Values are the glue that keeps us together. We need a value system built on virtue, integrity, and ethics if we want to grow old feeling good about what we've done in life, whether it was successful or not. Let's define some of the terms we are using here:

- Values—worth; that which renders anything useful or estimable; excellence
- Virtue—worth; moral excellence
- Integrity—completeness; wholeness; honesty; sincerity
- Ethics—standards of right and wrong; system of conduct or behavior; moral principles[6]

The decline of ethics and integrity in the United States has resulted in such a large number of nontrust systems that often the nontrust systems are more complex than the systems they are trying to protect. A nontrust system is a system established specifically for the purpose of making sure that the original system is not abused. For example, antifraud systems such as financial auditing systems exist in every organization.

From a psychological perspective, often we develop nontrust systems to protect us from having others do to us the types of things we are likely to be guilty of. Occasionally, through experience or stories, we also identify the need for such a system. Otherwise, we probably wouldn't have thought of setting up the nontrust system to begin with. It has been estimated that the nontrust systems in existence are costing us more than the occasional fraud that might be perpetrated. Our lack of ethics and integrity results in a lack of trust and leaves us morally and financially bankrupt. (Chapter 12 discusses these issues in detail.)

We can have a long, drawn out discussion about whether a bribe is less ethical than a tip. However, the distinction really isn't that complicated. If we feel good about ourselves and if the results leave everyone involved in a win-win situation, chances are the activity was ethical. Ethics is like pornography: we have difficulty defining it, but we know it when we see it.

Internationally, ethics become very confusing. United States citizens seem to see everything in the decision-making process as black or white, whereas most of the rest of the world sees shades of gray. For example, Malaysia and Thailand were having a border dispute in a region where a large reserve of oil had been discovered. The American solution would be to battle it out, but the Malaysia–Thailand solution was to draw a line around the region and bring in a private developer to develop the oil reserve. Then both countries shared equally in the profits. Which is more ethical, the U.S. way or the Southeast Asian way?

We are obsessed with the legalistic. The handshake is worthless, because our legal system has declared it worthless in court. Technically (on the books), the handshake has value, but in practice (in the courts) it has no value. This state of affairs has helped to destroy our ability to trust one another. If it isn't written down and spelled out in fine print, it legally doesn't have to happen. Another interesting ethics example involves the Southeast Asia region. North America and Southeast Asia both have free trade agreements. The North America Free Trade Agreement (NAFTA) binds three countries, the United States, Canada, and Mexico, in a free trade arrangement. The Association of Southeast Asian Nations (ASEAN) has formed a trade agreement involving six countries: Indonesia, Malaysia, Singapore, the Philippines, Brunei, and Thailand. The NAFTA agreement is 2,200 pages long, while the ASEAN agreement, involving twice as many countries, is 16 pages long. It's obvious that our lack of integrity and ethics has made us obsessed with nontrust systems. Show your employees a little more trust and respect, and they may surprise you by trusting and respecting you in return.

It's a shame that the reputation of an honorable profession like that of the legal profession has to be ruined by just five or six hundred thousand bad apples.

Rex Lee, attorney, president, Brigham Young University

Levi Strauss considers the company's most important asset to be its people's "aspirations." It has become famous for combining strong commercial success with a commitment to social values and to its work force. In 1987, the company developed the famous Levi Strauss Aspirations Statement, a major initiative that defines the shared values that will guide both management and the work force. This aspirations statement is reshaping how occupational roles and responsibilities are defined, how performance evaluations are conducted, how training is handled, and how business decisions are made. The aspirations statement, with its focus on the "people" and their values, is credited with making Levi Strauss a flexible and innovative company. More important, Levi Strauss has an exemplary record on issues like workforce diversity and worker dislocation benefits.

The Levi Strauss Aspirations Statement focuses on people who are proud and committed; on an environment where opportunity exists to contribute, learn and grow; and on a place where people are respected, treated fairly, listened to, and involved. It talks about the need to form friendships, to balance personal and professional lives, and "to have fun." The Levi Strauss Aspirations Statement identifies a new type of leadership focused on the following issues:

- New behaviors—directness, openness, honesty, commitment to the success of others, willingness to acknowledge problems and errors
- Diversity—diversity in age, sex, ethnicity, and so on in the work force
- Recognition—financial and nonfinancial recognition for individuals and teams that contribute to success
- Ethical management practices—"leadership that epitomizes the stated standards of ethical behavior"
- Communications—need for employees to know what is expected of them and to receive timely and honest feedback
- Empowerment—increase in the authority and responsibility granted by leadership to those employees closest to the products and customers

Levi Strauss has demonstrated the importance of people values and ethics and has taught that these values are critical to World Class Management (leadership) status.[7]

A company's values—what it stands for, what its people believe in—are crucial to its competitive success.

Robert Haas, CEO, Levi Strauss & Co.

Adding Value to Society as an Enterprise

Being world class refers to two opposite but equal activities:

Eliminating all waste

Focusing on value-added functions

Identifying non–value-added activities on a factory floor has always been relatively easy. But this chapter focuses on people— it focuses on us. How do we identify non–value-added activities in our own lives? Here are a couple of guidelines:

1. Does the activity help us achieve any of the goals that we established earlier in this chapter?
2. Does the activity we are engaged in benefit society or our family (our "circle") in any way?

A story will help you understand this concept. One time when I was working overseas, I got into a discussion of "what is wrong with the United States." Outsiders always have lots of ideas about what we should be doing differently. Sometimes, however, as on this occasion, such insights are thought-provoking. The answer given was that "the economic decay of the United States is be-ing caused by the fact that you are graduating more and more non–value-added graduates than you ever did before." So I asked for a definition of a non–value-added graduate. The answer was "anyone working in a profession that does not increase the output of the nation." Individuals who work at professions that simply move the existing resources of the nation around, placing some of them in their own pocket during the process without adding any value, are non–value-added workers.

On a smaller scale, many of the activities we are engaged in benefit only our own pocketbooks in the short term. We are not creating anything of value to society. And if we are engaged in activities that add no value, then we are actively engaged in creating waste. In our private or corporate life, we need to refocus our activities and the activities of our employees on adding value. We need to eliminate non–value-added processes. We need to add value to society as an enterprise, through the efforts of our employees.

Continuous Learning

It is only the intellectually lost who ever argue.

Oscar Wilde

A million different quotes could be selected for this section. I picked the Oscar Wilde quote because I believe that you can't learn if your mouth is open. You can learn only if you have your ears open and your mouth closed. Chapter 10 discusses training and education in detail, but in this section we focus on people learning or sharing between each other.

A lot of people are filled with good ideas, and we need to listen to them if we are to benefit from their wisdom. Additionally, being World Class means realizing that improvement comes about only if we open ourselves to changes in the form of new ideas. We need to learn new ideas in order to incorporate them into the things we do. Being World Class means offering everyone in the organization opportunities and the appropriate motivation to learn and develop through education and training. We need to build a learning organization.

In this category belongs the need for self-renewal, otherwise known as vacation time. Creativity is improved when pressure is removed and drudgery relieved. Employees need time to "get away from it all," and they need to be encouraged to get away from it often.

Innovation and Change Creation

Chaos often breeds life when order breeds habit.
Henry (Brooks) Adams, American historian

Being World Class involves breaking out of the ritualistic, mundane things in life. It's realizing that:

Professionals built the Titanic—amateurs the Ark.
Frank Pepper

Just because an employee is not an expert at something doesn't mean that he or she doesn't have worthwhile and valuable ideas. The expression of all ideas, whether by the professional or the amateur, needs to be encouraged. The trick in managing ideas is to not allow egos to get wrapped up in the innovation process. Every idea must be considered valuable, even if you really think it stinks, because you are a prejudiced observer and you don't want to discourage the creative process. Additionally, you need to be careful that the "professional" is not offended when the ideas of an amateur contradict his or her professional opinion.

World Class Management also includes the ability to laugh at yourself.

For the Wisdom of the World is foolishness with God.
1 Corinthians 3:19

The books by von Oech and Nadler and Hibion cited earlier stress that this point is critical in the creative process. Allow your ideas to be destroyed. In fact, do your best to destroy them yourself. How else can you be sure they are fool-proof?

Employees need to be involved in and understand the change process in order to effectively initiate changes. This process is explained in many models that share the following components:

1. Identifying/recognizing the need or opportunity for change as the first step in making any change
2. Defining the problem or opportunity that needs to be addressed
3. Identifying the current company position relative to the problem—you need to know where you are before you can determine where to go
4. Identifying alternative destinations
5. Identifying the desired destination
6. Defining a road map to get from where you are to where you want to be
7. Unfreezing the organization and preparing it for change—this includes training and empowerment
8. Change implementation
9. Stabilizing the organization under the new order—this includes the establishment of a new feedback mechanism that will monitor the new status quo

With an understanding of the change process, organizations and their employees are ready for innovation and change creation.[8]

This brings us to a critical element of World Class employee innovation and creativity. We need to develop an empowered work force that works together in teams, not groups, and has the authority to implement its ideas (this concept is expanded on in Chapter 14). Creativity works best through the synergy of effectively developed and empowered teams. One example of this is the Levi Strauss story, discussed earlier in this chapter. Another example is the Antilock Braking Systems Division (ABS) of General Motors in Dayton, Ohio (formerly Delco Products Company). They did what they were told would be impossible—they developed a World Class empowerment program, called Employee Involvement (EI), starting with a traditional United Auto Workers (UAW) contract. A covenant was established between the union and ABS. They felt that this agreement provided the only way they could still be in business in two years and that it was necessary if they were to keep pace with the continuous improvement programs of their competitors.

ABS supervisors were given new responsibility based on communication and training. A system of trust was established with the workers and forms the core of the EI program. Based on this trust, a set of guiding principles was established that included the following:

1. We will establish and maintain innovative systems that can compete in a World Class climate.
2. We will enact the cultural change necessary to ensure profitability and job security at the Dayton plants.
3. We will run the business as a joint activity seeking contribution from and sharing benefits with all.
4. We will provide mechanisms and incentives that promote continual improvement in customer satisfaction.
5. We will approach this covenant as a living agreement, continually reviewing our progress and proactively adjusting to maximize our competitiveness.

ABS truly has a World Class empowerment program worthy of study and emulation.[9]

Measuring/Rewarding

Treat people as if they were what they ought to be, and you help them become what they are capable of being.

Goethe

Innovation and creativity need to be stimulated. Recently I was working for a company that had an elaborate Total Quality Management (TQM) program. (TQM is discussed in detail in Chapter 11.) TQM is a tool for implementing change in an organization. However, the TQM program was failing, and the company couldn't understand why. I reviewed their measurement system and quickly learned that they were evaluating employee performance based on units-per-hour efficiency. Bonuses were paid when employee performance exceeded the standard rates of

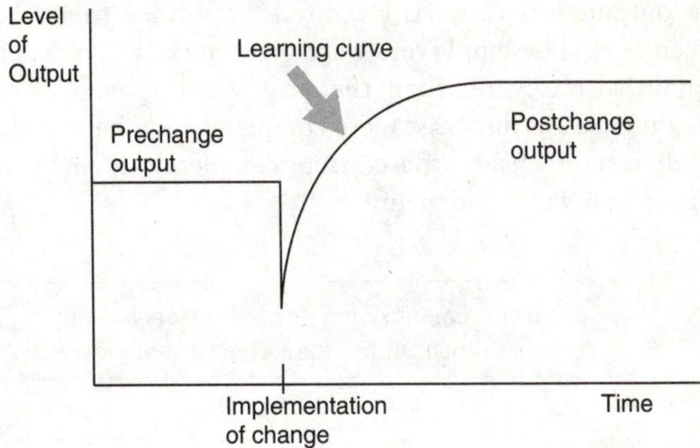

Figure 2.1   Change Function

production. Why would employees want to spend time implementing changes through TQM if:

1. They were being rewarded based on historical rates and historical methodologies.
2. There was no reward for implementing the change.
3. Changes would, in effect, decrease their productive output in the short term and therefore reduce their bonuses.

Let me explain point three in more detail. When change is implemented, the first thing that happens is a drop-off in efficiency. As Figure 2.1 shows, employees are working away at a certain level of output, and as change is introduced a loss of productive output immediately occurs. Then, through the process of the learning curve, employees slowly become better and better at the new process, eventually achieving a new, (hopefully) higher level of output. Unfortunately, in the short term, efficiency suffers—and so does the paycheck.

This company was asking employees to sacrifice their paycheck in order to implement changes. The company didn't want to lose output, but they still wanted employees to initiate improvements. The employees were given mixed signals, and the signal that motivated them the most was the paycheck signal (measurement is discussed more completely in Chapter 8).

To help you understand this concept completely, let me make a "hang on your wall" statement:

> A measurement system is not for management information; it's for motivating employees.

Any measurement system that exists simply for accounting purposes or information-gathering purposes is probably counter-effective and destructive to the company's ability to achieve its goals. A measurement system that is not focused on the goals of the organization distracts employees from those goals. Whether it is true or not, employees believe they are being graded by what they are being measured on, and they will focus their performance in those areas on which they are being measured. So select your measurement systems wisely—they may motivate the wrong actions.

Stake Holders

As a World Class Manager, you need to identify all the people involved in your circles. They include the following:

Family

Friends

Employees

Peers

Bosses

Customers (both internal and external)

Vendors

The community

Taking it from the top, can you satisfy your spouse's needs? Are you making him or her happy? Does he or she enjoy being with you? What about your children? What about your friends?

Do the people you work with come to you for help, or do they avoid you like the plague? Do your customers consider you someone who can get things done, or someone who puts things off or makes excuses? Do you identify both your immediate customer (the one you pass product to) and your final customer (the eventual end user) as someone who needs satisfaction?

Do you get involved? Do you look for ways to help out your fellow employees and your family and friends, or do you avoid challenging situations? Are you willing and eager to change? Do you avoid wearing shoes because it means you have to change? Simply put, are you World Class?

SUMMARY

In summary, I would like to recommend some reading material for those of you interested in this subject.[10] Without people who are willing and motivated to change, there can be no World Class organization. It is "we, the people"—you the manager, your bosses, your employees, your customers, and your vendors—that make your enterprise World Class, and just like Steve Young or Michael Jordan, you can't get there without your "circle."

Man is here for the sake of other men.
Albert Einstein, German-born Swiss-American scientist

CHAPTER 3

Goal-Based Strategies

> Only those who attempt the absurd
> can achieve the impossible.

Robin Hood was given a challenge. He was asked to take one bent arrow and with that arrow to hit three targets at the same time. If that wasn't bad enough, he was first blindfolded and spun around a few times. You may ask, "How can we expect him to hit a target he cannot see?" or "How can he hit multiple targets with the same arrow at the same time?" But as surprising as it may seem, we are asking our managers and employees to do what even Robin Hood couldn't do, and they are expected to do it every month. Read on and you'll see what I'm talking about.

IDENTIFY THE TARGET

> A journey of 1000 miles
> begins with a single step.

Goals give purpose and direction to what we are doing. We need to focus on a clearly defined target in order to be directed toward what we are trying to accomplish. The development of a goal involves the following stages:

1. Defining the core competencies
2. The vision
3. The mission
4. The strategy
5. The plan of operation

The first step is not really a goal as much as an introspective look at what you're good at. Are you good at sourcing, manufacturing, distribution, retailing, *and* customer service? Probably not. Which one are you really good at, and which are simply the necessary evils that you need to tolerate as part of your business? The core competency is the combination of individual technologies and production skills that underlie a company's productive processes. Some examples of core competencies (sometimes referred to as capabilities)[1] are:

Sony—miniaturization

Canon—optics, imaging, and microprocessor controls

Honda—engines and power trains

After defining the core competency (what you're really good at), we break down the core competency even more. For example, are you good at distributing everywhere, or just in the United States, or just in the Pacific Northwest? By going through this process of identification, you end up with a clear picture of what your core competencies are. Once you know what you're good at, capitalize on it and build your growth and future around it. This identification step gives you a basis for the development of your goals, which includes your vision, mission, and strategy.

To become a visionary company, you need two things:

1. A guiding philosophy and value system, that is, a vision
2. A challenging short-term goal or mission that quantifies the vision

In each stage of the goal-development process, we find more detail than at the level before it. For example, the vision consists of one or two sentences stating where the enterprise is going. It is an enterprise's sense of purpose, its reason for being, its guiding philosophy. A vision builds unity throughout the organization. It doesn't have to be lengthy, but it does have to give the organization purpose. The vision should provide employees with a clear image with which they can identify.[2] The following are examples of a company's vision:

. . . to make a contribution to the world by making tools for the mind that advance humankind.

Steve Jobs, Apple Computer

To make people happy.

Walt Disney

Unlike the vague, undefined, timeless vision statement, the mission statement is a series of defined goals that are aimed at the vision. The mission has a definite, measurable goal and should be date-stamped with a finish time. The mission should be challenging (see the section on the characteristics of good goals later in this chapter). Some examples of a mission are:

. . . achieving the goal, before this decade is out, of landing a man on the moon and returning him safely to earth.

President John F. Kennedy, 1962

Beat Coke!

Pepsi Co.

We will crush, squash, slaughter Yamaha!

Honda

The next stage of goal development, the strategy, identifies and quantifies goals for each strategic operating area and focuses on bringing that operating area in line with the mission of the enterprise. Strategy development is the topic of Chapter 4.

The final step in goal development, the plan of operation, is the operating plan for each strategic area detailing how each area will achieve its strategy, and thus its mission, and finally, in the long run, its vision. The plan of operation requires a detailed tactical plan for executing the strategy in the short term (over the next few months).

This chapter looks at the first big target, the vision, and then at the second, more focused target, the mission of the enterprise. Chapter 4 discusses the strategic plans. Later in the book we will discuss the operating plans.[3]

The process of establishing goals (visioning and missioning) takes a class-syllabus approach to business. When you take a college class, the professor doesn't come to you and say "Keep doing what you're doing, you're doing great, and at the end of the semester I'll evaluate you." Imagine that, as the semester progresses, the professor continues with his vague, directionless information. Then, when the end of the year rolls around, the professor says, "Well, you all did OK, so I'll pass some of you and flunk some of you," never indicating why some were passed and some were flunked. If this scenario were true, the students would be screaming and demanding the details of what is expected of them. But this directionless methodology seems to be an acceptable way to run a business (or the tenure and promotions process in some colleges and universities). In reality, when you take a college class, the professor gives you a class syllabus that defines what the requirements of the course are, what needs to be accomplished for successful completion of the course, and when the time to complete the course requirements is up. The class-syllabus approach gives everyone in the organization clear objectives and does not leave employees blindfolded, using crooked arrows. Everyone knows what he or she is shooting at.

In an empowered organization, it is a challenge of leadership to make sure each and every employee is involved in creating the vision.

James J. Mapes[4]

In order to discuss goals effectively, we need to discuss the types of goals that exist and their characteristics. One section of this chapter focuses on the types of goals. Another section focuses on the characteristics of good goals. It is also possible to have secondary goals, but they need to complement, not draw away from, the primary goal (see the discussion later in this chapter).

Where there is no vision, the people perish.

Proverbs 29:18

TYPES OF GOALS

The goals of an enterprise determine the value system of the organization. In the United States, we have grown accustomed to the idea that there is only one correct goal for a business enterprise—financial success. Interestingly, this goal is less prevalent from an international perspective. In my interaction with businesses around the world, I have found four major groupings of goals:

1. Financial goals
2. Operational goals
3. Employee-based goals
4. Customer-based goals

Each of these groupings has specific characteristics. For example, the goals are listed in order from short-term orientation to long-term orientation. We now discuss each of these goal types in detail.

Financial Goals

Financial goals include goals such as the following:

Increasing profits

Decreasing costs

Increasing sales

Increasing return on investment

> Increasing return on net assets
> Financial ratios

Financial goals are very shortsighted and tend to be oriented toward quarterly or annual results. The shortsightedness of these goals stems to a great deal from the nontrust that we have for one another (see the previous chapter for a discussion of nontrust systems). For example, stockholders don't trust the Board of Directors, the board does not trust the CEO, the CEO does not trust the VPs, the VPs don't trust middle management, and so on. The result is that each level monitors the level below it on the basis of short-term, financial measures. If, for example, the CEO wants to introduce massive technological changes that will take several years to show a return (see Figure 2.1), he or she will be out of a job after the first or second year of losses. The CEO will have difficulty convincing the board that "the benefits of the change are just around the corner."

That's exactly what happened to Florida Power and Light. The company implemented a total quality improvement–continuous change and improvement program called the Quality Improvement Program (QIP). The benefits from the improvements were so dramatic that Florida Power and Light was the first non-Japanese company to win the Deming Award, Japan's most prestigious national quality award. However, the implementation of this improvement program had extensive front-end costs, and the result was that after about three years of losses the board became impatient and nontrusting of the CEO. The board dismissed the CEO, along with his participative management style and all his continuous improvement ideas, and installed an authoritarian CEO who kept everything secret. Suddenly, employees who had previously been involved in the organization and its changes had no idea from one day to the next what was going on within the organization. Short-term financial measures ruled the day at Florida Power and Light, as they do in most U.S. organizations.

In spite of the shortsighted negatives, financial goals can, and often are, used to effect positive growth and change. The key to success seems to be in the realization that long-term visions and missions cannot be achieved if they are restricted by short-term measures that fail to focus on the long-term goals.

Operational Goals

Operational goals, which have caught on in some parts of Europe, tend to be more long-term than financial goals. Additionally, achieving operational goals tends to lead to, as a by-product, the achievement of financial objectives. Operational goals include:

Improved quality

Improved productivity

Reduced inventory

Increased throughput

Reduced scrap

Improved level of customer service

We can easily see how achieving each of these goals would improve profits. Additionally, these goals tend to be noncon-flicting (see the discussion and example of conflicting financial goals in the section of this chapter that discusses goal character-istics). Operational goals tend to be long-term, because success is generally measured incrementally. For example, a relatively small 10% inventory reduction each year for ten years would lead to an enormous (65% cumulative) inventory reduction after ten years, which would result in a similar increase in profitability.

Employee-Based Goals

Employee permanence and stability are important goals that are quite important in Japan. The primary reason for the popularity of these goals is that they support a participative relationship with the employees, rather than an authoritarian one. But there is a lot of misunderstanding about the meaning of these goals. For example, pursuing employee stability doesn't mean that a company should ignore profitability, any more than a successful, profit-oriented company can ignore its employees. It simply means that successful, happy employees create a successful happy company. I will explain, through a series of steps, how implementing this goal works:

1. The goal of the company is to offer its employees permanence and a steady growth path.
2. To accomplish this, you need to be in business longer than anyone else who is building your product.
3. Business longevity is achieved by being more successful with your product than any competitor.
4. Product success is measured in terms of market share control.
5. Market share control is captured by whatever means necessary.
6. Once market share control is achieved, you have control of the product pricing and therefore can recover any losses incurred in the attempt to gain market share, which enhances profitability.

Note that the key goal, the one that started this entire series of events, was employee satisfaction.

Federal Express, from its inception, has put its people first both because it is right to do so and because it is good business as well. Our corporate philosophy is succinctly stated: People-Service-Profit (P-S-P).

Frederick W. Smith, Chairman and CEO, Federal Express

Customer-Based Goals

A customer-based goal often is confused with a quality-based goal. Quality is a strategy for achieving any of the goals (see Chapter 5), but quality itself is not a goal, because it is defined and interpreted in so many different ways. For example, in the United States most companies who claim to have a "quality product" in fact have only satisfied some internal measure of quality. For most factories, a quality product is defined as one that meets engineering specifications; its quality has absolutely nothing to do with the customer. The international measure for quality, the ISO 9000 certification process, supports this "internal quality" perspective (see Chapter 5 for a more detailed discussion). In Europe, where the ISO 9000 process originated, the claim is made that Germany's quality is higher. Unfortunately, all this means is that its engineering standards are higher, not that the product is more customer-oriented. Therefore, a product can be "quality" and still not have satisfied a single customer.

World Class "quality" lies in customer satisfaction, not engineer satisfaction. A World Class quality product is one about which the following statement can be made:

> Customers are so excited about your product
> that they wouldn't think of going
> to anyone else to get it!

How do you know if you are customer-goal-oriented? You spend time with your customer, at your customer's location, and your customer spends time with you and your employees at your location. You share, discuss, interact, learn, and create ideas (innovate) together. The customer is an integral part of your planning circle. The reason for all this interaction is that you cannot satisfy a customer if you don't understand what the customer needs or wants (how can Robin Hood shoot a target he cannot see?)

Comparing the Targets

I have listed the targets from shortest-term to longest-term, from easiest to implement to hardest, and from most objective to most subjective. Let's take a look at the differences between these goals.

Financial and operational goals are easy to measure. Results are all in the data and can be displayed neatly on a graph. Working with employees and customers is vague and not as quantifiable. Maybe that's why we shy away from employee-based and customer-based goals. However, companies like FedEx and Toyota have found a very definite way to quantify their performance in these areas, as we will see later in the book. It just takes a little more effort. But is it worth it? All the Baldrige and Deming award winners seem to think so. They all place great importance in these last two categories.

What we have established, at this point, is the need to set a goal. The goal takes the form of a vision statement and a mission statement. As we discussed briefly in the last chapter, there are two ways to arrive at both of these statements:

Bottom-Up

Top-Down

The top-down approach is to have the CEO, in conjunction with the VPs, develop the vision statement. Then the mission statement is developed out of the vision generated by the top. The bottom-up approach is to have middle or lower management define what it sees the mission of the organization as being and then to define a vision out of this synergistic mission statement. This approach facilitates adapting the organization to its own capabilities, since what works well in one business rarely works perfectly in another. The bottom-up approach demonstrates ownership and commitment by the employees to the goals and has therefore become popular with companies that are employee- or customer-based in their goal structure.

No matter how the vision and mission statements are developed, the purpose of both is to develop a series of back-to-back targets that Robin Hood can shoot with only one arrow. These statements need to fit the employees, they need to be realistic, and they need to be communicated (see the section of this chapter that discusses the characteristics of a good target). We often find that employees, when given a say in the visioning process, are tougher on themselves than upper management would have been.

CHARACTERISTICS OF A GOOD TARGET

If Robin Hood were to pick the ideal target, what would it look like? It would be easy to see, focused (small enough so that he knows exactly what he's shooting for), well defined, and custom designed to challenge his abilities. Why am I making such a big deal out of setting a goal? Because the typical business plan of a company reads like a wish list of all good things and is totally worthless. Having many business goals is as useful as not having any if the goals are not focused on a common vision. The goals soon get in one another's way. Goal setting should not be a process of setting high goals to drive employees to unrealistic ends. Nor should goal attainment result in a compromise of easy-to-attain steps. A good target should be realistic and attainable. All goals should have several specific characteristics (most goals do not have all of these characteristics, but they should have as many as possible):

1. Participatively created by and matched to the employees
2. Shared
3. Nonconflicting
4. Allowing for and encouraging change
5. Simple but not simplistic
6. Precise
7. Measurable
8. Uncompromised
9. Focused
10. Achievable yet challenging

Goals Participatively Created By and Matched to the Employees

Employees who participate in the goal-development process maintain an ownership in the goals and feel personally challenged to achieve those goals. The goals are no longer "company" goals, rather they are "my" goals. This is what we meant when we discussed the process whereby employees develop the mission statement and then consolidate it into a vision. It is broader than the old concept of Management by Objectives (MBO), where the employees sit down with their supervisor and set goals for themselves. In participative goal setting, the employees establish corporate goals, not just individual goals. Recall the Tridon-Oakdale story in Chapter 1 and the case of the Antilock Braking Systems Division (ABS) of General Motors in Chapter 2. In both cases, the employees were actively involved in establishing corporate goals.

Shared Goals

One of the biggest "sins" of goal setting is failure to communicate the goal to the individuals responsible for achieving the goal. I have lost count of the number of companies that have related "We don't show our employees our business plan because it is confidential," meaning that only strategic management employees are allowed to see it (this is where Robin Hood is blindfolded). My question is "How can you expect the employees to hit a target they cannot see?" Even Robin Hood can't do that. Employees need to know what the goal is, how it is going to be measured, whether or not progress is being made toward the goal, and, one more step, that they will receive part of (share in) the reward of achieving the goal.

> A hidden goal is as useful as no goal,
> for no one will know if you succeeded.

Nonconflicting Goals

Financial goals are often conflicting, but nonfinancial goals can conflict as well. Let's consider a recent financial example that I encountered. The financial goals of this organization were:

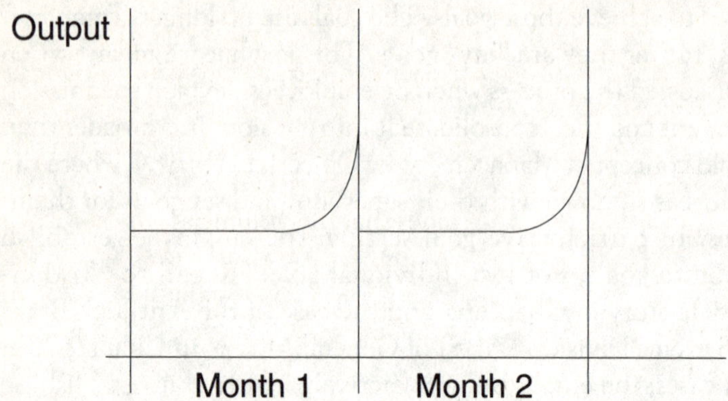

Figure 3.1   Conflicting Goals

Increase profits

Increase sales

Decrease costs

Increase return on net assets

On the surface, this set of goals seems reasonable. However, upon closer examination we see that these goals are conflicting and therefore impossible to achieve simultaneously. The result is similar to the situation depicted in Figure 3.1. For about the first 90% of the month, we have steady output and are working toward minimizing cost and maximizing profit. This happens because we are working efficiently. Then, during the last 10% of the month, we put on a rush, trying to push as much product out the door as possible. We have thrown efficiency, profit, and cost reduction to the wind. We send people scurrying around in an attempt to have employees work in smaller batch sizes so that we can push a few extra product units (orders) out the door. We are now working toward the goal of increased sales. Then we spend the first part of the next month trying to recover from the inefficient mess created near the end of the previous month.

Obviously, from this example, we see that the stated goals are in conflict. At one part of the month we are working toward one goal, while at another part of the month we are working toward another goal. We can't achieve both goals simultaneously.

For further explanation of this conflict, recall your elementary economics class, where you learned about the production function. This function teaches that the volume at which we produce to achieve maximum sales is not the same volume at which we produce to achieve maximum profits. So which is your goal: sales, profits, cost reductions, market share, or return on investment? Several are in conflict. You can't have them all as your goal (unless you're happy with not really achieving any of them), just as Robin Hood cannot hit multiple, unaligned targets with a single arrow.

Goals Allowing For and Encouraging Change

. . . because time and information don't exist or move fast enough for top management to make decisions from the top.
Alvin Toffler[5]

A well-developed World Class goals system takes into account the necessity for employees to be able to interact with and initiate change (empowerment). Employees can't wait for change decisions to come from the top. They need to participate in the change process (participative management). Employees need to be prepared for change (training and education) and motivated toward change (measurement systems). All these points are discussed in detail in later chapters.

Simple but Not Simplistic Goals

Goals should be simple—the shorter the better. Complex goals are harder to understand and are therefore ignored. Ideally, the vision portion of the goal should be short enough to be wall-plaque material and be easily remembered and stated by the employees. The vision should stress the core competency of the organization. The mission statement should also be simple, a collection of about ten sentences, stating how the vision can be operationalized. Similar rules apply to the strategies of the organization.

The vision, mission, and strategy should *not* be simplistic, for example; "We want to get better" or "We want to get richer." These statements are too vague, and employees have difficulty hanging their hat on them.

Precise Goals

Goals need to be precise, especially as you get into the strategies. Goal achievement needs to be measurable; an imprecise goal leads to confusion. The goal needs to be quantifiable and precisely related to each employee, telling them what is expected of them.

Measurable Goals

The enterprise needs competitive performance measures in order to ensure that it is staying on top of the competition. Measures like productivity, quality, time-to-market, and efficiency are excellent internal operational measures that demonstrate performance on a team basis. Measures of employee satisfaction and customer satisfaction are excellent departmental measures of performance. An entire chapter on measurement systems is coming up (Chapter 8).

One important lesson about measurement systems that needs to be learned if you are to achieve World Class status is that a measurement system does not exist for management information or for costing—it exists for motivation.

> What you measure is
> what you motivate!

Don't measure (and thus motivate) labor efficiency if what you really want is materials efficiency. And don't measure (motivate) labor efficiency if what you really want is quality. You'll receive results in what you measure, not in what you vocalize. Don't tell yourself that you can measure labor efficiency, materials efficiency, and quality all at the same time. The result would be to:

1. Confuse employees as to what you're really after
2. Receive average performance in each area, as opposed to achieving excellent performance in the area in which you really need performance, which should be your critical resource

A goal needs to be measured to ensure performance and goal achievement, and it needs to measure the right things in order to generate the proper motivation.

Uncompromised Goals

A goal needs to be uncompromised. Once established, it requires commitment. This is one reason why goal ownership by the employees is so important. Wishy-washy management commitment to goal achievement results in nonachievement. Goal downsizing also leads to nonachievement. If the employees were involved in goal development and fail to achieve the goal, we shouldn't go to them and say, "Well, you did OK and we'll give you your bonus anyway." Such downsizing will whitewash the goals and result in poor goal setting in the future. Goals need to be taken seriously, and they require commitment.

Focused Goals

The company of Figure 3.1 shows a lack of focus. It is basically running the plant in two different ways. Because the goals are in conflict, it is not possible to determine which measurement system is appropriate. The one used during the first 90% of the month would be efficiency, productivity, and cost of production;

the measurement system used during the last 10% of the month would be sales growth. Stressing both will result in the type of chaos shown in Figure 3.1. We need to have focused goals, which means we need a target that is well defined. Set your goal, build a measurement system around it, and stick to it.

Achievable yet Challenging Goals

The last characteristic of goal setting is that the goal should make us stretch ourselves, but not kill ourselves. We don't want last year's performance to be next year's goal. We want the new goal to be significantly but realistically better than last year's accomplishments, thereby making us better.

Now that we have discussed the characteristics of good goals, we discuss the role of secondary goals. Then we take a look at the implementation of a good set of goals.

THE SECOND AND THIRD TARGETS

Earlier in this chapter, we discussed multiple, conflicting goals. We also mentioned that we need a single, focused target to shoot at. Does this mean that secondary goals are bad? Definitely not! As long as they don't conflict with or interfere with the primary goal, they are desirable. Robin Hood can hit multiple targets if they are nicely laid on top of one another, but not if they go off in different directions.

There is nothing wrong with having secondary goals as long as they strengthen, rather than conflict with, the primary goal. Let me give an example. If your primary goal is employee permanence and stability, then it would be appropriate to ask what secondary goal would support this primary goal. If you want the employees to have jobs, then you want the plant to be around as long as possible. To do this, you need to make sure you manufacture the product as long as possible. You need to control the market and the production of the product. An appropriate secondary goal would be to control "market share." Then the next question is, how do you control market share? It may require some price cutting or gouging until you control the market. Then you can set the price at whatever level you want. A more important way to control market share reflects the definition of quality discussed earlier: to make a product customers enjoy, like, and appreciate so much that they wouldn't think of buying from anyone else. A recap of this chain of goals follows:

- Primary goal—employee permanence and stability
- Second goal—controlling market share
- Third goal—quality product

Another type of secondary goal involves breaking down a goal by departments or management levels. It would be helpful for each department to define a subgoal that would demonstrate that department's efforts toward the primary goal. This subgoal would be measurable within the organization and would be more useful to the specific department than the primary goal.

TARGET IMPLEMENTATION

Table 3.1 briefly outlines the form of the goal statements of an organization. Note the focus on the core competencies and the strengthening of these core competencies by developing goals around them. Also note the focus on goals and the development of supportive subgoals that will assist in the achievement of the primary goal.

As we implement the goals, we need to keep in mind:

1. Goal participation and ownership
2. Employee preparation and training
3. The corporate value system

Goal Participation and Ownership

Again it needs to be stressed that the most effective goal structure is a participative one in which the employees are involved in the setting of the goals and in their implementation. Only with employee participation do you achieve employee ownership. And

Table 3.1. Goal Development

Vision Statement

One or two sentences stating what the long-term vision of the enterprise is, focusing on the core competencies of the organization.

Mission Statement

A series of goal statements indicating how the organization plans to achieve the vision. This statement specifies what areas the organization plans to change (improve). Where do its strengths lie, and how does it plan to develop these strengths? The mission should be measurable, with a target completion date. The mission statement, like the vision statement, should focus on the core competencies of the enterprise.

Strategy

A focus on the various "strategic areas" of the organization and a quantifiable set of goals stating how each area plans to support and achieve the mission statement. (Strategy development is discussed in more detail in Chapter 4.)

---

only with employee ownership do you achieve a corporatewide commitment to succeed.

Employee Preparation and Training

It's one thing to set goals; it's another thing entirely to make sure that employees have the tools necessary to achieve the goals. Sometimes this means technology, but often it means training. For example, if quality improvement is a goal, then the employees need to be trained in quality improvement tools: what they are, how to use them, and how they can make a difference. I know a company that has been using statistical process tracking tools for many years to monitor quality. Recently I was brought in and asked "Why are we developing these control charts? What are we supposed to do with them?" Previous management had been on a quality control kick and had made employees fill out control charts. Most employees didn't know how to fill them out or why. They simply did it because they were told to. Is it any surprise that quality didn't improve, in spite of the quality control system?

The Corporate Value System

The corporate value system needs to be at the heart of all goals and their implementation. Values should be incorporated into, not take a back seat to, goal achievement. For example, honesty and integrity are often thrown to the wind in order to make the numbers look good. A company that loses its values to numbers will have a long road back trying to recover its lost integrity. And, since the numbers weren't realistic anyway, the company will also have trouble achieving its "realistic" goals.

Armed with the necessary commitment and tools, employees will be eager and interested in driving the enterprise toward World Class status.

WHEN GOALS DON'T WORK

If you fail to follow the basics of goal development, goals become nothing more than plaques on the wall. For example, a 1991 survey of over 300 electronics companies found that 63% had failed to improve quality defects by as much as 10%. The reason stated was that the programs were not "results-driven"; they did not have goals that were measured and motivated within a specific time frame. Another example of failure is the many companies who have identified so many activities in so many places in the change process that a complex chart is required just to describe them all. (I always leave out the name of the company when the news is bad.) In another case, successful change was measured by having 100% of the employees attend a quality training program. I wonder if anyone cares if they learned anything. In other cases, failure has occurred because credit wasn't given where credit was due; management took all the credit for what the employees accomplished.[6]

I was asked to visit a plant that had been officially notified of closure. Since the plant was going to close anyway, company management wanted to know "what went wrong." It didn't take long to discover a quality improvement system that had all the appropriate control charts and process control tools.

Employee training was in place. The plaques about quality were on the wall. So what went wrong? What we quickly learned was that employee performance was measured based on units of output. No one was measured on quality improvements, so no quality improvements occurred. Quality changes would interfere with productive units produced, which meant that quality improvements would actually reduce, rather than increase, the bonus. The employees weren't dumb; they knew how to play into the management fad of implementing quality control systems while at the same time maintaining the quality of their paychecks.

Another instance in which goal achievement fails is when the principles and values of the enterprise and its employees are compromised in order to achieve the goals. Goal achievement then becomes an unrewarding event rather than an exciting and celebrated one.

Goal achievement can occur only when it is based on the principles and characteristics outlined in this chapter. If they are absent, don't expect World Class results!

THE CHANGE PROCESS

Marriage should war incessantly with that monster that is the ruin of everything. This is the monster of habit.

Honoré de Balzac, French writer

Now we are ready to review the change process (mentioned in Chapter 2) in order to see how it ties into the goals and strategies we establish. Our vision and mission should focus on change (improvement). We implement this change through a series of strategic steps (Chapter 4). We then use any (or several) of a variety of change models in order to implement the changes (see Chapter 11).

In Chapter 1, we discussed two sources of change:

1. The changes you invoke yourself
2. The changes that are happening to you

This chapter has focused on the changes that you invoke yourself. However, there are still those changes that happen to you and that require contingency plans. You can't expect everything to roll along perfectly. Life is filled with surprises. The better you are prepared to "roll with the punches," the better you are prepared with contingency plans and the more likely you are to achieve your eventual enterprise goals.

SUMMARY

> To create a new
> we need to eliminate the old.

Robin Hood needs to have the blinders removed. He not only needs to know where the target is, he needs to participate in the selection and planning of the target as well. And he needs a target that challenges him yet is achievable. He needs to be excited about the target. He needs to feel that if he hits the target he will have improved himself.

Goals aren't just for the enterprise; goals should also be a part of your life and your family's life. What do you want to be when you grow up? What do you want to have accomplished in ten years? twenty years? How about the goals of your family? World Class means World Class in the home as well as on the job.

Managers, like Robin Hood, need targets in order to measure World Class performance. In this chapter, we discussed core competencies, vision statements, and mission statements. Next we identify the strategic areas in which we need to have quantifiable goals that in turn will focus on the vision and mission of the enterprise.

CHAPTER 4

Strategies for Change

> *Men fear thought as they fear nothing else on earth—more than death. Thought is subversive, and revolutionary, destructive and terrible; thought is merciless to privilege, established institutions, and comfortable habits; thought is anarchic and lawless, indifferent to authority, careless to the well-tried wisdom of the ages. Thought looks into the pit of hell and is not afraid. . . . Thought is great and swift and free, the light of the world, and the chief glory of man.*
>
> *But if thought is to become the possession of the many, and not the privilege of the few, we must have done with fear. It is fear that holds men back—fear that their cherished beliefs should prove delusions, fear lest the institutions by which they live should prove harmful, fear lest they themselves prove less worthy to the respect then they have supposed themselves to be.*
>
> Bertrand Russell, British mathematician and philosopher

Consider the diagram in Figure 4.1. What you are asked to do is determine the length of line *BD* in the rectangle *ABCD*, given that line *AE* (the radius) is 10 inches long. This is not intended to be a difficult problem. You can solve it with the basic geometry you learned in junior high school. It should take you about two minutes if you:

1. Understand the strategy
2. Follow through on the strategy

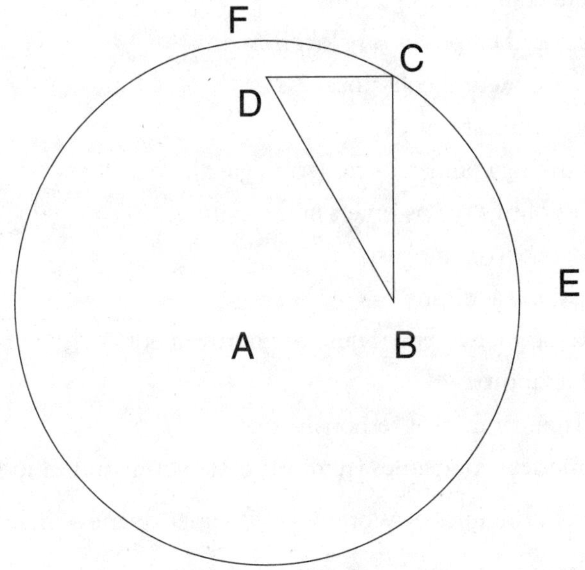

Figure 4.1   Find the Length of the Line *BD*

The point I am making is that without developing and understanding a strategy, you can not achieve even the simplest goal.
The solution to the problem appears at the end of the chapter.

The problem with strategy is that there are so many different
strategy models. I will present a few models and discuss some of
the features common to all of them. I will also suggest plenty of
good reading material for those interested in finding out more
about strategy development. However, my focus here is on World
Class Management, not on strategy development, so I will focus
primarily on those strategic areas that are most critical to helping you become a World Class Manager.

World Class strategies focus on World Class competitiveness.
Some of the competitive trends for the next decade are:

Rapid change in technology and markets

More competitors globally

Increased emphasis on globalization

Environmental consciousness

Decentralization

Shrinking company sizes (strategic alliances)

Closer links to customers and suppliers

Competitive emphasis on:

    Cost reduction

    Customer-oriented quality improvement

    Flexibility

    Time-to-market responsiveness

Borderless companies (removal of departmentalization)

The key principles of World Class competitiveness include:

Focus on the people (primary employees)

Focus on the customer

A quality and productivity stance

A global perspective

Time-based competition

A technological orientation

Information management

An integrative stance

Focused measurement

A value-added decision approach

Continuous training and education

These trends and principles are the focus of Parts I and II of this book. They need to be integrated into a strategic plan for the organization. What is a strategy? Figure 4.2 diagrams the traditional format of a corporate strategy. It shows business units, each of which develops its own strategies in each of the strategic areas. This strategy focuses first on the corporate strategy, which in turn

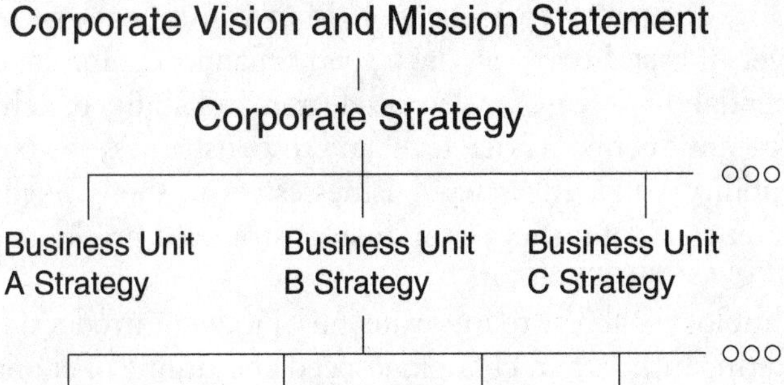

Figure 4.2   Strategy Development

should focus on the mission statement. Both the corporate and the business-unit strategies should identify quantifiable, time-based goals at their level. Although somewhat traditional, this process of strategy development is still heavily utilized today. However, the trend toward dropping internal corporate barriers suggests that the corporate strategy and the business-unit strategy might soon become one and the same.

The strategy, like the mission and vision statement, should focus on the core competencies of the business unit or corporation. It should contain all the characteristics of goals described in Chapter 3. The strategy specifies the scope and boundaries of the business unit. It identifies the basis for achieving and maintaining competitive advantage. It describes how the resources of the business unit will be utilized to achieve the focused corporate mission. It determines the competitive priorities of the business unit, which include:

- Cost competitiveness—e.g., K-Mart versus Sears; unit costs; delivery costs
- Time competitiveness—e.g., FedEx versus the U.S. postal system; responsive; time-to-market

- Quality competitiveness—e.g., K-Mart versus Sears; generics versus brand-name products; performance; conformance
- Dependability—e.g., fax versus telegram; reliability of delivery commitments; service level and responsiveness
- Flexibility—e.g., Taiwanese businesses versus the U.S. government; adaptability to change; customized products or services
- Technology—ability to innovate; new product introduction; tinkering rather than changing; speed and timing of change implementation

Although these competitive priorities are recognized and accepted as crucial elements in the development of an effective strategy, rarely do they become a part of the measurement/motivation system for the management of an enterprise (see Chapter 8). This is another example of verbalizing a goal without putting any power behind it. The strategy is only as valuable as the power and commitment that are devoted to it.

Now that we have determined what the characteristics of a competitive business strategy entail and what its competitive priorities should focus on, we are ready to look at some of the strategy models that exist. These models contain "areas of consideration" that an ideal World Class business strategy should contain.

MODELS OF MANAGEMENT COMPETITIVENESS AND CHANGE

. . . long range thinking is as rare in the board room as in the White House. . . .

. . . business is as confused as are the politicians. . . .

. . . we are moving from a brute force to a brain force economy. . . .

. . . knowledge is the new capital replacing stock or land holdings.

Alvin Toffler

I recently heard it said that behind every good man is a surprised mother-in-law. Similarly, behind every effective corporate strategy is a surprised manager.

There are numerous models of management competitiveness. Each model gives a slightly different insight into what our competitive strategies should be. However, all the models focus on corporate excellence through World Class Management strategies. These models are all valuable in helping us develop a strategic plan that translates our vision and mission into an area-by-area strategic process.

The Hall/Nakane Model

The Hall/Nakane model breaks competitiveness into four quadrants.[1]

1. Technical Factors—External and Worldwide Environment
   Government policies
   Fiscal and monetary policy
   Taxation system
   Trade policies
   Industrial development policies
   Regulatory policies
   Social and ecological policies
2. Technical Factors—Internal (within country)
   Technical capability
   Access to capital
   Technical advances for:
   Product design
   Process design
   Computer information systems
3. Cultures, Philosophy, and Customs—External and Worldwide Environment
   Socioeconomic environment
   Races, languages, cultures
   Religions, values
   Work ethic

       Educational systems and values
       Health of people
       Economic and legal systems
       Support for technical advance
       Concept of companies and management

4. Cultures, Philosophy, and Customs—Internal (within country)
       Management philosophy
       Concept and culture of the company
       Organization structure
       Human resources management
       Attitude toward change
       Competitive strategy
       Targeting of markets
       Method of manufacturing improvement

This model highlights the importance of the global strategy orientation. It also introduces the idea of a company culture that consists of the philosophy, values, aspirations, and beliefs the company has about itself and its people. This component is what differentiates it from the strategy of other firms in the industry.

The Burnham Model

Another model for World Class Management strategies, demonstrated by Burnham, breaks strategic planning into two areas:[2]

1. External Factors
       Competition
       Economic conditions
       Technology level
       Change in technology
       Government regulation
       Substitutions
       Product life cycle

2. Internal Factors
       Market share
       Profitability

Resources
Logistics management
Manufacturing

The Adler, McDonald, McDonald Model

A third model can be found in the publications of Adler, McDonald, and McDonald.[3] It suggests focusing on the following strategic areas:

1. Strategic Policies
    Personnel: recruitment, development, evaluation, and rewards
    Technical projects: selection, termination, and project management
    Quality assurance
    Intellectual properties
    Funding
    Facilities and equipment
    Structure: functional organization, authority
    Interfunctional linkages
    External linkages
    Regulatory compliance
2. Adjustment Processes
    Strengths and weaknesses
    Opportunities and threats

The Mojonnier Model

A fourth model for corporate strategy is the following:[4]

Customer and Markets

Technology and Its Characteristics

Performance Review Systems

Compensation Systems

Organizational Structure

Competition

Personnel Policies

Financial Position

Macro and Micro Economic Variables

Information Systems

The Porter Model

A fifth model for the development of a corporate strategy, formulated by Michael Porter, focuses on capitalizing on the competitive advantage (core competency) of an enterprise.[5] This model discusses the strategy of diversification and the need for each business unit to define its role (strategy) and fit it into the corporate strategy.

Corporate strategy is what makes the corporate whole add up to more than the sum of its business unit parts.

Michael E. Porter

World Class Strategy Model

If I were to suggest a model for a World Class corporate or business-unit strategic plan, I would suggest the following focus areas, all of which should have goals that point at the mission statement (or higher-level strategic plan) as their target. This plan probably includes more than any single business unit needs, but the idea is to pick and choose those areas for which it is important that your enterprise have a defined strategy. My plan would include the following strategic areas:

1. People
    First Employees
        Education and training
        Empowerment
        Teamwork
        Organizational structure, staff functions

> Then Customers
>> Involvement
> Then Vendors
>> Integration

2. Integration
   Elimination of barriers
   Information
3. Globalization
4. Measurement
   Internal performance
      Quality, productivity, efficiency
   External performance
      Are you adding value to society?
      Customer-perceived quality
      Market share
   Internal factors
      Capacity
      Equipment
      Operational performance
   External factors
      Competition
      Economic conditions
      Government regulation
   Focused
   Motivational
5. Continuous Change Process Focused on Adding Value
   Elimination of waste
   Identifying strengths and weaknesses
   Identifying opportunities and threats
6. Time-Based Competition
   Time-to-market strategy
7. Technology
   Funding
   Facilities and equipment

People   We need a strategy that identifies, incorporates, and empowers people, especially the employees of the business unit.

Chapter 2 discusses this topic in depth. Next, we need a strategy that relates to customers. Customer satisfaction is the second most important avenue to success. The third area of people to incorporate into our strategy is that of the suppliers. Their involvement and integration will help them make better products for us and will give us valuable insights into how to make our product better.

Integration   We need to drop internal and external barriers. These barriers include job titles, departments, and information barriers. Integration needs to exist in the following areas:

- Physical—Mix the different staff functions together in the same room.
- Informational—Don't have separate data bases for different departments; information also needs to flow easily from top to bottom and from bottom to top.
- Process—Your output (information or product, whatever it is you produce) needs to be passed from area to area, not thrown "over the wall" to one another organizationally; keep the employee designations and titles vague; treat everyone as an equal.

Chapter 8 focuses on integration issues.

Globalization   We are part of a big world that is affected by international transactions. We need to be aware of how these transactions affect us. Chapter 6 spends time discussing this process.

Measurement   Defining a measurement/motivational system is at the root of developing a strategic plan. We need to be able to demonstrate, over a defined period of time, that we are able to do our part in achieving the mission of the organization.

Continuous Change Process Focused on Adding Value
We need to add value to ourselves, our organization, and society as a whole. Our strategic plan should motivate us toward adding

value, which also involves the identification and elimination of waste.

Time-Based Competition   Time, like change, can be either our enemy or our friend. Presently, for most U.S. firms, time is an enemy because time-to-market performance is so poor. We are enormously effective at developing technology, but we are terrible at implementing it. For example, who developed the air bag (the United States), and who was first in installing it in their cars (Japan and Europe)?

Technology   Technology is often the most effective tool for positive change. We need to develop a strategy that defines our organization and that focuses on long-term technological improvements, as opposed to short-term "patch-it-up and keep-it-running" technologies.

Whatever strategy model you decide to adopt, the following rules apply:

1. No one should be left without a goal (strategy). Everyone from janitor to CEO should have a goal. For example, Walt Disney Company orients all employees into the big corporate picture and teaches them how they fit in, even if they are only a temporary, six-week employee.

2. Strategies should have short-term (less than one year), mid-term (one to five years), and long-term (more than ten years) targets. Each strategic area needs a one-year and a twenty-year target to focus on.

3. The best strategy model to fit your enterprise does not yet exist. You'll have to develop it yourself. You can use the ideas from the example models in this section, but you need to develop your own model.

4. Contingencies need to be established. A strategy is only as good as external influences (changes) allow it to be. Contingent strategies are strategies that help you plan for external changes without giving up the focus of our goals. A contingency is an alternative route to reach your destination. The more thought

that is put into contingency strategies (the more you plan for potential problems), the more likely it is that you will achieve your goal.

> A philosopher was asked, "What do you do when you reach a fork in the road?"
> He answered very simply, "Take it."

At this point, you should have a good feel for the types of areas and goals that your strategy should include. In the next section of this chapter, we discuss one of the most difficult strategies of all—difficult primarily because of its complexity. This is the manufacturing strategy, which we will use as an example of a functional business-unit strategy.

THE MANUFACTURING STRATEGY

[The great society] is a place where men are more concerned with the quality of their goals than with the quantity of their goods.

Lyndon B. Johnson

Now it's time to combine all we've learned about World Class strategy. It should:

- Be developed at multiple levels, involving both corporate strategy and business-unit strategy
- Focus on the mission statement or higher-level business strategy
- Identify areas of competitiveness within each of the functional strategic areas of your selected strategic model
- Focus on the competitive trends and priorities listed at the start of this chapter

- Integrate the key competitive principles for strategy development listed early in this chapter
- Contain quantifiable, time-stamped goals that exhibit the characteristics of goals discussed in Chapter 3

Perhaps one of the easiest ways to explain strategies is by using an example. Referring to Figure 4.2, I will discuss what elements should be present in the manufacturing strategy for business unit B. A manufacturing strategy is designed to support the business-unit strategy. It needs to complement the other functional strategies. The major areas of a manufacturing strategy (goals) include (expanding on my model):

1. People
     Employees
          Selection and training
          Involvement/empowerment
          Compensation
          Job security
          Team development
          Organizational structure, staff functions
     Customers
          Involvement
          Internal to the organization
          The final end user
     Vendors
          Integration
          Extent, number, relationships
2. Integration
     Vertical integration—direction
     Elimination of barriers
     Information
3. Globalization
4. Measurement
     Internal performance
     Quality
          Definition, role, responsibility

      Productivity, efficiency
      Capital budgeting process
   External performance
      Are you adding value to society?
      Customer-perceived quality
      Market share
   Internal factors
      Capacity—amount, timing, type
      Equipment and process technologies
         Scale and level of automation
         Flexibility versus specialization
      Facilities—size and location
         Specialization
      Operational performance
         Production control
            Flow, inventory levels
            Scheduling
   External factors
      Competition
      Economic conditions
      Government regulation
   Focused
   Motivational

5. Continuous Change Process Focused on Adding Value
   Elimination of waste
   Identifying strengths and weaknesses
   Identifying opportunities and threats

6. Time-Based Competition
   Time-to-market strategy

7. Technology
   Funding
   Facilities and equipment
   New product development
      Interface with engineering, marketing, and
        the customer

> *The measure of success is not whether you have a tough problem to deal with, but whether it's the same problem you had last year.*
>
> John Foster Dulles

A manufacturing strategy would have short-, medium-, and long-range goals in each of the major categories in our model, focusing on the business-unit strategy and the corporate strategy and identifying each issue in the above list.

Hayes and Wheelwright developed a model based on what they call the four stages of manufacturing's strategic-effectiveness role.[6] Manufacturing's role should be to move from Stage 1 to Stage 4, at which stage it is making a significant, value-added difference. The stages are described as follows:

- Stage 1—Internally Neutral
  The role of a manufacturing strategy is to minimize the negative impact that manufacturing has on the overall organization. Manufacturing is a necessary evil.
- Stage 2—Externally Neutral
  Here the strategic role of manufacturing is to achieve a parity with its competitors. U.S. manufacturing falls primarily into this category. Manufacturing is strategically competitive as long as the competition plays the same game.
- Stage 3—Internally Supportive
  In this stage, manufacturing needs to provide a credible supportive role to the overall business strategy. This role should focus on continuous positive change and overall goal contribution.
- Stage 4—Externally Supportive
  In this role, manufacturing has become a significant contributor to the overall corporate competitive advantage. Manufacturing is a major innovator.

At Stage 4, in-house process-development capabilities exist that enable manufacturing to do things that competitors can't do. Internal innovation for modifications and adaptations is motivated. Continuous improvement programs are operational and are effective. Integration of the functions at low levels leads to short product-introduction cycles. External benchmarks ensure that manufacturing performance is ahead of the competition. You find out who is the best, learn from them, and then use the innovativeness of your internal work force to accelerate past the competition.

Stage 4 fully utilizes all its manufacturing resources. At this stage, manufacturing knows what its critical resource is and motivates plant operations to effectively utilize this critical resource.[7] Manufacturing is integrated with the other functions of the company to the point that they see one another as peers; no one function is king. Manufacturing has moved from being a fire fighter to being a strategic planner.

The largest gap exists between Stage 3 and Stage 4. Achieving Stage 4 means that you need to continuously focus on creative change processes. Companies like Apple Computer have been known to achieve Stage 4 status and then, through a lack of innovative manufacturing, fall back to a Stage 2 position.

Within the stages of strategic effectiveness, Wheelwright and Hayes list the major types of manufacturing choices. These are the areas in which World Class strategies should be developed:

- Capacity—amount, timing, and type
- Facilities—size, location, and specialization
- Equipment and Process Technologies—scale, flexibility, and interconnectedness
- Vertical Integration—direction, extent, and balance
- Vendors—number, structure, and relationship
- New Products—hand-off, start-up, and modification
- Human Resources—selection and training, compensation, and security
- Quality—definition, role, and responsibility
- Systems—organization, schedules, and control

Numerous excellent articles and books contain valuable information on manufacturing strategy development. For example, Walters discusses the integration of engineering, Computer Integrated Manufacturing (CIM), and automated manufacturing technology into the strategy, with the focus on change.[8] Burton stresses globalization, global competition, and the development of strategic alliances as the first strategic priority.[9] Landvater, Souza, and Wallace focus on the importance of a strategic measurement tool.[10] Gregoire and Delaney stress the development of good strategy as the key to competitive and World Class success and the need for future vision in the strategy.[11] One of the classics in manufacturing strategy is Wickham Skinner's article, focusing on developing a competitive advantage by task and thereby focusing the factory. He stresses the following points, among others:

1. There are many ways to compete besides producing at low cost.
2. A factory cannot perform well on every yardstick.
3. Simplicity and repetition breed competence.[12]

Many other books contain information on manufacturing strategy development.[13]

Additional valuable information that can assist in the development of a manufacturing strategy is available from the many national and international quality awards programs that exist. These include the Baldrige (U.S. national quality award), the Shingo Prize (U.S. award for manufacturing excellence), the NASA (U.S. award for government contractor manufacturing excellence), and the Deming Award (Japan's national quality award). You need not apply for these awards to be World Class. However, you need to be a contender. By examining the award criteria, you can improve your strategies for change. These award criteria highlight the areas of World Class manufacturing excellence.[14]

The manufacturing strategy example outlined above should help you with ideas for the development of your own corporate or business-unit strategy. No model is perfect, but the manufacturing example is a good case study. Every business area has criteria for excellence available to it, including awards programs that assist in defining World Class status.

Another complex area that offers enormous opportunities for World Class changes is the logistics.[15] The area of customer service and support also tends to need an overhaul. Whatever area you are in, innovation and competitive change are sure to be needed. So move forward and take on the challenge of turning your business unit into a Stage 4 World Class enterprise.

STRATEGIC EFFECTIVENESS

. . . seek ye earnestly the best gifts, . . .

Doctrine and Covenants 46:8

When I think of strategy development, I think of the following saying (one of my favorites):

> If you're not green and growing,
> you're ripe and rotting.

Many organizations seem to be rotting rather than growing. You hear comments like "they've always done it this way" or "they don't see any need for change." They're ripe and rotting. When you are looking for improvement, you always need to be "green and growing"—never thinking you have it all figured out, always looking for a better way or a new idea.

The Saturn automobile manufacturing facility in Spring Hill, Tennessee, is one of the premier models of effectively developed and implemented strategies at both the corporate level and the business-unit level. The goal of this facility is to build a World Class car, which includes all aspects of the product: sales, service, the entertainment value of the car, the shipping and delivery of the vehicle to the customer, problem correction, and employee empowerment. The key elements of Saturn's strategy are:

1. The importance of people. Employees are salaried and involved. Five percent of an employee's time is spent in training.

2. Commitment to customer satisfaction. They'll travel around the world to fix a problem. They offer no discounting because their customers told them they want the best price the first time, not after extensive negotiations. Additionally, customers don't want to be "hassled" when they walk into a car dealership, so Saturn has "no hassle" dealerships.

3. A redefinition of the "product" to include the people, the vehicle, and the way people are treated.

4. An emphasis on building brand equity. Their vehicles have the highest residual value, even higher than the Lexus and the Mercedes.

5. A reliance on partnerships, on people working together. This is true within and outside the organization. In meetings, they pride themselves on not knowing who's who in terms of job titles and levels within the company.

Saturn focuses on problem acceptance, which means identifying the problem, accepting responsibility for it rather than trying to blame someone else, and fixing the problem correctly the first time.

Esso Japan has taken a jump ahead in its strategy development. Company managers have developed a strategy that focuses on a goal beyond "commitment to excellence" (CTE). Feeling that they needed a program that took the next step, they developed a strategy that focuses on:

Creativity and response to changes

Vision and participation

Entrepreneurship and dynamics

The new strategy program they developed was labeled "power to succeed" (PTS). A diagram similar to the one in Figure 4.3 is used to chart their utilization of power circles to develop, grow, and

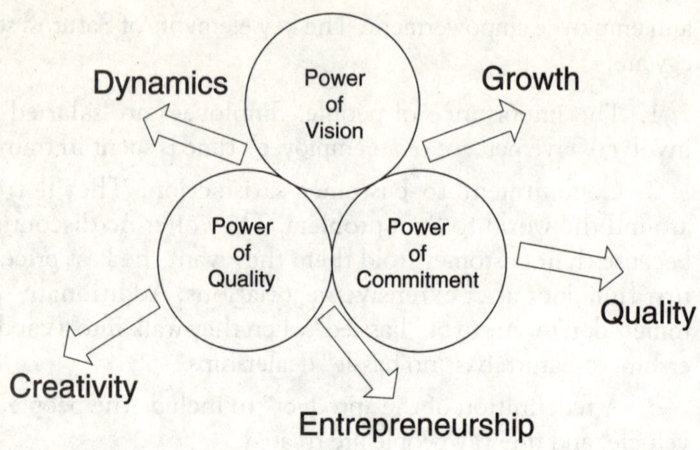

Figure 4.3   Esso Japan PTS Program

explode beyond these into PTS. The new challenges they have integrated into their strategies include:

Swift technological changes

"Smart" machines

Low-cost factory operations

Value-added performance

Developing easier new market entries

Generating stiffer competition

They feel that the keys to meeting these challenges are the innovation and entrepreneurship abilities of their employees. They focus on empowerment based on a shared vision with a minimum amount of bureaucracy. They believe that people need to grow in order for the organization to grow. They focus their strategy on teams, utilizing a Total Quality Management (TQM—see Chapter 11) process to move employees from a status of "work" to a status of "create." They want employees to be able to "think again."

The Saturn and Esso examples are two examples of World Class enterprise strategy development. By benchmarking (comparing and analyzing) how far these organizations have already come, we can see how far we still have to go in order to become World Class competitors ourselves.

STRATEGY IMPLEMENTATION

. . . press toward the mark for the prize.
Philippians 3:14

Strategy implementation focuses on the same considerations that goal implementation focuses on (see Chapter 3):

1. Goal participation and ownership
2. Employee preparation and training
3. The corporate value system

Some additional concerns of strategy implementation are:

4. Integration
5. Measurement/motivation
6. Innovation

The strategy should not lose sight of the need for integration. The separate business strategies should not create barriers; rather they should focus on barrier removal.

People are important to strategy implementation. The strategy gets closer to the people than do the vision and mission statements. Therefore, the measurement and motivation process is also more important.

Strategy is the level at which innovation and change occur the most. Innovation and change need to be driven by the appropriate tools and motivations. Refer to the books by Nadler and Hibino mentioned in earlier chapters to open your mind to innovative thinking.

Additionally, some key situational variables need to be considered in strategy implementation:

- The amount and type of resistance
- The trust and power levels of the initiators and resistors of the plan
- The availability of the resources necessary for implementation (data, energy, etc.)
- The stakes involved[16]

While planning for implementation of the strategy, all players need to be involved in its design and committed to its success, just as they were in the development of the strategy. Otherwise, they will be passive as to the results. Without commitment, a power struggle may develop and soon territorialism may arise. When this happens, strategy implementation turns into a contest of wills. Involvement needs to build into commitment, and commitment builds success. This reminds me of the remark about a bacon and eggs breakfast: the chicken is involved in the breakfast, but the pig is committed to it. We need commitment in both the goal-setting process and its implementation, not just commitment—and definitely not resistance.

STRATEGY SUMMARY

. . . it is expedient that he should be diligent, that thereby he might win the prize.

Mosiah 4:27, *Book of Mormon*

Strategy development is the critical fourth step in the development of goals in an enterprise, the first three being defining the core competencies, the vision, and the mission. The strategy gets closer to the employees and is more detailed, identifying specific targets for each business unit. The strategy thus is the key measurement and motivation tool for each business unit.[17] With strategies, we have a tool to handle internally generated changes. With contingencies built into the strategy, we have the capability to defeat imposed (externally generated) changes.

At this point, the World Class Manager should have defined competitive targets for growth, both personally and as part of a corporate entity. In Chapter 1, we discussed where we are now. In Chapters 3 and 4, we have established the target we want to reach. Now we need to detail the road map to direct us on our journey. Part II focuses on the key competitive strategic areas on which a World Class Manager should focus (not forgetting the most important, discussed in Chapter 2). Part III focuses on the World Class Management tools that need to be used within the enterprise setting. Let's move forward, fleshing out the areas that make a manager World Class.

That's one small step for a man, one great leap for mankind.

Neil Armstrong, first words spoken on the moon

SOLUTION TO FIGURE 4.1 PROBLEM

The solution to the problem posed in Figure 4.1 is easier than you think. The trick is to realize that the line *BD* is the same length as the line *AC*, because both are diagonals in a rectangle (see Figure 4.4). Next we see that line *AC* is the same length as line *AE*, since both are a radius to the circle. Therefore:

$$BD = AC = AE = 10 \text{ inches}$$

Now that you know the strategy (the trick), you should have no difficulty solving for line *BD* in Figure 4.5, given that line *AE* is 20 inches. (*BD* is 20 inches, of course.)

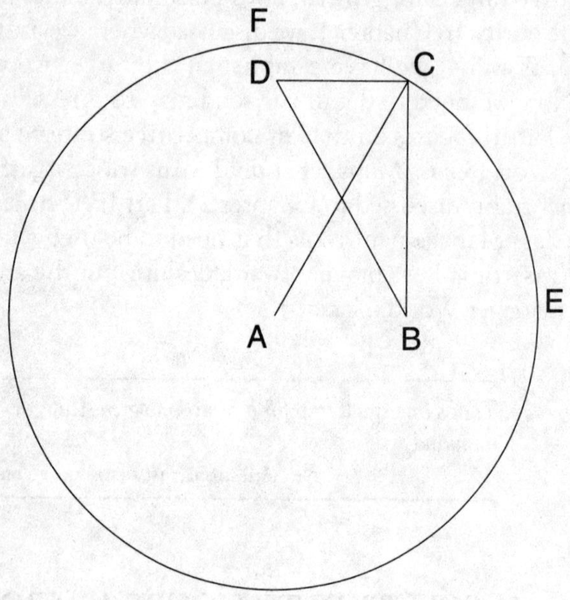

Figure 4.4　Length of the Line *BD*

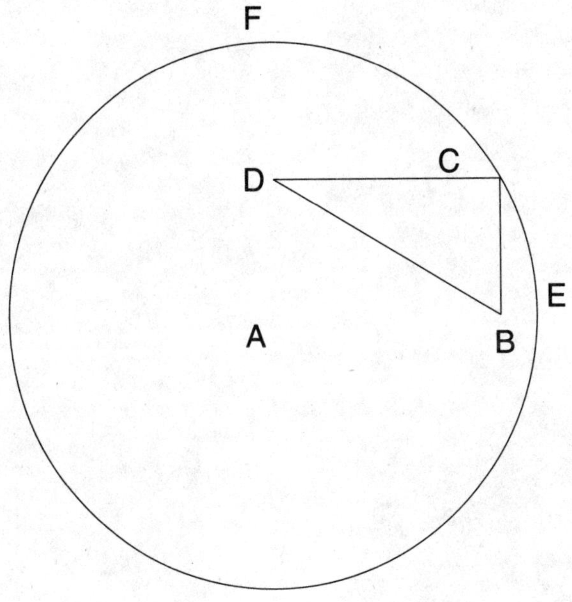

Figure 4.5   The New Length of Line *BD*

PART TWO

World Class Strategies

CHAPTER 5

Quality or Productivity— Which Strategy Is Best?

If you have a job without aggravations, you don't have a job.

Malcolm Forbes

What performance strategy is the best? Some claim productivity, others quality, but most organizations still evaluate performance based on efficiency or cost. We will look at and compare all these strategies. But first let's consider the man whose house was next to a river. The river started to flood. A truck came by to pick him up, and the man refused the ride and said, "Faith will save me." As the water worked its way up to the level of the windows, a boat came by to pick up the man and again, refusing the ride, he said, "Faith will save me." Eventually the water reached the level of the roof. As the man sat on the roof, a helicopter came by and offered him a ride. And guess what? He refused the ride, saying "Faith will save me." The man eventually drowned. As he met Peter at the pearly gates, he asked him, "Why didn't I get saved? I had faith."

Peter responded, "I sent you a truck, a boat, and a helicopter, but you wouldn't take any of them!"

Performance strategies require a lot of faith. Most managers think that if you "believe" in quality or productivity strongly enough, you'll eventually "be saved." You believe in them because they are right, and eventually right has to win out over evil. Well, the true believer learns that religion and faith in God are a lot more than just believing. They require a lot of work, too. If you don't act on your faith, your faith is worthless.

Even so faith, if it hath not works, is dead, being alone.

James 2:17

When we look at the performance evaluators quality, productivity, cost, and efficiency and try to implement them into our strategy, we need to do more than just hang plaques on the wall. We need to understand them, define them, and then implement them through goals, strategies, and measures. Let's start by defining and exploring each of them.

QUALITY

Quality is a funny concept. For some organizations, quality means a plaque on the wall that quotes some clever slogan. For other organizations, quality means a sticker on the bag you give your drive-through customers that says that their order has been double-checked. In reality, nothing has changed internally for either of these types of organization. Both work to the same level of quality as they did before the plaque or the sticker. And you still have to do your own double-check of the double-checked drive-through order, because invariably one out of two orders will be wrong. The sticker didn't seem to motivate any change in the behavior of the employees. Why should it? No one ever asked the customer how the employees were performing. The measure of quality performance seems to be determined by the number of stickers that are used up and has nothing to do with the customer.

> The best quality manager is
> no quality manager.

Don't get the idea that I'm anti-quality! I am opposed to some defined individual being responsible for quality. Everyone in the enterprise should be responsible for quality. The role of quality managers should be to work themselves out of a job. The World Class Quality Manager should develop such a corporate fever and quality-consciousness that everyone becomes a quality manager. Unfortunately, most quality managers see their role as one of "trying to keep their job and get a raise," and therefore their intentions are somewhat suspect. Before we fire the quality manager, let's define what quality really is.

You never get promoted when no one else knows your current job. The best basis for being advanced is to organize yourself out of every job you're put into. Most people are advanced because they're pushed up by the people underneath them rather than pulled up by the top.

Donald David, former dean, Harvard Business School

The traditional definition of quality in most parts of the world is the following:

A quality product is one that meets internal specifications.

If you're a manufacturer, quality means that the end product meets engineering specifications. If you're a service organization, quality means that you're doing the job the way the boss wants it done. That expectation of what the output should be becomes your quality "standard," and you proceed to set up elaborate measurement and nontrust systems to make sure you achieve your internal measure of quality. Under these conditions, quality is measured by using measures similar to the number of rejects coming from the "internal" quality department.

World Class quality is quite different. World Class quality is customer excitement. A definition would be:

Quality is when your customers are so thrilled with your product that they would go out of their way to get your product from you.

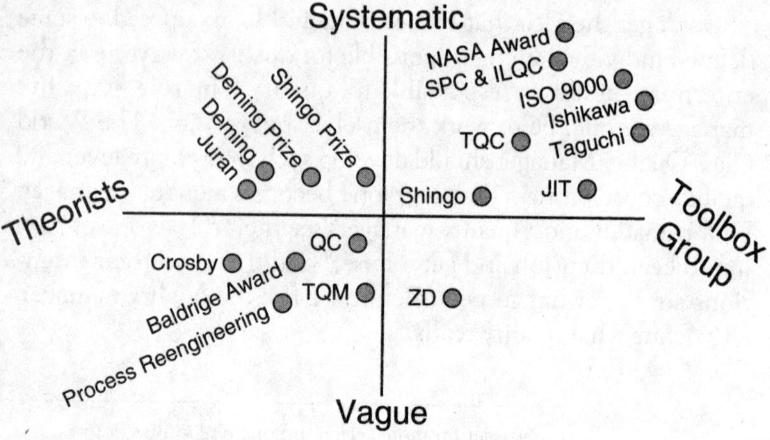

Figure 5.1   Quality Definition Line

How do you measure quality under this definition? You ask your customers, and your competitors' customers, what they think of your product. Once you have defined what is important to your customers, that becomes your "customer expectation standard." You then measure your performance against this standard. For example, if quick response is important, you measure response time. It is the conformance to this standard that allows, for example, the Saturn to be of equal quality in many customers' eyes, as the Lexus or the Mercedes (see Chapter 4).

To measure quality performance against "standard," numerous gurus and systems have established their mark in quality literature. Figure 5.1 is a quality definition line that shows how several of the gurus and systems stack up against one another. The figure plots the systematic against the vague and the theoretical against the "tool box" approach to quality for the following:

Quality Gurus:
    Deming
    Juran
    Crosby

    Ishikawa
    Taguchi
    Shingo
Quality Systems:
    Total Quality Control (TQC)
    Just-in-Time Production (JIT)
    ISO 9000
    SPC
    ILQC
    QC
    ZD
Change Systems:
    Total Quality Management (TQM)
    Process Reengineering
Quality Awards:
    Baldrige Award (U.S. government)
    Deming Prize (Japan)
    Shingo Prize (U.S. manufacturing)
    NASA Award (U.S. government)

Appendix 5.1 offers some insights into the focus of each of these quality gurus. The quality systems and change systems options are discussed below. The quality awards were discussed in Chapter 4.

Does it seem reasonable for the United States government to be the issuer of a quality award, when they, with their characteristic rudeness and unresponsiveness, are the epitome of non-quality? Wouldn't we prefer that our congratulations come from someone who knows something about, or can at least spell, quality?

Gerhard Plenert

Quality Levels

Quality, in the narrow sense ("C"-level quality), is what you as an enterprise feel your product should be. In a slightly broader sense ("B"-level quality), quality is what your customers feel your product should be. And, in the broadest sense, quality is what society as a whole feels your product should be ("A"-level quality).

Quality is added value. In the narrow sense, quality is adding value to (eliminating waste from) the internal organization. A quality product is one that fits as closely to specifications as possible, generating as little waste as possible during the process (i.e., making as few mistakes as possible in the creation of the output).

Similarly, in a "B" sense, quality is maximizing the value added to the customer. This level of quality means your customers go out of their way to buy your product because they feel confident that you will maximize the value added for them.

In the broadest sense, "A"-level quality includes "C"-level quality (internal value added) and "B"-level quality (customer-added value). In addition, "A"-level quality incorporates issues such as environmental consciousness, developing the infrastructure (schools and roadways), and utilizing home-country employees and vendors as much as possible. "A"-level quality is especially important internationally, where the acceptance of your business into the community can be critically important (see Chapter 6).

Unfortunately, there is also a "D" level of quality, which a large number (probably the majority) of companies utilize. At this level, companies have no quality program, no quality goals, and no quality measures at all.

The Cost of Quality

Is there a cost of quality? Definitely! Quality exacts a cost in terms of time, commitment, risk, dollars, and control.

- Time—Quality systems take years, not weeks or months, to implement. In addition, quality systems take the time of numerous personnel who are committed to being educated and to making a quality difference.
- Commitment—Quality systems require the commitment, not just the involvement (remember the bacon and eggs

breakfast!), of top management, or else no one will take the quality change process seriously.

- Risk—A quality change is risky. All change requires risk. As in the Florida Power and Light story, implementing change may cost you your job.
- Dollars—As demonstrated in Figure 2.1, there is a very definite short-term cost involved in any change program. A quality program requires training and the time of employees, both of which carry a price tag. The benefit of the quality change process is long term, and, just as in Figure 2.1, in the long term the benefits will far outweigh the initial costs.
- Control—A World Class Quality Management system results in the loss of control. A manager who enjoys power will rebel at the need to empower the employees. The management role is changed into one of facilitator rather than one of traffic cop. The employees are the creators of quality improvements.

Quality Systems and Change Systems

The amount and variety of quality systems that exist are absolutely astounding. What generally happens is that we copy some little piece of a much larger quality system (usually from the Japanese), give it an Americanized name, try it out for about six months to a year, decide that it doesn't bring about a sufficient amount of improvement in that short length of time, throw out the system, and start the cycle all over again, searching for some little piece to copy. We have a black-and-white approach to these quality processes. Either they prove themselves in the short run, or they're no good. We don't even seem to consider the possibility that these systems might be building blocks that need to be used together, rather than as isolated entities. We will discuss a collection of these systems, most of which originated in Japan and most of which have been dropped by the United States but are still alive and well in Japan.

One of the prime copycat processes that we are trying to imitate is the Japanese JIT production process. More factories have thrown out this process than have implemented it in the United States. Rarely will a company give the system more than two years to prove itself. However, Toyota will readily state that it took them thirty years to fully implement the JIT process. Why do we think we can do it in two years?

Another example of short-sighted quality implementation is the Florida Power and Light example discussed in Chapter 3. Again, they were plagued by the short-sighted hurry-up bug, believing that "faith would save them."

For purposes of definition, we list some of the more popular quality and change systems that have come and gone (some linger on):

- Quality Circles (QC)—These management teams focus on quality improvements. The team concept has come and gone in a variety of forms. Lately we've been calling it empowerment. Chapter 14 discusses teaming in detail.
- In-Line Quality Control (ILQC)—This system utilizes the Japanese concept of having everyone trained in quality so that all employees understand and can inspect the quality of the products they are receiving and also of those they are sending out. This usually encompasses some of Deming's statistical processes for quality monitoring.
- Zero Defects (ZD)—This system focuses on error elimination by catching the problem as it occurs and then continuously improving the process so that the error will not occur again.
- Statistical Process Control (SPC)—This system uses statistical sampling and control charts to monitor the process so that corrective action can be taken immediately when (or even before) the error occurs.
- Total Quality Control (TQC)—This system involves the control of quality in all aspects of the organization, using a variety of systems tools and statistical control tools.
- Just-in-Time (JIT)—JIT is the Toyota production philosophy that focuses on materials efficiency and waste elimination in the production process.

- Total Quality Management (TQM)—This system moves the quality process out of the realm of "controlling" (baby-sitting) quality and into the realm of "managing" (motivating) quality. TQM is discussed in detail in Chapter 11.*
- Process Reengineering (PR)—PR is a change system that promotes "rapid, radical change" throughout the organization. This change model is also discussed in detail in Chapter 11.
- ISO 9000—ISO is a certification process initiated by the European Community. It requires anyone who wishes to bring product into Europe to be certified. ISO 9000 is a procedurization of the quality process. It documents that what you say you are going to produce is what you produce. It is not customer-oriented but rather procedure-oriented. Some of the more progressive (in terms of quality) organizations have seen it as a bureaucratic step backward. Other, not so leading edge, companies see it as a positive step that formalizes their quality process.[1]
- Quality Functional Deployment (QFD); sometimes referred to as Quality Systems Deployment (QSD). This is the buzzword that has been given to the organized Japanese way of implementing a goal-directed quality change process. More is said about this change tool in Chapter 11.

Quality buzzwords are floating around by the dozens. If you don't see your favorite in this list, check the glossary at the end of the book.

Quality systems are building blocks and should be treated as such. They are not isolated entities. An enterprise should

---

*Change systems and quality systems have become confused and mixed together. Change systems such as TQM and PR are also included in the grouping of quality systems in an attempt to focus on quality improvements or quality changes. However, change systems change more than just quality, as discussed in Chapter 11. I have included TQM and PR here because they are important tools in improving quality.

custom-design a quality system for its use, utilizing the systems listed above along with other tools such as systems analysis and process documentation.

The Role of the Manager in Quality

Quality is not the function of a department; it is the function of the company. As long as we consider quality to be someone else's job (e.g., a quality manager), we will never become involved in it ourselves. However, being World Class in today's competitive market requires that we be totally involved in quality. This means involvement on the part of every department, every employee, and every job function. *You have to want to be involved* in quality before a quality program will work. Involvement requires time— time spent in training, time spent in teams and in meetings discussing quality improvements, and time spent sharing and coordinating the quality effort.

Two types of customers must be dealt with: the internal customer and the external customer. Internal customer quality is employee-conscious, empowered, and participative quality. The employee is the internal customer of the company and should be treated as such. This means that you as a manager need to think of fellow employees as your customers in that you pass on information and product to them. The quality of what you pass on to them needs to be a quality product, and you should expect to receive a quality product from those who pass on information and product to you.

External customer quality is customer-participative quality, as described earlier. End-user customers are consulted to find out how they perceive quality, and we then satisfy their perceptions with our performance.

Is quality a good measure of strategy performance? Definitely, especially when it's tied internally to the employee and externally to the customer. Several quality organizations exist that would be delighted to help you prepare your quality initiative. There is a listing of them in Appendix 5.2.

The Measure of Quality

Defining what quality is for you and for your customer is the first step in the development of a quality measure. Are you focusing on "A"-level, "B"-level, or "C"-level quality? Next you need to devise ways to measure quality based on your definition. Some examples of quality measures will help you see how some "A"- and "B"-level companies have approached the issue.

Canadian National measures the following quality items in the service sector:

On-time delivery, punctuality

Competitive prices

No damaged goods

Right container equipment available

Correct billing

Good communication

FedEx measures the following items and attaches the corresponding weights to them. The weights, which are determined by customer service based on "what is important to the customer," are part of the FedEx Service Quality Indicators (SQI). The items measured are:

Lost packages (10 points)

Damaged packages (10 points)

Delivery on the wrong day (5 points)

Tracing required (3 points)

Late pickup (3 points)

Complaints reopened (3 points)

Delivery late on the right day (1 point)

Invoice adjustment requested (1 point)

Missing proof of delivery information (1 point)

In the FedEx system, the customer is often unaware of a failure. Some things may be troublesome to one customer but not of concern to another. But because FedEx has stated that its quality goal is 100% customer satisfaction, it has established a standard that strives to satisfy all customers.

United Parcel Service (UPS) is looking for financial returns in terms of increased sales. It is trying to accomplish this by giving its drivers free time to "talk to the customer." It believes that the customer wants interaction and that this "hand-holding" aspect of customer service will develop sales leads.

World Class Quality

In moving from the role of general manager to World Class Quality Manager, we need to address several issues:

1. We need to establish a *quality culture* where all of management, from top management to the clean-up crew, is trained in how to recognize and improve quality. Management needs to have quality goals established, and these quality goals need to focus on the business strategy. The work force needs to think, feel, eat, sleep, and breathe quality. Employees need to be motivated to be on constant lookout for quality improvements. They need to be excited about opportunities to make a quality difference in the organization.

2. Quality needs *direction*. It needs to be part of a strategic plan that focuses on a specific objective.

3. Quality is not short term; it requires a *long-term commitment*.

4. Funding and staffing need to be available to do the necessary *training*. (Remember the learning curve of Figure 2.1.)

5. The workers, not the managers, produce quality. *Empowerment* of the employees, allowing them to improve quality and rewarding them by giving them the benefits of the improvements (recognition, financial rewards), is the only way to motivate quality change. For example, Jan Carlzon, when he took over Scandinavian Airline System (SAS), gave the frontline employees the freedom and authority to do whatever it takes to improve quality service. He kept them informed, opened up communication lines, and gave them direction.

World Class Management requires a strong focus on quality, both internal and external to the organization. Quality is customer satisfaction, and customer satisfaction is World Class.[2]

PRODUCTIVITY

During an age when Christianity dominated Rome, a devastating plague was destroying the population of the city. St. Augustine testified to the population that the only way to end the plague was to close all theaters, because they displeased the Lord. The theaters were closed, but the plague continued. Faith in the wrong messenger caused useless effort to be placed in the wrong area. Similarly, faith in the wrong types of productivity can cause us to expend a tremendous amount of effort trying to correct a symptom while at the same time totally ignoring the real problem. Let's take a closer look.

What is productivity? It is defined as follows:

$$\text{Productivity} = \frac{\text{Output}}{\text{Input}}$$

The output part of the equation is easy to define. It's net sales (gross sales adjusted by returns). The input part of the equation, however, can be confusing. For example, the United States uses labor productivity as its measure of productivity performance in comparing itself with other countries, and the United States is by far the best in the world based on this measure. We generate more output per productive labor hour than any other work force in the world. Just look at our agriculture output. Less than 3% of the U.S. labor force, which is about one-tenth of one percent (00.1%) of the world's population, generates about 25% of the world's agricultural output. The United States is similarly impressive in technology development, but here meaningful numbers are much harder to come by. So why, if our productivity is so impressive, do we have an ever-increasing deficit? Simply because we are measuring the wrong type of productivity. We are putting our faith in closing theaters.

The United States, although best at labor productivity, is rapidly losing ground. It is best in absolute productivity terms, but is near the bottom in terms of labor productivity trend (year-to-year improvements in labor productivity). The trend race is currently being won by Singapore, with several other countries, primarily Asian, falling close behind.

Alternative types of productivity calculations exist, and they should be considered. For example:

1. *Labor Dollar Productivity*—Labor dollars rather than labor hours are used as the input number; this model adjusts for our high cost of labor and brings the productivity numbers down slightly. However, when compared to some countries where the exchange rate with the United States is disfavorable we can still look artificially good. For example, in Germany we find the labor wage rate is $US 25 per hour (and getting worse) compared with the United States average of $US 17, which makes the United States look better than it should.

2. *Total Factor Productivity*—which is never measured on a level basis, only on a trend (change) basis, includes the costs of all input factors, such as materials, energy, equipment, and so on, in the productivity calculation. This model is discounted in the United States because of the claim that materials and energy cost the same for everyone and wouldn't significantly affect the calculation. However, in a global economy, this assumption is not valid. Globally, material costs and energy costs can vary dramatically. For example, Japan does not have the desired natural resources and has to import both the materials and energy generating resources. Total Factor Productivity, although considered an effective measure by some countries, is not sufficiently understood to be used globally.

3. *Value-Added Productivity*—The input is the difference between the purchased materials cost and the sold materials cost divided by labor. The best way to describe this process is to use an example. Suppose we are building a radio, and in the radio we have a tuner and a power supply. Both components cost $10 in

raw materials, but the tuner can be sold on the open market for $15 and the power supply can be sold for $20. We earn $10 for every power supply and only $5 for every tuner. Value-added productivity would suggest that we have someone else produce the tuner and build the power supply ourselves, thereby maximizing the value-added productivity. The value-added productivity model is a favorite with several foreign firms (primarily Asian).

4. *Change Productivity*—Measures the change (as opposed to absolute number values) in output over the change in input. Total Factor Productivity, and most productivity measures, should be treated as Change Productivity measures, rather than the level measures used for labor productivity in the United States. This model shows labor productivity improvement, or value-added improvement—an area in which the United States is weak. The United States has high total productivity, but we are losing ground to the rest of the world. By comparing our productivity growth with the productivity growth of the rest of the world, we would get a better feel for where we are going (future) rather than where we are or where we have been (present or past). The risk with change productivity is the exchange rate problem, discussed in the Labor Dollar Productivity paragraph. Exchange rates artificially inflate or deflate the comparison. Purchasing-power-parity, a comparison of the purchasing power (number of eggs, hamburgers, or loaves of bread you can buy for an hour's work) resolves some of this problem but creates other problems (what if the Hindu country doesn't eat beef, or the Moslem country doesn't eat pork, etc.).

Given so many productivity measures, does productivity really have any meaning? There is no perfect global productivity measure. Unfortunately, it has very little meaning as an external measure. However, internally it can be an extremely useful measure. If we monitor our own total factor productivity or value-added productivity from one year to the next, we can learn much about our ability to remain competitive.

Productivity Improvements

The key to productivity improvement is to improve the performance of your input, whatever it might be. Hopefully, you are using a meaningful productivity measure such as total factor productivity or value-added productivity. If that is the case, productivity improvements revolve around the value-added factors. You need to add value to the output in every step of the enterprise while at the same time reducing the inputs. Reducing the inputs primarily means reducing waste in the inputs—unnecessary processing steps, unnecessary time, and so on. You need to minimize or eliminate functions that do not add value to the output product. You need to eliminate waste in as many resource areas as possible, a waste being any non–value-added activity.[3]

World Class Productivity

Is productivity a World Class performance measurement tool? Definitely, as long as we focus on our own internal productivity improvements and don't become overconfident by comparing ourselves with other countries. Value-added or total factor productivity, especially changes in productivity measures, is enormously valuable in letting us know whether we are becoming competitively better at utilizing our resources to maximize the benefit to our customers and to our organization.

We need to foster high-productivity performance workplaces. For example, the National Productivity Board of Singapore claims that 62% of Singapore's economic growth is the direct result of productivity gains since the 1970s.[4] We need high-productivity performance that is focused on the right productivity measures. For more details on productivity improvements, see Appendix 5.2, which lists productivity improvement organizations that sell literature and offer seminars and conferences on the subject.

EFFICIENCY AND COST

The lash may force men to physical labor; it cannot force them to spiritual creativity.

Sholem Asch

Efficiency and cost are internal (to the organization) measures of performance to standard. Almost always, efficiency measures labor performance against some standard rate of production. For example, if you produce 100 units per hour but the standard rate of production, based on some historical average for your function, is to produce 80 units per hour, then your efficiency is 125% and you should receive a substantial bonus.

Cost is a measure of reducing the inputs into a process, primarily by reducing the labor force or the materials purchasing costs. Most companies develop costs around three categories: materials, labor, and burden. Materials is considered to be an uncontrollable cost that is minimized by price-bidding the vendors. It is uncontrolled because all the competitors can achieve the same materials cost minimizations. Burden is also considered to be uncontrollable and is simply allocated over all the enterprise's output. That leaves labor as, theoretically, the only controllable cost that can be minimized, so cost cutting as a performance measurement tool usually means labor cost minimization.

An example may help illustrate the fallacy of this cost evaluation process. In most forms of discrete manufacturing, we have the following cost breakdown:

Labor: 8–10%

Materials: 50–60%

Burden: 30–40%

Cost reduction would focus on improving the 10% labor cost component. However, using these numbers, if we focus on a 10% improvement in labor cost, we will achieve an overall cost improvement of less than 1%. However, if we were to reduce burden cost by 10%, we would achieve a 3–4% cost reduction overall. Obviously, the benefit in cost reduction is in the larger-percentage players—materials and burden. The traditional focus on cutting labor cost is misdirected.

Also, by improving labor cost by 10%, we may end up costing ourselves more than the 1% overall cost savings we thought we had gained. To understand this, consider a production line where the focus is on labor efficiency (minimizing labor cost). In order to keep labor busy, we need to have plenty for them to work on (more materials). The more materials we have, the more inventory carrying costs we incur. I have experienced numerous situations in which this inventory carrying cost has increased materials cost by more than the labor savings that were gained. The result is that improved labor efficiency has resulted in increasing the total cost of production.

Similarly, improving materials efficiency decreases labor efficiency. In order to be materials-efficient, which means keeping the materials in the production process as much as possible and minimizing inventories, we can't always keep everyone busy (labor inefficiency). However, a 10% increase in materials efficiency earns us a 5–6% overall improvement. Even if this results in a 10% loss in labor efficiency, we will have a net gain in overall efficiency of 4–5%.

Unfortunately, American management finds it very easy to tolerate inventory standing around and doing nothing but incurring cost (financing costs), but it goes absolutely crazy if labor is standing around doing nothing but incurring cost (wages). Someday we will wake up and realize that the inventory standing around is costing us more than the labor that is standing around.

Another example of a confused focus on efficiency is the relocation of factories overseas in an attempt to take advantage of labor cost reduction. I am familiar with a plant that was transferred from Michigan to Mexico for this reason. The result was that, indeed, labor cost was reduced. Unfortunately, material carrying cost increased so dramatically because of the material transfer time of one to two months between the two locations that the labor cost reduction was far outweighed by the cost increases buried in burden (interest costs). Even today, the plant relocation is considered a good move, because the cost of labor is the only measure of performance that is used. However, the plant has been in the red every year since the move.[5]

Efficiency and cost are outdated forms of strategy performance measurement. Unfortunately, of the four measures under discussion (quality, productivity, cost, and efficiency), efficiency and cost are used most often. For example, I know of several companies that put their employees through elaborate quality and productivity training improvement programs. Yet incentive pay and bonuses are based on employee efficiency and cost performance. Obviously, if the paycheck is based on number of units output, regardless of whether the units are quality units, the employee is motivated to produce quantity, not quality, output.

Wickham Skinner also agrees with this assessment of the use of efficiency and cost. He states that the use of efficiency and cost measures is keeping us from being productive. He stresses that the use of cost and efficiency as measurement tools hinders competitiveness.[6]

World Class Management understands the inefficiency of using efficiency and cost as strategic performance measurement tools. The focus on labor performance to standard ignores the larger, more value-added resource components of the organization's processes, such as technology and materials. The use of cost performance also tends to hide the real opportunities for adding value and eliminating waste. If you are still measuring efficiency and cost performance, you need to rethink what measure might more rapidly elevate your organization to World Class status.

> You get what you pay for.

WHAT MEASURE IS BEST?

On my honor I will do my best . . .
                          Boy Scout oath

Why is the Boy Scout oath so important to us as children and so ignored by us as adults? Is being "best" no longer important? Maybe we are just giving it a new name—now we are trying to be "World Class."

At New United Motor Manufacturing, Inc. (NUMMI) in Fremont, California, workers are trained on problem-solving skills before they are put to work on the production line. The reason: new people breed new ideas, and you can't find quality or productivity improvement opportunities if you're not trained to recognize them. Part of this training includes team participation training. Employees learn to recognize safety, quality, productivity, and cost-saving opportunities. They are cross-trained to learn a variety of functions so that they understand "their fit" in the big picture and understand their internal customers better. NUMMI has become a Stage 4 (see Chapter 4) company with effective, empowered involvement of employees in the quality and productivity improvement process. The result is that in 1992 the average number of defects per 100 cars manufactured was as follows:

United States—125 defects

Asia—105 defects

NUMMI—83 defects

The answer to "what strategic performance measure is best" is actually very simple. In a move to World Class Management status, you should use the measures of:

Customer-based quality

Total factor or value-added productivity change

Quality and productivity are not achieved at the expense of the other. They go hand in hand, like two sides of a coin. Improving quality can be done in such a way as to simultaneously improve productivity. It goes back to the slogan:

> Work smarter, not harder.

Warner-Lambert's Technical Operations Division shifted to a focus on quality and productivity improvement. In 1983, they formally instituted what they referred to as their Total Production System (TPS), which incorporated extensive training programs, Just-in-Time (JIT) production, and Statistical Process Control (SPC) quality tools. The TPS program contained three essentials:

1. A focus on the improvement of production and administrative processes
2. The use of multidiscipline teams trained in problem solving and statistical methods
3. The direction and management of local projects by the local management

The TPS program focused on total productive output and, in their words, "was really a total success."

In 1988 Warner-Lambert shifted its focus to a Total Customer Satisfaction (TCS) system. The movement from TPS to TCS is seen as a migration process, not as a replacement of bad to good. TPS was needed and made a difference, but there came a point where TCS was needed in order to take that final, competitive, leading-edge step. TCS was a step toward a continuous quality improvement process. It incorporated the 3M quality process, which identifies five essentials of quality improvement:

1. Quality is defined as conformance to customer expectations.
2. Measurement of quality is done through indicators of customer satisfaction.
3. The objective is conformance to expectations 100% of the time.

4. Quality is attained through prevention and specific improvement projects.
5. Management commitment leads the quality process.

In developing the TCS program, Warner-Lambert started by developing a vision and mission statement focusing on the customer perspective. They then developed an implementation strategy for TCS, using eight elements:

1. Management leadership—open communication, empowerment, motivating innovation
2. Organization—quality steering and improvement teams similar to the TQM process described in Chapter 11
3. Education—quality education; training in skills, methods, and techniques
4. Developing a sensitivity for customer expectations—information analysis, customer surveys
5. Quantifying conformance—identifying measurement criteria; goal setting; improvement toward 100% conformance
6. Communication of achievements—awareness and recognition
7. Action—projects and systems that bring visible improvements
8. Annual plan—annually refocusing the quality effort

Some of the results of this migratory improvement process from TPS to TCS are shown in the following table:

	1984	1990
Cost of goods as a percent of sales	38.4	32.3
Inventory as a percent of sales	14.1	8.4
Inventory turnover	2.7	3.8
Dollar sales per employee	75.7	134.3
Dollar after-tax profit per employee	5.4	13.9

> *The way we deal with each other, the way we respond to our phones and memos—everything in the process is designed to show our concern for our customers—internal and external.*[7]
>
> Dr. Elias Hebeka, Vice President of Technical Operations,
> Warner-Lambert Technical Operations Division

WHERE TO BEGIN

If you think you're on the road to being World Class, first take a little test.

- Question 1—How good are you at satisfying your most crucial internal customers—your family members?
- Question 2—When was the last time you asked these important internal customers how satisfied they are with you?

If you can't add value to the lives of the people you love, how can you bring meaning to the lives of those you work with? Quality begins in the home. Achieve success there, and you'll also feel good about yourself at work!

SUMMARY

Good performance in both of the strategic areas of productivity and quality on a continuing basis won't guarantee a competitive position, but it is definitely a sign that you are moving in the right direction. Both productivity and quality in a World Class setting, if they are goal-directed toward customer satisfaction, will focus on waste elimination (value-added increases). The two strategies work together to simultaneously drive your enterprise toward World Class competitive status.

With a handle on the strategic performance measures we should use if we are to become World Class Managers, we now move forward to investigate the other areas of strategic competitive advantage.

To find out how to improve productivity, quality, and per-
formance, ask the people who do the work.

Peter F. Drucker

APPENDIX 5.1—QUALITY GURUS

The quality gurus all agree on the need for a focused and con-
centrated effort aimed at achieving quality improvements in
order to be a World Class competitor. However, they disagree dramatically on the best road to getting there. This appendix will
not attempt to explain each of their philosophies in detail; rather,
it will give you background in each philosophy and offer you tools
to research each guru further.

Ishikawa bases his quality program on seven in-process tools
that monitor the ongoing flow of the process. The tools are:

Pareto charts

Cause-and-effect diagrams

Stratification

Check sheets

Histograms

Scatter diagrams

Control charts

Taguchi uses "off-line" methods for quality improvement. He
focuses on what can be done to improve the product or the
process through off-line studies.

Shingo focuses on the Toyota production philosophy known as
Just-in-Time (JIT) production.[8]

Deming uses a series of fourteen "points" that he feels are the
quality tools of success.[9] They are not so much tools as a pre-
scription for quality systems reform. The points are:

1. Create consistency of purpose toward improvement of
   product and service. Develop a plan to become competitive, stay in business, and provide jobs.

2. Adopt a new philosophy. We are in a new economic age and can no longer live with commonly accepted levels of delays and mistakes.
3. Cease dependence on mass inspection. Require statistical evidence that quality is built-in that eliminates the need for mass inspections.
4. End the practice of awarding business to vendors based on the price tag. Instead, depend on meaningful measures of quality along with price. Move toward single suppliers for any one item.
5. Improve constantly and forever the system of production and service, thereby improving quality and productivity and decreasing costs.
6. Institute modern training methods.
7. Supervise never-ending improvement through leadership.
8. Drive out fear so that everyone can work effectively for the company.
9. Break down organizational barriers so that everyone works on problem solving as a team.
10. Eliminate arbitrary numerical goals, posters, and slogans for the work force that seek new levels of productivity without providing the means.
11. Replace management by-the-numbers with never-ending improvement.
12. Remove barriers that rob employees of their pride of workmanship.
13. Educate and retrain everyone.
14. Create a structure that will push the prior thirteen points every day.

Deming has also identified the deadly diseases of the quality process. They are:

1. Lack of constancy of purpose, lack of goals
2. Emphasis on short-term profits
3. Evaluation by performance, merit rating, or annual review of performance
4. Job-hopping managers
5. Running a company on visible figures only

Deming focuses on people working smarter, not harder. Managers need to remove 85% of the defect-creating elements that are "systematic" and require management intervention. The work force will eliminate the rest if they are allowed, and motivated, to do so.

Juran has developed a "breakthrough sequence" of quality improvement steps.[10] They are:

1. Achieve a breakthrough in attitudes by proving to the employees that changes are needed.
2. Identify the vital few projects using Pareto analysis.
3. Organize for a breakthrough in knowledge using a steering group and a diagnostic group.
4. Conduct the analysis.
5. Determine how to overcome resistance to change.
6. Institute the change.
7. Institute controls to monitor and follow up on the changes.

Crosby also has a series of fourteen points for quality improvement.[11] He focuses on showing that quality control is something that happens in the management office, not just on the factory floor. Quality begins with the people—all the people! His fourteen points are:

1. Management commitment
2. Quality improvement team
3. Quality measurement
4. Cost of quality evaluation
5. Quality awareness
6. Corrective action
7. Establishment of an ad hoc committee for a zero defects program
8. Supervisor training
9. Zero-defects day to kick off the program
10. Goal setting
11. Error-cause removal by error acknowledgement within twenty-four hours
12. Recognition through nonfinancial prizes and rewards

13. Quality councils
14. Repetition of the process every twelve to eighteen months

APPENDIX 5.2—PRODUCTIVITY AND QUALITY CENTERS

For your reference, I have included a listing of productivity and quality centers.

The American Production and Inventory Control Society (APICS)
500 West Annandale Road
Falls Church, VA 22046-4274
(703) 237-8344

Quality and Productivity Management Association (QPMA)
300 N. Martingale Road, Suite 230
Schaumburg, IL 60173
(708) 619-2909

GOAL/QPC
13 Branch Street
Methuen, MA 01844-1953
(800) 643-4316

Association for Quality and Participation (AQP)
801-B West Eighth Street
Cincinnati, OH 45203
(513) 381-1959

American Society of Quality Control (ASQC)
611 East Wisconsin Avenue
Milwaukee, WI 53201-3005
(800) 248-1946

Council of Logistics Management
2803 Butterfield Road, #380
Oak Brook, IL 60521-1156
(708) 574-0985

American Productivity and Quality Center (APQC)
123 N. Post Oak Lane
Houston, TX 77024
(713) 681-4020

Jarrett Thor International, Inc.
771 Battery Place
Alexandria, VA 22314
(703) 548-7306

Work In Northeast Ohio Council (WINOC)
6200 Rockside Woods Blvd., Ste. 300
Independence, OH 44131
(216) 520-0770

Maryland Center for Quality and Productivity
College of Business and Management
CBM/SPA Building, 4th Floor
University of Maryland
4321 Hartwick Road, #308
College Park, MD 20742-1815
(301) 405-7099

International Productivity Service
200 Constitution Avenue NW, Room N5409
Washington, DC 20210
(202) 523-7464

Productivity and Quality Research Group (PQRG)
Brigham Young University
680 TNRB
Provo, UT 84602
(801) 378-7338

If you can't get the help you need from any of these sources, contact the Network of Productivity and Quality Centers. They will help you find the type of organization you need.

Network of Productivity and Quality Centers (NQPC)
300 N. Martingale Road, Suite 230
Schaumberg, IL 60173
(708) 619-2909

Global Management Strategies

I was made to work; if you are equally industrious, you will be equally successful.

Johann Sebastian Bach

A friend of mine had been working at a lumber mill for years. Every Friday night, he would go home from the factory with a wheelbarrow full of sawdust. The security guard at the plant gate became suspicious about this friend of mine and his sawdust and questioned him. The guard had a hard time believing that anyone could find a use for that much sawdust. The guard would search through the sawdust, expecting to find something hidden, but he always came up empty handed.

After my friend had been retired for several years, the security guard came to him and asked him, "I know you were stealing something from the plant all those years; what was it you were stealing?"

My friend answered, "Wheelbarrows!"

Do you ever spend time digging around in the sawdust and not seeing the wheelbarrows of competitiveness? One of the great wheelbarrows of industry today that keeps it from being World Class is globalization. We dig around trying to find competitive opportunities in the sawdust and miss the really big opportunity. Let me test your ability to spot a wheelbarrow. Connect all nine dots in Figure 6.1 using only four straight lines. You can't lift up

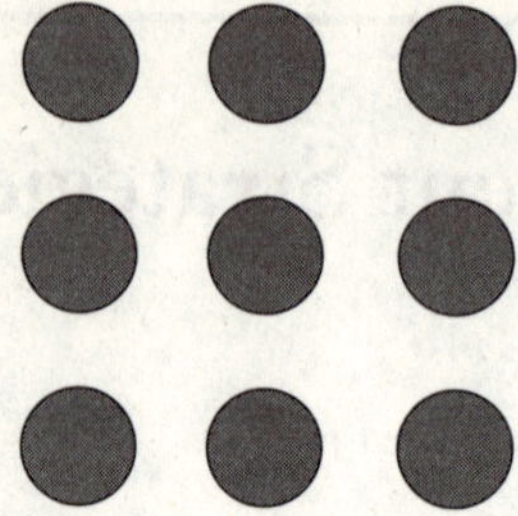

Figure 6.1   Nine Dots

your pencil between lines (the lines must be connected). The solution is found at the end of this chapter.

> If you don't want to win,
> no one will stop you.

GLOBALIZATION DEFINED

Globalization means looking beyond the nine dots. It's realizing that there's a big world out there, geographically, that reaches far beyond our small community and that this world is getting closer to us all the time. Globalization is the realization that, whether we like it or not, this big world is becoming an ever-increasing factor in our daily lives. Being World Class in this global environment means looking beyond the sawdust to see the wheelbarrows; it means looking beyond our small, isolated environment to identify competitive opportunities on a much larger scale than we ever previously imagined.

In this chapter, we offer a brief outline of globalization and its dynamics. As with many of the topics of this book, I can offer only a brief "big-picture" perspective of the topic of globalization. Numerous books exist that offer detailed explanations of the topic.[1] Globalization requires careful strategic planning, because it can become very complex depending on where you are working and what you are working with. However, the benefits are enormous, as you will see. Globalization is a critical strategic requirement in your drive to become World Class.

The wise learn many things from their foes.

Aristophanes, Athenian poet

THE GLOBAL ENTERPRISE

A global enterprise is one that is involved in international transactions. These transactions can take many forms, including:

Vendors

Subcontractors

Customers

Subsidiaries

Plants

Financing (banks and private investors)

Almost every company, no matter how small, is globally influenced in some way, either directly or indirectly. Even if you don't have direct international transactions, it is highly likely that either components of what you purchase or the end user of your output will be internationally influenced. Often one of your primary competitors will be an international enterprise.

Ignoring the global perspective is not seeing the wheelbarrow or not connecting the nine dots. A global manager understands and effectively manipulates foreign markets, whether they are consumer markets, labor markets, or vendor markets. Ohmac goes so far as to say that seeing and thinking globally comprise the World Class Manager's first task.[2] Information technology has allowed global managers around the world to speak a common business language.

Globalization does not remove the need for localization. The products and services we provide still need to be culturally distinct. For example, when Mexico decided to market shoes called "Jesus boots" (a direct translation from the Spanish) in the United States, sales went stale. However, renaming the sandals made sales quickly take off. When U.S. auto manufacturers were faced with the kimono regulations of Japan, which required bumpers to be wrapped back into the body of the car so that long kimonos would not get caught in them, they cried "trade barrier" and fought the regulations all the way. A global enterprise, and a World Class Global Manager, understands the need for product and service localization within a global environment.

The global enterprise is an "insider," not an outsider. It understands how a localized market works from the inside, whether it is in North America, Europe, Japan, Latin America, or some other location. It realizes that differences exist within each region (compare the United States, Canada, and Mexico) and within each country (compare the United States West with the Northeast, the South, Alaska, and so on). A global enterprise focuses on the localization within each of these subregions.

The result is that a global enterprise develops a global strategy that builds on localized independence. It develops global visions and missions but realizes that home-office solutions seldom work locally and that local organizations need to be empowered to make their own decisions. A global enterprise recognizes that all customers, including those rarely or never heard of in the home office, are equally important.

When things go really well—or very badly [in your business]—misplaced home-country reflexes start to intervene. . . . Too many entrenched systems work against collaborative efforts. . . . Customer needs have globalized, and we must globalize to meet them.

Kenichi Ohmae

Global management has been the focus of numerous studies. For example, thirty-one major trends shaping the future of American business have been listed. Industrial globalization is affected by the majority of these trends directly, including issues such as:

Time control/time responsiveness

Dramatic growth of home shopping

The environment

Labor relations changes

Defense spending shifts

Increasing government regulations

Permanent damage to the nuclear industry

The budget deficit's persistence

Reversal of tax cuts for wealthy[3]

Another study suggests that the first characteristic of twenty-first century industry is the emergence of the global corporation. Some features of the global corporation are:

- Virtually instantaneous operations—A customer enters a custom-designed order based on something seen on the home shopping network, and instantaneously the customized production of that product begins in a plant in Chile. Companies like FedEx handle the shipment of the product, and three days later the customer has the product in hand.
- Integration of the supply chain
- Flat, unstructured, modular organizations
- Growth of strategic alliances
- Renewed focus on quality[4]

Another study stresses four critical success dimensions, each focusing on the global effects:

1. Business strategy
2. Product strategy
3. Market-mix strategy
4. Country strategy[5]

The big issue today is not whether to go global but how to tailor the global marketing concept to fit each business.

Quelch & Hoff

Still another study stresses that the effective global competitor must understand the nature of the global customer, including:

- Cultural differences (discussed later in this chapter)
- The political ideology—government stability and degree of government control, tariffs
- The business climate—business practices and protocol, banking, technological sophistication
- The demographic infrastructure—population makeup, education, health, urbanization[6]

The World Class Global Manager realizes that he or she does not have all the answers. Global managers realize that they do not have a localized perspective for every region in which their enterprise is involved. For example, Whirlpool International's management committee is made up of six people from six different nations; this arrangement is typical of most World Class global enterprises. Asea Brown Boveri (ABB), the European electrical engineering giant based in Zurich, Switzerland, has grouped its entire product line of thousands of products into fifty business categories or business areas (BA). The leadership team for each BA is given global responsibility for developing the business-unit strategy for its area, including incorporating global responsibility, selecting product development priorities, and allocating production among countries. None of the BA teams are located in Zurich; rather, they are distributed throughout the world.[7]

Other examples abound. Hewlett-Packard moved the headquarters of its personal computer business to Grenoble, France. Siemens A. G., Germany's electronics giant, moved its medical electronics division to Chicago, Illinois. Ford's engine factory, at which Mexican engineers and technicians produce 1,000 engines per day at World Class quality levels, is located in Chihuahua, Mexico. Texas Instruments' most complex wafer production facility is in Sendai, Japan. Intel is establishing one of its prime strategic research centers in Penang, Malaysia. Most consumer electronics products marketed in the United States by American companies such as General Electric, RCA, and Zenith are manufactured abroad. Chrysler has reduced its domestic capacity to 40% and now buys the majority of the automobiles it markets under its brand name from Mitsubishi in Japan. Sears, K-Mart, and J. C. Penney procure a large percentage of their merchandise from foreign manufacturers. Non–U.S. companies such as Shell, British Petroleum, Hoechst, Toyota, Nissan, Honda, Sony, and Mitsushita have, through acquisitions and new facilities, introduced production facilities in North America. Other successful global competitors include IBM, GE, McDonalds, Philips, Toys-R-Us, KFC, NCR, AT&T, Unilever, Procter & Gamble, and many others. These companies have discovered the globalization advantage and are focusing on strategic global relocations. They are becoming global citizens. World Class Management requires that you become a global citizen as well.

. . . change is the nursery
of musicke, joy, life, and eternity.

John Donne, English poet

REASONS FOR GLOBALIZATION

So far in this chapter, we have discussed why it makes good sense to be globally oriented. We now review some specific strategic reasons why you might want to make globalization a part of your corporate or business-unit strategy. My own personal list of specific strategic reasons for globalization includes:

Cost competitiveness

Time-to-market competitiveness

Manufacturing processes

Information processes

Government policy

Competitive markets

Technology transfer

Competitive lessons we can learn

Cost Competitiveness   Cost competitiveness is usually the first, and often the wrong, reason for globalization. As we have already discussed in previous chapters, cost cutting is a short-term financially oriented decision motivator. Almost always, the relocation decision is based on labor cost, and labor cost is typically 10% or less of the value-added cost of the production process. Relocation decisions based only on cutting labor costs can detrimentally affect the total cost reduction. In the past, labor cost competitiveness has caused plants to be shifted to Latin America, East Asia, and, more recently, Southeast Asia. Fortunately, the mistake of labor cost competitiveness has been recognized and labor-cost-only shifts do not occur as frequently as before.

The truth is that many accounting systems are not designed to provide information to answer the questions managers face in today's market. Worse, the information is still used and catastrophic decisions are made because the accounting information indicates it is the smart thing to do.

Howell & Soucy[8]

If total cost or value-added cost competitiveness is the basis for globalization, however, then the global strategy, although still short-term oriented, at least has potential merit. Often, in these cases, materials sourcing costs are the dominating factor in the decision. For example, if locating a plant in Asia, in spite of increased shipping and inventory carrying costs and in spite of potentially lower productivity and quality levels, results in a net production-cost reduction, then the move is a good one. Products such as electrical components, compressors, electric motors, metals, agricultural materials, some chemicals, petroleum and its products, and so on are cheaper to purchase overseas than in the United States.

Other cost-competitiveness issues that have motivated globalization are transportation, shipping, tariffs, and exchange rates. For example, Coca Cola and Pepsi bottle their product as close to the consumer as possible. The only thing that is imported is the syrup, a high value-added item. Bulky items such as the bottles and the soda water are locally sourced and bottled. Similarly, Japanese companies have decided to manufacture in the United States or Canada because of the Japanese yen–U.S. dollar relationship (exchange rates are discussed later in this chapter).

Recently, with the introduction of NAFTA, there have been many surprises in global marketing. For example, the movement of Toys-R-Us and Walmart into Canada has resulted in the closure of some major Canadian toy retailers. Labor-intensive production processes like agriculture, which should favor the low labor costs of Mexico, have in fact seen agricultural products being shipped from the United States to Mexico, and Mexican farmers, rather than U.S. farmers, have been displaced. In both the Canada and Mexico cases, cost competitiveness was the issue. The producer with the lowest total cost won the lion's share of the market.

Time-to-Market Competitiveness   One strategic disadvantage of the United States is its inability to react quickly to market changes (this topic will be discussed in detail in Chapter 7). However, some Asian countries, such as Taiwan and Hong Kong, have developed a strategic niche by being able to react quickly. For example, if you are trying to produce fad clothing items or if you are trying to react to a sudden trend shift in the toy market, these Asian producers can quickly adjust their production output to meet your needs. A similar shift in the productive output of a U.S., European, or Japanese plant could take months.

Manufacturing Processes   Improvements in manufacturing processes have created mini-factories that are more efficient and less costly than their earlier counterparts. These mini-factories are easily relocated overseas, opening the door for new market opportunities.

As discussed in Chapter 5, World Class global quality is level "A," societally oriented quality. World Class productivity is value-added, waste-eliminated productivity. Productivity and quality strategies need to be integrated into a global strategy.

Information Processes   Tools such as telecommunications, faxes, teleconferencing, and computer networking have reduced or eliminated distance barriers. These tools have become increasingly important to the financial and retailing industries (see Chapter 8).

Government Policy   Countries such as Mexico and many of the previously communist countries have initiated enormous privatization programs. These programs offer opportunities for new markets and have become part of the globalization strategy of many companies. Also, many countries, including Malaysia, Singapore, Mexico, and Ireland, offer enormous incentives and attractive packages for companies interested in developing operations in their country. These packages often include tax incentives and duty-free trade zones for the manufactured products.

Competitive Markets   Markets for your products exist all over the world. Globalization is often driven by the desire to enter these markets. Often, opening new markets also requires the globalization of the manufacturing process. For example, in Europe you need to have a production facility within the borders of the European Economic Community (EEC) in order to avoid certain tariffs and trade restrictions. Therefore, a European production facility becomes part of the marketing globalization strategy for companies who want to access European markets.

. . . the [international] service sector will become a major target of productivity improvements in the 1990s.

Blumberg[9]

Technology Transfer   The exchange of technology between countries is often the primary basis for globalization. For a long time, Japanese firms have transferred technology to Japan by establishing a facility in the United States and staffing that facility with the best of America's work force. The Japanese learn the technology and transfer it back home.

Ideally, however, the exchange of technology is not as one-sided as the Japanese example. World Class technology transfer is a two-way exchange whereby the United States shares with Europe and Asia, and they in turn share their insights with the United States. This strategy forces us into a discussion of perspectives. Many different perspectives exist on what technology should be transferred and when. We explore just a few.

1. *United States, Japan, or Europe out to a Less Developed Country*—The U.S. perspective on why we should transfer to a Less Developed Country (LDC) is that we should be kind and generous, giving the LDC a chance for its economy to grow. We are providing jobs and a market for the products that are produced. In return, we receive cheaper products.

2. *Less Developed Country in from the United States, Japan, or Europe*—The LDC sees the United States (or Japan or Europe) as an opportunist looking for cheap labor that can be utilized to operate outdated technologies. For example, Malaysia has a negative unemployment rate, that is, it has more jobs than people and imports people from other countries to cover increasing labor demand.[10] As another example, Thailand, like many Less Developed Countries, has a positive trade balance. It wonders why, if manufacturing is so good for the economy, the United States doesn't keep its manufacturing and build up its own economy.

These LDCs feel that the United States and Japan are systematically trying to keep them twenty years behind technologically. For example, when the United States wants to transfer a plant to an LDC, it transfers old, inefficient technology in the hopes that cheaper labor rates will turn the inefficient machinery to a positive financial gain. Using this twenty-year-old technology, the United States systematically holds down the LDC's level of technology.

Japan is more open about keeping the Less Developed Country behind. When the Japanese transfer technology to an LDC, they bring in their own technocrats and never give the LDC any leading-edge technology. For example, the Proton Saga is a Malaysian-built car being produced in a plant that is the combined effort of Mitsubishi and the Malaysian government. However, rather than bringing in the leading-edge manufacturing technology used in Japan, the Japanese set up the plant using outdated technological production methods similar to those used in older U.S. plants. The Japanese didn't want the Proton Saga to become an international competitor.

In a technology exchange, both sides of the exchange should benefit. We would assist the LDC in technological growth, and it in turn would help the United States develop new technologies. These types of exchanges motivate companies to set up technology development centers in many parts of the world. An interesting, though controversial, book discussing the LDC point of view is *Small Is Beautiful*.[11]

Technology is such an important topic that the entire next chapter is devoted to discussing it in detail. Technology transfer is an important element of a globalization strategy and needs to be considered carefully in ways familiar to every newspaper reporter:

- Who—to transfer to
  Some countries offer financial incentives, and others offer a highly educated work force (Malaysia and Hong Kong).
- What—to transfer
  Some companies select to transfer only their support functions and not their core competencies. Others transfer in areas where they hope to learn from the country transferred to (Europe or Japan).
- When—the timing or turn-around of the transfer
  Some countries are quicker at technology implementation (e.g., Taiwan). On other occasions, the technology

> transfer may be timed to specific events, such as market entries (e.g., Mexico and NAFTA).
>
> - Where—location of the transfer
>   The location of some countries offers strategic opportunities (Singapore, shipping; Hong Kong, banking).
> - How—the transfer process
>   Does transferring require the movement of large amounts of equipment or personnel? Does the new location require large amounts of resources (heavy equipment or energy)?
> - Why—does technology transfer make strategic sense
>   Is the transfer justified financially, logistically, and so on?

A recent study looked at the transfer of bicycle technology within three classes of countries—the Developed Countries (DC; e.g., United States, Japan), Newly Industrialized Economies (NIE; e.g., South Korea, Singapore), and Less Developed Countries (LDC; e.g., Mexico, Indonesia).[12] A comparison was made based on several criteria, including cost. The results showed that NIEs are the most cost-competitive countries for bicycle manufacturing. The introduction of state-of-the-art technology has detrimental consequences for LDCs. The complex machine technology introduced should be oriented toward more mass production rather than hi-tech advances. Large production gains occurred in each category of country after the introduction of advanced technology processes, such as the quality control process discussed in Chapters 5 and 11 and the introduction of flexible production methodologies. None of these findings are surprising, but the study quantifies the results with supportive data.

Competitive Lessons We Can Learn Post–World War II Japan and Germany both went through all three stages of development, from LDC to NIE to DC. If we learn no other lesson, we should at least recognize the competitive characteristics of enthusiasm, drive, and commitment shown by these countries.

One of the greatest pains to human nature is the pain of a new idea.

Walter Bagehot, English economist

One of the primary tools used for analyzing the growth of nations, and of the development of industries within these nations, is benchmarking. Benchmarking is an analysis of national, industrial, or corporate numbers to compare different industries. The main basis for comparison is financial and operational numbers; however, these numbers don't always tell the complete story. For example, the innovative potential of employees is hard to quantify. The American Productivity and Quality Center (APQC) and the International Productivity Service (IPS) have data collection services that can be utilized to help you compare your industry to the rest of the world (addresses for both are listed in Appendix 5.2). Additional in-country services are available, for example, Canadian Interfirm Comparisons Program or the U.S. SIC classified financial statistics.[13] The Interfirm Comparison Program, sponsored by the Industry, Science and Technology Canada organization (see Appendix 6.1), focuses on benchmarking for Canadian firms. Similar programs exist in many other countries.

Harley-Davidson was in serious trouble in the early 1980s. In fact, the company wasn't expected to survive. This last surviving U.S. motorcycle manufacturer was being devastated by the Japanese, with a market share decline from 75% in 1973 to less than 25%. But Harley has recovered and has come back to control 50% of the market share. Here is an example of a banker (Citicorp) badly misjudging a company's potential by looking only at the numbers. What happened? It's simple—Harley learned from the competition, and it learned its lessons well.

In the early 1980s, Harley quality was awful and manufacturing was a mess. The company thought it could rely on its dedicated and committed customers forever. Unfortunately, it was wrong. Managers bought the company and made a dramatic turnaround. They tell their story in the book *Well-Made in America*.[14]

We were being wiped out by the Japanese because they were better managers. It wasn't robotics, or culture, or morning calisthenics and company songs—it was professional managers who understood their business and paid attention to detail.

Vaughn Beals, Harley-Davidson

Harley-Davidson used World Class Management tools such as empowerment and globalization to make a difference, and they see the difference in increases in sales, profits, and return on equity. But the numbers that eventually made Citicorp happy came only after Harley understood and beat the competition.

One lesson that we learn from globalization is that most countries have moved away from the concept that there is one perfect right answer to all problems. The "one right answer" way of thinking seems to be characteristic of Christian cultures. In the Middle East and Asia, there is a realization that "one right answer" does not exist—rather, alternatives exist. Two plants running side by side producing the same product may have different "right" answers to the same problem. One may have an authoritarian management style, and the other may have a participative management style.

In the United States and Europe, the search for the "one right answer" leaves us with an all-or-nothing attitude toward changes. For example, in our attempt to copy Japan, we went through a series of all-or-nothing right answers. About ten years ago, quality circles were the fad. Everyone thought that implementing Quality Control (QC) circles would be the perfect answer to competing with the Japanese. When this strategy didn't provide the desired results within two years, it was thrown out, and Statistical Process Control (SPC) was deemed the perfect solution. Again, after two years, this strategy was thrown out and the next fad was introduced. We went through In-Line Quality Control (ILQC), Just-in-Time production (JIT), Total Quality Management (TQM), and many more fads, trying, implementing, short-term testing, and then rejecting each technique. But in our search for the perfect answer—the search for the trick of the Japanese—we never asked the Japanese what their secret was. The Japanese would have eagerly told us that their secret is none of the above, rather, it is all of the above. The integration of all these processes over a long period of time (twenty to thirty years) brings about the desired results. But we in the United States still go on looking for the one perfect, two-year answer to our differences.

Many developing countries have learned the building-block approach to improvement. They have given up on the idea of a quick fix; rather, they are looking at alternatives for improvement, implementing the change, saving and incorporating the elements that work, integrating them into the process, and finally moving on to another idea for change. Tools such as SPC, QC, or JIT are not tested and rejected; instead, the good elements of each are accepted and integrated into the process. They take the approach that all these tools are building blocks in a long-term, planned-out solution, not a quick-fix solution.

Developing countries have also learned another lesson from change implementation: changes don't work unless you follow them through to completion. A change is not fully implemented until it achieves Stage E of the implementation process (see Figure 6.2). Stage E may take two months, two years, or twenty years to achieve, but you don't reject the change process, the way Florida Power and Light did, just because your two years are up and you're still in Stage C or Stage D. This is a lesson that all World Class Managers need to integrate into their way of thinking:

1. Change processes need to be followed through to completion.

2. Each change needs to be thought of as a building block in achieving some larger goal, not as the total solution in and of itself.

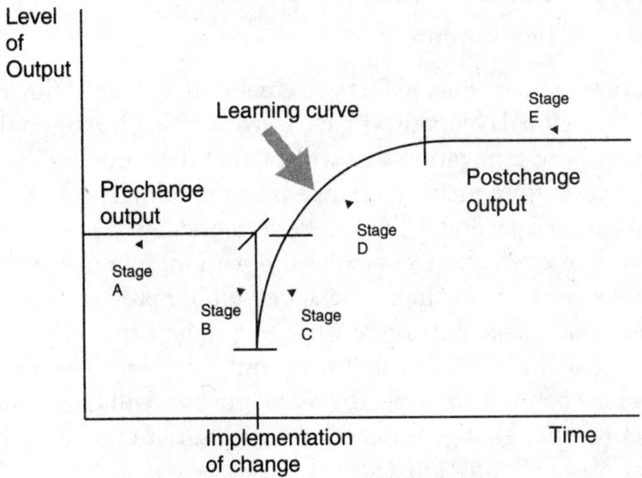

Figure 6.2 Change Function

Globalization has taught us another lesson:

> As long as you're playing catch-up,
> the best you can ever do is get caught up.
> And that's just not good enough.[15]

As long as we're playing copycat, we won't get ahead. Playing catch-up has value only if you're way behind or just beginning. In head-to-head competition, you need to innovate yourself ahead of the competition. This innovation can take many forms including:

Product innovation

Process innovation (what the Japanese are good at)

Technology innovation

Time-to-market innovation (Taiwan)

Marketing innovation

Innovation, not copying, makes you competitive. Part of the lesson that the global competitors have learned is that it is often the unique, surprise innovation that will capture the customer's eye.

The reason for continual change is to unendingly add value to the output we generate. Time erodes value added through competition. However, change, such as innovation, increases value added. We can not stay in business and sell our product at cost. It is the value-added portion of what we produce that allows us to cover our mistakes, breakdowns, and surprises. The more value-added content we have, the more profit we will have. Similarly, continual change is necessary to eliminate waste in the process. Waste elimination adds value.

We can learn an unlimited number of lessons from globalization. A few important ones have been highlighted. You should incorporate these lessons in your drive to become a World Class Manager.

When asked what he thought of Western civilization,
Mahatma Gandhi replied, "I think it would be a good idea."

GLOBAL CULTURAL DIFFERENCES

We often use "culture" as the excuse for our lack of a competitive stance. We say that "culture" is the reason why the Japanese are better at teaming, or that "culture" is the reason why the Chinese are the business entrepreneurs of Asia. We say that "culture" explains differences in the work ethic of one country compared to another. Unfortunately, most of these "cultural" excuses are nothing more than that—*excuses*. The key to cultural differences and to taking advantage of these differences is in understanding them. We will discuss some of them, and when you consider them you will have a better understanding of why business transactions and ethical systems work differently.

The biggest component of cultural differentiation is religion. My statements about religions are not an attempt to correctly interpret a religious philosophy. Rather, I am saying that a business attitude and culture can be seen as having developed around a particular aspect of a particular religion.

The religious basis of the United States, Canada, most of Europe, Australia, South Africa, and a few other countries, including many East-Bloc countries (former Soviet Union countries such as Russia) tends to be right-wing Christianity. Right-wing Christianity is characterized by belief in Jesus Christ and claims of the one true religion, the one right answer, and the one God. But this God is a God that we use as a tool to help us get what we want. In this environment, the individual, and individual rights, is paramount.

The religious basis for most Latin American countries, Spain, Portugal, and Italy is left-wing Christianity. This is characterized by belief in Jehovah of the Old Testament and the one God who is a condemning God who will punish you if you don't stay on track. In this culture, the family unit tends to be most influential.

The Middle East, North Africa, Indonesia, Malaysia, and a few other countries are predominantly Moslem. The Moslem God is a God of fear. Strict rules must be complied with. Allah wants us to fight for what is right, often to the obliteration of all that is considered to be wrong. In this culture, religion is most important, and an attack on religious doctrine is suicide.

The Jewish God Jehovah is also a God of fear. He is quick to destroy evildoers. However, in the end, He will forgive all. You find a strategy of "don't do unto others what you don't want them to do unto you." Judaism is also characterized by "it is easier to get forgiven than to get permission." This attitude encourages aggressive and adventurous risk taking.

In the Far East, such as Thailand and surrounding areas, we find Buddhism. Here we tend to find a compromising, second-chance attitude to life—if you mess up the first time and don't achieve Nirvana, you'll come back to earth and get a second chance. The little stresses of day-to-day life don't matter much in the big picture of the eternities. What matters most is the larger (family or societal) unit.

In China, we find communism tainted with Buddhism and Taoism. The success of the societal unit is what's important, and an individual who is not contributing to society is a disgrace.

In India and surrounding regions, the dominant religion is Hinduism. Hinduism is a world of many Gods and finds acceptance and good in all Gods. Hindu culture is characterized by tolerance and compromise. The most important unit is the clan or caste (extended family).

Looking at these religious differences, we see a few things immediately. One observation is that the individual dominates in importance only in right-wing Christianity. An individual-rights-oriented ethical system is not universal. There are even extreme cases in which the religion requires that an individual who is an embarrassment to the larger unit by not being an active participant and adding value to the unit be removed (cast out).

A friend in Southeast Asia suggested to me that the reason for the decline in U.S. economic strength is that we are graduating more and more non–value-added graduates than ever before. A non–value-added graduate is one who graduates and then works only to fill his or her own pocket. The jobs they perform do nothing to increase the resources or the output of the country. Their jobs simply shuffle the existing resources around and may even waste some resources in the process. This Asian friend suggested that in order to improve the economic strength of a country you need a value-added labor force in which each job function adds value to society as a whole. I'll let you decide whether your job function adds value to society.

Considering the religious influence, we also notice that some cultures focus on compromise as opposed to a fight-for-what-is-right attitude. For example, a piece of land on the border between Malaysia and Thailand was disputed. Both countries laid claim to it. Then oil was found in the region. The American way would be to fight over this piece of land. The Asian way was to draw a line around the region and set up a separate entity to manage the region and the oil. Both countries then shared in the profit.

Often, in societal-oriented cultures, the relationship is the focus of business transactions. The trust between individuals is more important than the transaction. The "word" is more important than the paper (contract). In the United States, we have developed such elaborate nontrust systems (accounting, finance, auditing, personal, information, legal, and so on) that the cost of these nontrust systems is often higher than if we were to get rid of them all and suffer an occasional fraud. The U.S. way to handle business transactions is to not let anyone get away with anything. We protect ourselves by crafting elaborate documents. For example, the NAFTA agreement, a trade agreement between three countries (the United States, Canada, and Mexico), is 2,200 pages long, while the APEC agreement, a trade agreement between six countries (Malaysia, Indonesia, Brunei, Thailand, the Philippines, and Singapore), is only 16 pages long.

As stated, in societal cultures the word is more powerful than the paper. This is true even in court. It is not the contract but rather the "understanding" that influences court decisions. In addition, no matter how complete you think your contract is, if you are not willing to demonstrate your trustworthiness by spending time with those with whom you are trying to do business, then you're simply not going to win the business.

This discussion of cultural differences is not intended to be close to complete. It is meant to be enlightening and to open your eyes to the diversity that exists. Cultures vary dramatically between countries as well as between regions within a country (for example, compare the U.S. Southeastern Bible Belt with the hippies of the Pacific Northwest). A more complete study of the localized culture of the specific country is important in order for you to be an effective World Class player.

DEFINING A GLOBALIZATION STRATEGY

A globalization strategy is an element of the corporate or business strategy that focuses on internationalization. As discussed at the beginning of this chapter, internationalization can take many forms. In one study of internationalization practices, it was found that nearly all the globalized companies required major organizational changes, primarily involving decentralizing. Ninety-four percent of the globalized companies strongly agreed that competition is heating up globally and the pace of innovation has quickened.[16] Additional points of the study included:

1. Half of the companies feel that exports are the best globalization strategy, and the other half feel that investment is the best strategy.
2. About three-fourths of the companies feel that globalization is best accomplished using joint ventures.
3. Relationships with customers and suppliers must change dramatically to the point where they work much more closely with each.
4. That empowerment is not a buzzword and should be used for decision making is supported by 85% of the surveyed companies.

Another study stresses that the competitive advantage of a company determines the value added in the global marketplace. The existence of both determines a successful globalization strategy.[17]

In yet a third study, successful global (referred to as transnational) companies are shown to require the integration of efficiency, customer responsiveness, and the ability to exploit learning (employee training and innovation) in order to be successful.[18]

Having defined a globalization strategy, we also need to recognize some risks. The biggest risk is pushing too much toward one of the extreme ends of the integration–diversification spectrum. Too much diversification will cause segmentation. Over-diversified organizations tend to have separate foreign and domestic branches, each with its own objectives and value system. The other extreme is equally bad. If the global and domestic arms of the company are too integrated, effective localization is lost. Over-integrated organizations treat everyone the same and expect everyone to act the same as in the good old United States of America. A happy balance between these extremes is needed in which globalization is part of the vision, mission, and strategy of the corporation while, at the same time, the localization aspects, whereby we work closely with the country and the culture, are not lost.

ELEMENTS OF A GLOBALIZATION STRATEGY

We do not attempt here to dictate what is required in a globalization strategy but rather suggest a list of elements that should be included:

Ethical considerations

International trade theory

International financial transactions

Political and legal environments

Types of international relationships

Modification of goals

Relocation decisions

Ethical Considerations   Ethics are discussed in Chapter 12; however, in a globalization strategy it is important to recognize that cultural differences translate into ethical differences. For example, we often encounter the age-old debate over why a tip is considered ethical and a bribe unethical in American culture, whereas this conflict does not exist in other cultures.

Other ethical issues also come into play in a globalization strategy. Is it ethical to relocate a plant to India so that we don't have to be concerned about health risks to the employees? Is it ethical to move a plant to Latin America so that we don't have to comply with stringent pollution regulations? Are employee safety and pollution cost reductions considered legitimate cost savings for plant relocations?

Another ethical dilemma is that of nationalism. At home, offshore plant relocations cost American jobs but save American consumers money. Overseas, nationalism may mean that the relocated plants lead to the building of schools, roads, or other infrastructure items in order to support the community and thereby become an integral and accepted part of the society.

When in Rome, do as the Romans do.

St. Ambrose

Determining what is ethical is a judgmental evaluation based on background and experience. However, we must adhere to some ethical legal basis for our activities. The important point is not that we should disregard our ethics but that we should recognize that we don't possess the one right ethical system, any more than we have the one right way to run a factory.[19]

International Trade Theory   International trade theory stresses the law of comparative advantage, whch basically states that if I'm better at growing apples (if I can grow them more cheaply) than you are and you're better at building boxes than I am, then each of us should do what we are comparatively better at, and then trade. In the end, we will both end up with the desired number of boxes and apples, but the total cost of boxes and apples for each of us will be cheaper than if we each grew our own apples and built our own boxes. The principle of comparative advantage supports the benefits of job specialization and economic efficiency.

International Financial Transactions   Numerous forms of international financial transactions need consideration by the global enterprise; for example, what form of investment is best. The forms of foreign investment that are preferred differ dramatically from one country to the next. Within each country is a U.S. embassy, and within each embassy is a foreign commercial officer. The role of this officer is to help U.S. investors determine the best form of foreign investment for them. Investment may involve the direct investment of capital in resources such as plants or equipment, or it may mean the development of partnerships or the establishment of strategic alliances.

The foreign commercial officer can also help you contact existing businesses that have already taken part in the foreign investment experience. For example, in Malaysia the foreign commercial officer arranges monthly "breakfasts" where foreign visitors can meet with many of the leaders of American businesses in Malaysia and discuss their experiences. You can't get any better information than that directly related by those who have already gone through the experience.

Another critical element of the foreign financial transaction is the foreign exchange process. This process is a lot like playing the stock market. Foreign currencies are much more sporadic in their activities than the U.S. dollar. Exchanging dollars for Mexican pesos, Malaysian ringgits, or any other currency can create a boom or a bust. Timing the investment correctly, like timing in the stock market, is the key to success or disaster. Because of this volatility, many companies require all transactions to be made in U.S. dollars, thereby assuring some level of protection.

Currency exchanges become especially risky in countries where the inflation rate is enormous, as in many Latin America countries, or where the government is unstable. For example, in one day the Turkish lira experienced a 28% plunge in value—and that's just one of many recent examples.[20] However, investment in the currencies of aggressively growing countries, such as countries of Southeast Asia, can generate substantial profits beyond what U.S. investments would have returned. Currency exchange transactions need to be managed carefully. Recently, one (unnamed) developing country nearly lost its entire treasury because of a poor currency investment decision.

Political and Legal Environments   The political and legal environments play a large role in strategic globalization. The instability of a government may discourage commitment. For example, China's lack of consistent policy has made some companies gun-shy. Other countries have been known to nationalize (take over) companies. On the other hand, countries like Mexico and many East-Bloc nations are privatizing (eliminating government control of) many of their industries, opening opportunities for foreign investment.

As discussed earlier, the legal environment in many countries focuses on trust, not on contracts. Having it "in writing" may be important in the United States, but the "understanding" is more important in many other countries.

The government also becomes involved in control issues such as regulations, taxes, and tariffs. In some countries, like Brazil, it is extremely difficult to bring product in and take profits out. Other countries, like Singapore, are extremely open, with tariff- and tax-free zones for export production.

Some countries require partnerships. For example, Mexican coastal properties can be owned only by Mexicans. Therefore, if you want to build a coastal resort, you need to arrange a partnership with a Mexican national.

Trading partnerships are springing up all over. The initial trading partnership was the European Economic Community (EEC), in which the European nations banded together to eliminate barriers to the flow of goods across national borders within Europe. The North America Free Trade Agreement (NAFTA) is a trading partnership between the United States, Canada, and Mexico. NAFTA has so far been a real boon for American industries. Industries such as agriculture, which the United States was expecting to lose ground, turned out to be gainers. Other trading partnerships are springing up in Southeast Asia, Africa, and Latin America. The advantage of the partnerships is that, for example, if you want to trade within Europe, you need to establish a relationship with only one country in order to be able to trade with them all. The disadvantage of the partnerships is that each has its own political agenda, for example, ISO 9000 certification in Europe, and this agenda has to be worked with.

Unfortunately, whenever a trading partnership is formed and two countries agree to trade more with each other, they are also, by default, agreeing to trade less with other countries. Some alliances even set up barriers to trade with countries outside the partnership. For example, the EEC's ISO 9000 quality certification program requires that anyone who wants to trade within the EEC must be certified. This program blocks many countries from trading in Europe. Economically, however, anytime a trading barrier is dropped through a partnership, it is ultimately the consumer who benefits through cheaper products.

The world's major trade liberalization program is the General Agreement on Tariffs and Trade (GATT), which has 117 member nations. GATT has generated a basic set of rules for trade negotiations and offers a mechanism for ensuring that the rules are implemented. The most recent round of negotiations, the Uruguay Round, which lasted eight years ending in 1993, agreed on provisions that will take effect in mid-1995. The GATT process has equalized trade between nations and has significantly reduced the average tariffs of industrialized countries (from about 40% in 1947 to around 5% currently). The result of these negotiations has been to significantly reduce the cost of consumer goods and to offer open and freer trading for developing countries, which is vital for their economic growth.

Types of International Relationships   Many different forms of international partnerships have been developed, such as company buy-outs or joint ventures. The partnership arrangement that currently is being given the most attention is the formation of strategic alliances. In a strategic alliance, an enterprise focuses on its core competencies and then orients its business strategy around that core competency. There are many examples of recently established strategic alliances. For example, FedEx is utilizing its logistics capability to act as the inventory and distribution agent for other enterprises whose core competency is manufacturing. Federal Express has established a Business Logistics Services division, which forms a unique alliance with companies such as Laura Ashley to restructure and manage its distributions systems. FedEx is the master of logistics, and Laura Ashley is the master at producing products with English charm. Neither could perform the other function well. The strategic alliance formed between the two companies gave each the best of both worlds. The result: Laura Ashley can resupply any of its 540 shops around the world within 24 to 48 hours.

FedEx provides similar services for National Semiconductor Corporation, which wanted to stay within its core competency, building semiconductors. FedEx also provides logistics services for the House of Windsor. The logistics services provided by FedEx offer time-definite delivery within two working days. Additionally, they offer inventory tracking and control, including pulling, packing, shipping, and monitoring the inventory movement process.

Another company that has developed a strategic alliance is Solectron, a Malcolm Baldrige Award winner and one of the world's premier electronics companies. It has shunned advertising, minimized product research and development, and focused entirely on manufacturing and customer service. Because they're so good at it, they're getting more business than they can handle and are becoming choosy about who they accept as a partner.[21]

Strategic alliances mean sharing control of some aspects of the company, a difficult condition for some managers to accept. However, backing off from the things you're not good at and doing even better at those things you are good at is the focus of the strategic alliance gamble, and most companies that have attempted these alliances have found them to be successful. For example, the FedEx strategic alliances have become a critical element of customer service and satisfaction for the companies FedEx supports.

Company buy-outs or joint ventures involve an enterprise in new areas that are often not part of its core competency. This may be a good strategy for maintaining control, but it is often not as profitable as forming strategic alliances, in which the enterprise focuses on its core competency. Unfortunately, strategic alliances work not on the basis of ownership or control, but on the basis of partnership, effort, and commitment.

To compete in the global arena, you have to incur—and defray—immense fixed costs. You need partners. . . .
With enough time, money, and luck, you can do everything yourself. But who has enough? . . . Having control does not necessarily mean better management.

Kenichi Ohmae[22]

Collaboration is the best form of education. By working in strategic alliances you benefit financially and learn strategically—and you save a lot of time and money in the process.

It's not devious to absorb skills from your partner—that's the whole idea.

Hamel, Doz & Prahalad[23]

Modification of Goals   When globalizing, we need to rethink our goals. The vision, mission, and strategy of the enterprise need to reflect the focus on globalization. Our core competencies and core processes need to be evaluated in light of the new global agenda.

Relocation Decisions   The vision, mission, and corporate strategy need to be centralized, but the business strategy needs to be diversified (localized). The localization process needs to be done carefully, with consideration given to local attitudes and cultures, or the investment will be a failure. For example, in the case of plant relocations, the approach taken in justifying a plant relocation can mean the difference between success and failure. Most relocations are still based on a labor-cost approach, forgetting issues such as increased inventory carrying costs or relocation overhead costs. Much better approaches exist, including the total-cost approach, the value-added approach, and the critical resource approach. In the total-cost approach, all costs of relocation are considered, including overhead and burden costs. In the value-added approach, the products selected for relocation are those that contribute least to overall corporate profitability. The high-value-added products are kept at home so that the home company and country can maximize the profitability of these products. In the critical resource approach, the resource that is most critical to adding value to the product is evaluated to determine whether the relocation will reduce the costs of this critical element. If so, then relocation is considered desirable.[24]

The balance between centralization of goals and diversification of control is critical. All business units need to be focused on the same targets, but not all will achieve those targets using the same types of bows and arrows.

Developing the Strategy   Several excellent sources specifically assist in the development of a globalization strategy. They should be used if you need more detailed information than what has been presented here. Yip's article was written specifically to "globalize an individual firm's corporate strategy."[25] The Daniels and Radebaugh book listed in note 1 of this chapter offers a detailed explanation of global strategy development.

CHARACTERISTICS OF A WORLD CLASS GLOBAL MANAGER

The World Class Global Manager incorporates all the strengths discussed in this chapter:

1. A "big picture" perspective
2. Globalizing the vision, mission, and corporate strategy
3. Utilizing international transactions to add value and minimize waste
4. Understanding global markets and competitors
5. Centralizing with a localized perspective
6. Develop global thinking corporations
7. Understanding cultural, political, demographic, and business climate differences and their effects on the business transaction
8. Understanding when globalization is good and when it isn't
9. Understanding differences in perspective
10. Understanding technology transfer
11. Utilizing comparative tools such as benchmarking
12. Moving from a copycat to an innovation mentality
13. Learning from competitors
14. Utilizing strategic alliances
15. Utilizing step-by-step building blocks toward improvements
16. Supporting free trade and avoiding protectionism

The *Harvard Business Review* has conducted a number of surveys on the characteristics of a World Class Global Manager. The one common characteristic is that "change is indeed everywhere—regardless of country, culture, or corporation." The surveys also show that culture, more than geography, is the major determinant of a manager's views.[26] These studies are ongoing and reinforce many of the points made in this chapter.

ADDITIONAL SOURCES OF INFORMATION

For a general-information publication on what's happening in the world, I recommend the *Christian Science Monitor*. For a business look at the world, I recommend the magazine *International Business*, which includes articles focused on the events within specific countries or regions as well as summary information such as the Dave Savona articles about trade and trade changes. For example, the August 1994 issue gave information about U.S. trade and the import-increase rankings of countries and featured China. In September 1994, the Caribbean was featured and information was supplied comparing the export trends of countries. In November 1994, India's growth was discussed and country imports were ranked.[27] International Cultural Enterprises in Deerfield, Illinois, puts out a useful *Worldwide Business Practices Report*.

The productivity and quality organizations listed in Appendix 5.2 can open the door to courses, consultants, and certification programs. I have listed a few more North America regional organizations in Appendix 6.1. Such organizations also offer excellent conferences and conference proceedings. Hundreds of helpful conference articles are available, such as the Albin article from an APICS conference that comments on *Fortune Magazine*'s global competitors and discusses ten successful global strategies, or the Peters article that describes the business strategy for the rapidly developing Asia-Pacific nations.[28] The Academy of International Business (AIB) is also an excellent source for international business conferences and proceedings.

A few books are also worth mentioning: *International Business—Environments and Operations, International Management and*

Production: Survival Techniques for Corporate America, and *Global Operations Perspectives.*[29]

SUMMARY

A bus driver and a minister died at the same time, and both met Peter at the pearly gates of heaven. Peter interviewed each of them; then he sent the bus driver to the highest place in heaven and the minister to the lowest. The minister protested and asked: "I dedicated my whole life to spreading the word of God. Why does a bus driver get the high place and I get such a low place?"

Peter answered, "When you preached, everyone slept. But when the bus driver drove his bus, everyone prayed."

I'm a little worried that I might be like the preacher when it comes to globalization. I would prefer this chapter (and the entire book) to affect you in the manner of the bus driver. I want you to feel as if you are on a whirlwind tour-bus ride that motivates you to pray for a rebirth. I want you to be reborn into a World Class Management realization that without a globalization strategy your enterprise will have difficulty achieving and maintaining a competitive stance.

SOLUTION TO FIGURE 6.1

The solution to Figure 6.1 is easy once you see the strategy involved. A tendency to limit the scope of our vision seems to be a common problem in attempting to solve Figure 6.1. Looking at Figure 6.3, we can see how, by looking beyond the isolated world of the nine dots and extending the lines beyond this region, we can easily connect the dots with four continuous lines by drawing them in the sequence A–B–C–A–D.

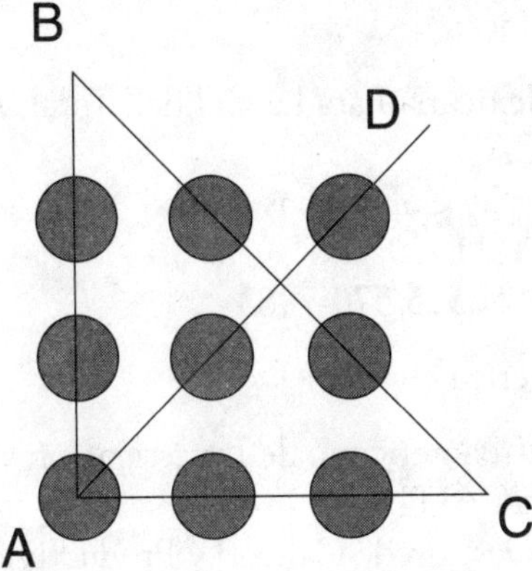

Figure 6.3   Nine Dots Solution

APPENDIX 6.1 NORTH AMERICA REGIONAL QUALITY AND PRODUCTIVITY ORGANIZATIONS

For Canada, contact one of the following:

Interfirm Comparison Program
Industry, Science and Technology Canada (ISTC)
Ottawa, Ontario K1A 0H5
Canada
(613) 954-4971

Productivity Improvement Service
Services to Business Branch
Industry, Science and Technology Canada (ISTC)
235 Queen Street
Ottawa, Ontario K1A 0H5
Canada
(613) 954-4969

For Mexico contact:

Fundacion Mexicana Para La Calidad Total, A. C.
FUNDAMECA
Loma Bonita #24 Col. Lomas Altas
Mexico, DFCP 11950
525/570-3989 & 525/570-7483

For Central America contact:

Instituto Centroamericano de Investigacion y Tecnologia
    Industrial (ICAITI)
Programa de Gestion de Calidad y Productividad (PGCP)
Ave. La Reforma 4-47, Zona 10
Gautemala 01010
Central America
502/2 31 06 31

CHAPTER 7

Technology Management/ Time-to-Market Strategies

The guts to attack yourself mercilessly is what counts.

Tom Peters

The computer is an utter and complete failure—or is it? If the development of a piece of technology does not achieve its initial goal, is it a failure? Often the initial reason for development of a piece of technology does not turn out to be its primary area of usefulness. NASA technology centers have developed hundreds of devices—medical advances such as incubators, fire-retardant materials such as fire suits, and optical materials such as night vision, for example—that have little to do with the initial reason for their development. The initial reason for the development of the computer was to predict the weather. We all know how accurate weather prediction has become since the introduction of the computer. So is the computer a failure? You be the judge.

Technology development has always been a strong point of the United States. The U.S. government, through its technology development centers, develops more technology than any other organization in the world. Unfortunately, the development of all this technology has little worth if it can't be turned into consumer products. For example, the United States was the developer of the air bag, but the Japanese and the Germans installed it in their cars first.

Technology developed in the United States is, by law, available to anyone and everyone who wants to copy it. There is an enormous library in Washington, D.C. where anyone can go to learn about developed technology. The function of the employees of the U.S. federal government who work for this library is to assist anyone interested in finding the desired technology. Unfortunately, the biggest users of this library are foreign businesses and foreign governments, not U.S. businesses or U.S. state and local governments. The U.S. government develops the technology, but U.S. business never gets around to applying its share of the technology. We can't seem to get it to market in time to be competitive.

In today's new business order, the spoils of corporate warfare belong not to the biggest companies, but to the quickest—those firms that consistently speed quality products or services to the marketplace and respond instantly to their customers' needs.

Philip R. Thomas

AREAS OF TECHNOLOGY COMPETITIVENESS

Technology is improvement, and leading-edge technology requires change. In the operation of a World Class Enterprise, technology improvement and its rapid implementation are continuously required in all areas. World Class Management involves continuous change through innovative technological improvement.

There are several areas of technology competitiveness. Few countries are competitive in all of them. They are:

Pure research technology

Time-to-market technology

Product technology

Process technology

Technology transfer

Facilities and equipment technology

Systems and procedures technology

Information technology

Services and customer support technology

Pure Research Technology   This area is the primary area of U.S. technological leadership. The U.S. technology data banks develop so much technology that it would take more resources than we have available to develop it all. However, U.S. industries tend to avoid this technology because they cannot maintain proprietary rights. Anyone can copy it, including international competitors who don't honor our patent laws. However, in today's high-speed competitive world, self-development of technology takes too long. We should let the experts in technology development create the technology for us, as they are so willing to do (similar to strategic alliances). This strategy would generate faster technology implementation, one of the keys to World Class competitiveness.

A network organization links all the federal technology centers. This network, the Federal Laboratory Consortium for Technology Transfer (FLC) exists solely to assist businesses in finding already developed technology that can be applied to satisfy their needs. It publishes a free newsletter, called *News Link*, that updates available resources for technology users. The FLC receives funding from each of the technology labs and matching grants from the White House. Some examples of the technology available are:

Fiberoptic connector advances

Vaccine improvements

Electromagnetic analysis tools

Airborne mapping systems for agriculture

Integrated circuit technology

Improved lasers for manufacturing

Solid oxide fuel cells to power electric cars

Computer security systems

NASA is one of the many technology labs. NASA has a library of 3,000 patents available for licensing by businesses and individuals in aerodynamics, chemicals, electronics, optics, medical research, test and measurement equipment, sensors, computer software, materials, mechanics, mathematics, life sciences, fabrication technology, machinery, manufacturing, physical sciences, and more. NASA publishes a free monthly summary of a small part of the technology that is developed and available for private industry called *NASA Tech Briefs*. This magazine contains a list of NASA technology transfer services (including contact names, addresses, and phone numbers). Technology transfer centers are located all over the country. Some recent examples of the hundreds of thousands of NASA technological developments are:

- COSMIC, a NASA library of thousands of computer software applications (for example, CARES, which is used by Mitsubishi Motors to predict the probability of failure for a rotating ceramic turbine rotor)
- Medical advances such as a cool suit for MS patients that improves vision and reduces fatigue
- Robotics so dexterous they can play the piano
- Icing buildup sensors for aircraft

Appendix 7.1 lists contact information for the FLC, NASA, and other technology organizations.

Time-to-Market Technology   As we already mentioned, this is the primary area of weakness for the United States and the primary strength of many Asian countries. In today's competitive World Class environment:

> Timing is everything.

The development of technology is only one small step for mankind. The second step is to find commercial application for the technology. The third step is to engineer the technology into a consumer product. The fourth step is to engineer manufacturing of the product so that it is producible rapidly, flexibly, and at low cost. The final steps are to produce the product and deliver it to the customer. Delays in any of these steps will destroy competitiveness. All areas need innoveering (innovative engineering—see Chapter 1).

Volumes have been written about the importance of an innoveered time-to-market effort for U.S. industry, and I can't attempt to reproduce it all here. However, when it takes U.S. manufacturers three to four months to build a bicycle—the same bicycle that can be produced in a couple of hours in an Asian plant—we can envision the magnitude of the problem. Another example of time differences involves the automotive fender-forming machine used in the United States, Sweden, and Japan. The setup time for this machine in the United States is six hours, in Sweden it's five hours, and in Japan it's 12 minutes. Consider also the new-product introduction time of four to five years in the United States versus less than a year in most Asian countries (a couple of months in Taiwan). The United States clearly has a long way to go, but we can do it, and many examples prove it. For example, Motorola reduced its invoice processing from 3.6 days to 30 minutes.

World Class enterprises realize that long-term strategies and short-term technology implementation and operations are the competitive advantage for the next decade. The opposite—short-term strategies and long-term technology implementation—is currently an ingrained part of the United States' method of operation. The most difficult part of this shift is effecting a change in attitudes and culture.[1] For example, IBM, with its development of the IBM Proprinter, was being hammered by its Japanese competitors. Recognizing that they had to "find another way of doing things," they redesigned with a "fast to market" philosophy. Among the changes was a Design for Automated Assembly (DFAA), which included a new set of rules such as the "no-fasteners" rule, needed in order to satisfy robotics limitations. IBM incorporated concurrent development, knocking eighteen months off the product development time. They adjusted the testing process so that it started and ended sooner. The bid-and-quote purchasing practices of tooling were suspended because they delayed tooling availability. The changes affected all areas of technology deployment. In the end, the Proprinter cut 40% off normal development time.[2]

You can do it! Remember:

> Be bold and courageous. When you look back
> on your life or the life of your company,
> you'll regret the things you didn't do more
> than the things you did.

Product Technology   Product technology ideas originate from several sources. For example, the customer may define a need that we try to fill, or the vendor may determine an improvement to our products. Employees are also an excellent source for product innovations, if we just ask them for their ideas. Sometimes product ideas come from pure research technology just begging for consumer application. Whatever the source of the technology, it needs to be transformed into a consumer product through the efforts of the product engineering people.

A World Class product technology strategy must satisfy several important requirements:

- Time—Time-to-market efficiency is crucial.
- Quality—The product must be exciting to the customer and satisfy customer requirements.
- Productivity—The product needs to be efficiently producible in our production environment.
- Teaming—It's not only engineers who develop a World Class product, but also customers, vendors, and employees. This implies a new culture.

Numerous strategies can affect and improve the product design process. One good example is described in the Henrickson article, which lists "forty things to do for more competitive product designs."[3]

A fundamental change must occur in your company culture and in the way you conduct business.

Dave Henrickson

Another example of product technology development is detailed in the Adler/Riggs/Wheelwright article, which stresses improving competitive position. This article focuses on management frustration with product development projects and suggests improvement strategies.[4]

Product technology development needs to have a faster time-to-market and be more focused on customer satisfaction (quality and productivity). And it needs to be a team effort in order to be World Class.

Process Technology   Whereas product technology development has always been a strength in the United States, process technology development has always been a strength in Japan. The Japanese have been known to copy U.S. products exactly, but they improve the methodology and speed of production to the point that they obliterate their American competitors in terms of cost and quality. This is true in the automotive and electronics industries as well as in many other industries. Process has simply never been a focus of concern in U.S. manufacturing. We always left it to the process engineers to come up with the best way to build products, and we never did what the Japanese do so very well—ask the employees who carry out the production process if they can think of any improvements. The difference is demonstrated in the setup times for the fender-forming machines mentioned earlier—six hours compared to twelve minutes. As another example, Sony has zero changeover time. New products begin on the assembly line while preceding models are still coming off the end of the line. Tool and die changes are made in minutes, as the assembly line is running.

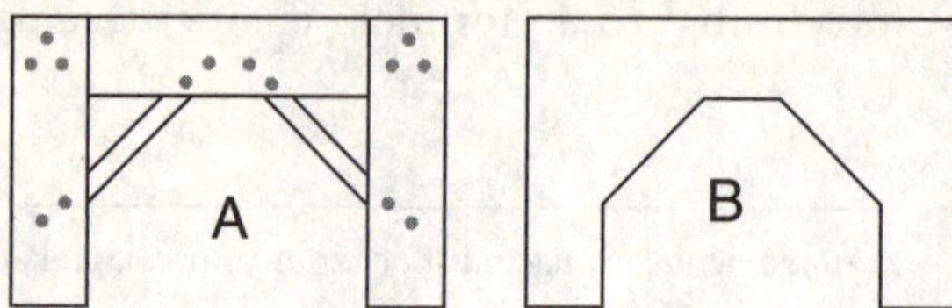

Figure 7.1   Worktable Design

Let us consider another example where process technology (also affecting product technology) was significantly transformed when the employees became involved. In this case, the engineers were made to work side-by-side with the production employees for a period of time, making their own products. The engineers learned much from their temporary co-workers. They also learned from the frustrations they personally felt while building their own products. Figure 7.1 shows a small example of one of the effects of this project. Product A shows an initial worktable that was part of a much larger product. The worktable was composed of sixteen structural pieces (four legs, eight angle braces, and four sides, no top). It was spot-welded at each of the overlapping connection points. Product B shows the redesign of this table using one sheet of folded sheet metal (folding down the legs at the corners) and requiring only one line of spot welds where the ends are joined. Product B is both cheaper to produce and much stronger.

Obsolete processes need updating and innovating; they need to be changed.

> You won't become
>   World Class
>   utilizing obsolescence!

Nearly all of the information available about process improvements comes from two sources:

1. The theories of the Americans
2. The tools of the Japanese

American theorists who are experts in process improvements go back to Henry Ford and his assembly line and to Frederick Taylor and his book *The Principles of Scientific Management*.[5] Although these individuals have fallen into some disfavor, a reading of their original teachings will show that their philosophies, especially with regard to employee relations, aren't that different from what we are trying to copy from the Japanese today. It's the abuse of their philosophies over time that has caused them to seem outdated. More recently, American authors such as Deming, Juran, and Crosby and Japanese authors such as Shingo, Ishikawa, and Taguchi have taught us a great deal about process improvements (see Appendix 5.1).

Some more recent publications focus on process changes. For example, Belt discusses the tools available for process technology change implementation. Camp has written a book that discusses the benchmarking of the process (comparing the process with that of other organizations). Mody, Suri, and Sanders focus on the organizational changes required for effective process change implementation to maintain a steady pace of change.[6]

One dilemma that seems to be a contradiction and exists in process technology is the speed of technological change. The Japanese look for small, incremental changes developed and implemented by their employees through the process of empowerment. The United States tends to think of change as a surge of innovation effected by replacing production lines and even factories. Is rapid change better than incremental steps toward improvement? (See Chapter 10 for a discussion of the alternative change methods.) One thing is sure: change is critically necessary. The U.S. approach of looking for the big innovative step, unfortunately, often results in no change being made at all because of the long-term payback of large changes.

Behold the turtle. He only makes progress when he sticks his neck out.

James B. Conant

Is American industry a turtle looking for the big innovation that never happens?

Technology Transfer   Technology transfer, or technology exchange, has become a critical World Class strategy. As discussed in Chapter 6, technology partnerships with other companies or countries, like the use of strategic alliances, allow a company to focus on its core competencies, letting it do what it's best at. Refer to the discussion of the types of technology transfer in Chapter 6.

Surprisingly, some of the poorest technology transfers occur within our own company or country. Intercompany communications need "rapid, radical change." There is still too much of an "over the wall," departmentalized mentality within companies. We waste a lot of time, money, and effort when two facilities develop similar software packages or work out technology implementation procedures independently.

Technology substitution is an excellent form of technology transfer. For example, a process developed in Russia, known in the United States as group technology, focuses on identifying similar parts that could be used interchangeably as substitutes for each other. Group technology avoids the unnecessary design, development, and production of similar, interchangeable products by different parts of the organization. I have encountered situations in which engineers working right next to each other have designed very similar (interchangeable) products and have triggered the making of tools and dies and the cataloging of procedures to make these similar products. They both had their own setups and schedules. This situation adds no value and is a blatant waste of resources.

Facilities and Equipment Technology   In considering areas for technological advances, we often consider only product technologies. We have already discussed the importance of time-to-market and process technologies. However, facilities and equipment technology is another forgotten area of technology that can make a big difference in World Class performance. The building, the materials movement equipment, and the preventive maintenance program all improve the productivity of an organization. For example, the Japanese focus on factories that are one-third to one-half the size of American plants. They use equipment that is small and specifically task-functional (and much cheaper) and avoid the megamachine that does everything. They produce the same output and have the same size labor force. However, they use less space for materials movement and materials storage.

The organization of the facilities and equipment is also a factor. The United States tends to departmentalize similar equipment within the same area. The Japanese tend to organize the equipment in the sequence in which it will be utilized by the manufactured product. A World Class technology strategy should consider alternatives in facilities and equipment technology.

Systems and Procedures Technology   A focus on systems improvement is not new. Systems include production planning, logistics planning, inventory planning, accounting and billing systems, and so on. Systems technology means having the systems tools available for product and process improvements. Most Deming Award winners focus on systems improvements, for example, the documentation of all processes including reporting and feedback mechanisms. They continually study what, why, and how a process is carried out. They look for value added, trying to eliminate wasted steps in any procedure. They use tools such as flowcharting and wall pasting to review all the steps in a process and the length of time a particular process takes. Process improvement often includes the implementation of quality process control tools.*

The Japanese stress that "big systems mean big trouble" and that the movement into robotics or other sophisticated, automated technologies should occur only after the operating "bugs"

---

*Wall pasting refers to when you use a wall to diagram all the details of a process. You tape sample documents and procedures on the wall to show all the steps in an information process, and draw the appropriate connecting lines.

have been worked out. Often, in the United States, the implementation of a system is based on the philosophy that the "system" will solve the "bug." In actuality, the only thing most systems do is speed up the error creation process. Things can now go wrong faster. I have been involved in numerous implementations in which a computer and a software tool were introduced with the promise of improving employee discipline and reducing the number of errors. However, employees didn't understand that they needed to do things differently, and in the end the system failed. The "system," not the poor installation process, was blamed for the failure. The Japanese would suggest that until the employees understand and perform the process correctly, speeding up the process will only speed up the errors. The focus should be on understanding, training, and "keeping it simple."

Information Technology   For many organizations, information technology is beyond being a solution—it has become an obsession. We hurry to automate everything and anything, losing any focus on why we should automate. Goals and caution are thrown to the wind. Software technologies are brought in and out of companies as if they were toys. An information technology strategy needs to be a part of the overall company strategy and focused on the mission and vision of the company.

Having expressed my word of caution, let me stress that numerous areas of information technology can be extremely helpful and time saving. For example (these are just a few):

- Electronic Data Interchange (EDI)—the ability to transfer order and billing information between customers and vendors without extensive written documents
- Networking—the interconnection and data sharing among all organizations and people within a company
- The Personal Computer (PC)—computer power at every desk for analysis and planning
- Image Processing—the ability for anyone to review source documents on the computer screen from anywhere in the computer network

- Digital Technology—improved accuracy in the data collection and storage process, for example voice messaging

Tools such as multimedia marketing allow flexible information technology. However, the high price of this technology may make it prohibitive.[7] Other information technology tools provide international data sharing and information integration. In a recent research study, 82% of the companies studied indicated plans to increase their information technology, a higher percentage than for any other type of technology.[8]

Information technology is a very positive growth influence, but it needs to be focused on value-added and waste-elimination opportunities. I was recently asked to review a company's Statistical Process Control (SPC) process. Apparently they had been collecting data for about a year. Some consultant had told them that SPC was a good thing, so they implemented it. Each department had set up its own data collection criteria, but only a few departments had any idea why they were going through the process. Data collection for the sake of data collection is a waste; it adds no value. Similarly, I have worked in factories where, every once in a while, we would not deliver the month-end reports or would deliver them late on purpose, just to see who would scream. Those who screamed were those who actually used the reports. For the others (about 80%), we were generating waste. Perhaps it's time to review the value-added influence of your information system.

Common sense is not common.
Will Rogers

Services and Customer Support Technology   Ultimately, technology advances should be focused on the customer. However, we often forget about technology interfaces with the customer. Improved customer communication, whether it's an 800 number for complaints or problems or an arrangement whereby people from our organization work at the customer site to better understand the customer's needs, is a form of technology that can be just as critical as any other form of technology discussed. Often, this is the only thing the customer sees, and it is a vital element in achieving customer satisfaction and repeat business. We need to make a good impression on the customer via an effective customer interface.

A TECHNOLOGY STRATEGY

I never did anything worth doing by accident, nor did any of my inventions come by accident. They came by work.

Thomas A. Edison

The key to a technology strategy is the customer. Occasionally, technology development for the sake of technology (like the Post-it Notes) generates benefits, but most often it is technology development focused on customer satisfaction that brings the biggest rewards. This emphasis translates into a technology strategy that focuses on:

Quality

Timeliness

Productivity

Service

Competitiveness

A customer-oriented technology strategy requires:

Customer tie-ins

Employee tie-ins

Vendor tie-ins

A keep-it-simple strategy

A focus on:

How much technology

When to introduce the technology

Where, or in what areas, to introduce the technology

A corporate culture shift toward motivating innovation and invention

One of the toughest areas for technology strategy development is the area of new product development. However, numerous recent studies assist with planning such a strategy. For example, Roberts and Berry stress a framework for a new-product entry strategy that focuses on the enterprise's future growth and profitability. Wheelwright focuses on why development projects go wrong and suggests that failed projects tend to be reactionary (responding to problems) rather than planned strategies for technological implementation.[9]

. . . the organization fails to plan sufficiently for the requisite skills and resources, to define the project and its purposes appropriately, and to integrate the development project with other basic strategies.

Steven C. Wheelwright

Another study, by Lewis and Linden, stresses that we sometimes waste time and money unnecessarily by focusing on technological development when it is not part of our core competency.[10]

Much of the money and effort spent today on research and development at the corporate level is wasted. . . . [It is] necessary only if a company is following a technology leadership strategy . . .

Lewis & Linden

There is also the concern, addressed by Erickson, Magee, Roussel, and Saad, that the focus on short-term profitability may derail vital research and development programs. This study states that incremental, innovative technological improvements in existing product lines and innovating to adapt old products to new markets tend to be most profitable.[11]

A program to develop a radically new technology must be approached with great caution; it can be a strategic trap.

Erickson, Magee, Roussel & Saad

The Economist has conducted an interesting survey of manufacturing and process technologies in order to identify cutting-edge technology strategies. This study stresses that information technologies tend to be the technology that is most fruitful. It also focuses on the effective utilization of time-to-market technologies and process technologies such as robotics as a strategic advantage.[12]

Integrated engineering change management, which eliminates over-the-wall technology or engineering departments, promotes interaction and time-focused change. Time-focused change is the World Class competitive strategy of the future.

Positive, goal-focused technology development is change, and change is competitive advantage. Without an aggressive technology development strategy, whether it focuses on all the technological areas listed or just on one core competency area, we cannot stay competitive.

It is a bad plan that admits of no modification.

Publilius Syrus

A TIME-TO-MARKET STRATEGY

A time-to-market strategy should really be part of a technology strategy. However, it is so competitively critical that I want to emphasize it by addressing it all by itself. A corporate and business-unit strategy must incorporate a plan for being time-competitive. This plan must define the time elements for all the technology areas discussed in this chapter, including:

- Time to develop pure research technology
- Time to develop product technology
- Time to incorporate the necessary process technology
- Time savings through technology transfer
- Time savings and waste elimination through facilities and equipment technology
- Time savings with systems and procedures technology
- Time-improved information technology, avoiding waste-generating data and reports
- Time-response-oriented services and customer support technology

Supportive literature includes recent conference articles, such as those by Arenberg and Vesey, which stress engineering focus and efficiency in the time-to-market process.[13] The Thomas book focuses on time-to-market reduction in the production and process technologies areas.[14] The Peters article stresses ten "must-dos" for a World Class Manager in a time-competitive environment. These are:[15]

1. Pioneering the application of information technology inside and outside the firm
2. A revolution in organization structure—a flatter organization with no borders or barriers
3. Total Process Revision (TPR)—eliminating administrivia
4. Measurement—making time the principal basis for measurement
5. Wholesale empowerment
6. Decentralization
7. Shift from adversary to partner—networking through strategic alliances based on trust (see Chapter 6)
8. Eliminating job descriptions (see Chapter 14)
9. Focusing on wholes, not parts—networking and the big picture
10. Time-focused way of life—time-obsessed competition entrenched into the enterprise

> *To compete in time, the average front-line employee must*
> *be encouraged to go anywhere, talk to anybody, to get*
> *any information.*
>
> Tom Peters

ADDITIONAL READINGS

Consult the following books to find out more about competitive strategies in technology. *Strategic Technology Management*, by Frederick Betz (New York: McGraw-Hill Engineering and Technology Management Series, 1993), discusses core competencies, goal setting, and technology planning. It goes through all potential areas that a technology strategy might cover. *World Class Manufacturing*, by Thomas F. Wallace (Essex Junction, Vt.: Oliver Wight Publications, Inc., 1994), offers a chapter on infrastructure and technology.

SUMMARY

Did the microwave oven replace the traditional oven, as was initially planned? No! But most kitchens won't be caught without it. It has become too useful for defrosting meat and making popcorn. In the end, do we care whether the microwave replaced the oven? Yes! Because we now need to focus the microwave on what the customer expects from it. We need to focus on technological advances that will satisfy the customer and possibly open the door to new, expanded—yet undiscovered—technological opportunities. After all, before the microwave existed, no one knew they wanted it. The key question at this point is not whether the microwave is valuable but whether the United States can innovate and technologically advance the microwave into new, unfounded product and process territory before foreign competitors do it and we lose the market completely. That is the real time-to-market competitive technology strategy issue that needs to be addressed by the World Class Manager.

APPENDIX 7.1
U.S. GOVERNMENT TECHNOLOGY
DATA SOURCES

Federal Laboratory Consortium for Technology Transfer (FLC) and *News Link* newsletter:

> FLC
> P.O. Box 545
> Sequim, WA 98382-0545
> (206) 683-1828

National Aeronautics and Space Administration (NASA):

> *NASA Tech Briefs* magazine:

> > NASA Tech Briefs
> > 41 E. 42nd St., Suite 921
> > New York, NY 10017-5391

> Technology Transfer Division:

> > P.O. Box 8757
> > Baltimore/Washington International Airport, MD 21240

> COSMIC (software):

> > Suite 112, Barrow Hall
> > University of Georgia
> > Athens, GA 30602
> > (404) 542-3265

> NASA Industrial Applications Center:

> > 823 William Pitt Union
> > University of Pittsburgh
> > Pittsburgh, PA 15260
> > (412) 648-7000

> NASA Industrial Applications Center:

> > University of Southern California
> > 3716 S. Hope St., Suite 200
> > Los Angeles, CA 90007-4344
> > (213) 743-6132

U.S. Army Electronics Research and Development Command:

U.S. Army Electronics R & D Command
Night Vision and Electro-optics Laboratory
Fort Belvoir, VA 22060

Lawrence Livermore National Laboratory:

Lawrence Livermore National Laboratory
Technology Information System
P.O. Box 808, Mail Stop L-275
Livermore, CA 94550

Naval Weapons Center:

Naval Weapons Center
China Lake, CA 93555
(619) 939-9011

Journal of Technology Transfer:

The Technology Transfer Society
611 North Capital Ave.
Indianapolis, IN 46204
(317) 262-5022

Integration, Information, and Measurement Strategies

The measure of success is not whether you had a tough problem to deal with, but whether it's the same problem you had last year.

John Foster Dulles

Dorothy arrived at a crossroad in the *Wizard of Oz* and asked the Scarecrow which way she should go. His response was "That all depends on where you are headed; if you don't know, then any road will do!"

In developing the road map that will guide us on our journey to World Class Management status, we started with a vision statement and a mission statement, both focusing on our core competencies. Then we developed a corporate and business-unit strategy focused on what we are trying to accomplish. Now we need to develop a measurement/motivation strategy that conveys to the work force what it is that we are trying to achieve. This measurement system is the primary focus of this chapter, but before we discuss the measurement system, we discuss two elements that are closely tied to the measurement process: integration and information.

AN INTEGRATION STRATEGY

> Everything was said,
>   that needs to be said—
> But since no one was listening
>   it needs to be said again.

Integration is a topic that reminds me of the speaker who needs no introduction but demands one. One major shortcoming of this book is that it segments World Class Management tools (in the American way). In reality, none of these tools have stand-alone value; they all need to be integrated. We need to involve (integrate) people and systems, utilizing the best of each and eliminating the waste in each, thereby maximizing the value added.

Several changes need to be made within our organizations in order for us to overcome the barriers to integration. Areas of change include:

- Focused goals
- Over-the-wall organizations
- Organizational structure
- Physical environment
- Process/technology
- Employees' abilities
- Team/empowerment culture
- Information systems
- Measurement/motivational systems

The last two items in this list are discussed in the second and third sections of this chapter. The team/empowerment culture is the subject of Chapter 14. We will briefly discuss the first six items in the list in this section.

Focused Goals   Chapters 3 and 4 thoroughly discussed goals, including the development of goals using:

Core competencies

Vision statement

Mission statement

Corporate strategy

Business-unit strategy

Plan of operation

Chapter 3 also discussed the measurement of goal performance using measurement tools such as:

Quality

Productivity

Efficiency

In this chapter we reemphasize the importance of focusing these goals and measures on the same target (remember Robin Hood). Being World Class means having a focused integration strategy in which all parts of the company are aiming for the same target yet each is empowered to develop its own road map to get there.

Focused goals also necessitate integration of people, as discussed in Chapter 2 and again in Chapter 14. World Class integration incorporates:

Customers

Vendors

Employees (from CEO to line workers)

An integration plan should also include focusing goals on a time-based strategy, as discussed in Chapter 7.[1] With correctly defined goals, we won't need the help of the Scarecrow to direct us down the best path to World Class performance.

Over-the-Wall Organizations   We've heard the story before, but we still haven't learned the lesson.

> Departmentalized,
>   hierarchical
>   organizations
>   don't communicate,
>   and
>   can't compete.

Enterprises have numerous internal barriers. One of the biggest barriers is an over-the-wall organization. In this type of organization, each department works independently. For example, marketing generates a forecast without regard to customer wants. Engineering designs a product without integrating its design with marketing or the customer. Engineering throws its design, and marketing its forecast, over the wall to production, which in turn modifies both sets of numbers to satisfy capacity and producibility, again communicating with neither. This of game of independency goes on throughout the enterprise.

World Class Enterprises have realized that integration is the key to success. The organization needs to be borderless, both vertically and horizontally. Vertically borderless organizations have dropped job titles and hierarchical definitions (see the discussion below of organizational structure). Horizontally borderless organizations no longer define departments along functional lines but rather organize themselves along process lines. Such organizations don't have a marketing department, a production department, and so on; rather, they have an automotive department, a television department, and the like. Within this process department structure, all employees are encouraged to work together, eliminating traditional functional barriers. The marketing and engineering employees' desks are on the shop floor right next to the people who are producing the product. The process group is empowered, as a team, to change almost anything, as long as it focuses on the target goals given to them.

Borderless organizations are organic. This means that they are not rigid but instead grow and evolve as the needs of the organization change. Employees may change functions and roles. They are encouraged to communicate with anyone within or outside the organization—customers, competitors, vendors—whatever it takes to get the job done and get it done right.

Integration requires teaming across functional boundaries (see Chapter 14). Teaming encourages communication, and communication encourages integration. In World Class borderless, organic organizations, integration processes are part of the strategic plan.[2]

Organizational Structure   Hierarchical organizations have a rigid and proceduralized structure for communication. The rapid move toward World Class high-speed time-to-market strategies, which involve employee empowerment, requires breaking down these traditional barriers. Employees shouldn't have to talk to their boss, who talks to his or her boss, who communicates with another functional area to the boss there, who communicates to a subordinate supervisor, who communicates with his or her employee, who gives the information to the supervisor, who communicates with his or her boss, who . . . you get the picture. The result of time-to-market strategies has been to eliminate as many levels of the hierarchical structure as possible.

The elimination of power levels has generated concern about the span of control. A manager is supposed to be able to manage only four or five employees effectively. However, by reducing the number of levels, managers now have ten, fifteen, or more direct subordinates. The solution is to change the role of the manager from drill sergeant to facilitator. The manager no longer directs activity. Now the manager leads, or orchestrates activity, and empowers the employees to run their own organization.

The issue of centralization versus distribution also comes into play. With fewer levels, the CEO is much closer to the line employees. This situation encourages increased centralization. However, empowerment offers the localized teams of employees the opportunity to make localized decisions, which encourages decentralization. If the CEO's role is defined correctly, he or she will realize that it also involves being a facilitator, and the new centralization should not obstruct localized efforts at making the company successful.

Physical Environment   Physical integration means physically putting the CEO's and plant manager's desks in the middle of the factory floor. It means removing walls, suits and ties, and other physical distinctions that draw attention away from empowerment, teaming, and integration. It may mean physical relocation of plants or of machines within the plants so that the enterprise can become process, rather than functionally, focused.

Process/Technology   In process integration, the company organizes around a process that it accomplishes. For example, if one of our processes is building televisions, then all aspects of the organization that go into building televisions are organized together. For example, we would house:

Information systems

Accounting

Marketing

Engineering

Production

Purchasing

Customer support

Logistics

Technology development (see Chapter 7)

This is not to suggest that we should eliminate the synergistic benefits of large purchasing, accounting, or information systems groups. However, we need representation from each group involved in our functionally empowered team.

Employees' Abilities

People are lonely because they build walls instead of bridges.

Joseph Fort Newton

We tend to be so busy driving our employees that we forget to communicate with them. If we would do the unheard of—sit down with our employees during working hours and find out what they think, feel, like, dislike, and so on—we just might learn something about ourselves and the enterprise. We need to interview our employees on a regular basis, not just those we want to reprimand but also those who are doing a good job for us. We can learn a lot from all our employees. Communication should involve a personal, one-on-one interview searching for ideas, opinions, and feelings. Don't be disappointed if the first one or two times do not seem fruitful. The employees are still trying to figure out what you are up to; they don't trust you any more than you trust them. Give it time, and you'll be amazed at what you learn.

To see our people talking about something that they know more about than anyone else—their jobs, and how to make them better—is exciting. It gets to you. . . . We've got people here who are stars—who really want the opportunity to participate and to plot their own course.

Shigeo Shingo, Toyota

Another key step in the employee integration process is teaming, which is discussed in detail in Chapter 14. The interaction and synergy of teaming to focus on problem solving has long been an effective method of change improvement in Japan. Teaming taps the employees' abilities to solve problems and integrates them into the overall operation of the enterprise. But it takes time. For example, looking at the teaming process for Toyota, we see in Table 8.1 that it has taken thirteen years to increase the number of suggestions per employee from ten to forty-seven. However, the total history for the small-group (team) improvement process at Toyota goes back much farther, and the effectiveness of the process is now obvious. Employees are integrated into the process, and their abilities are an integral part of the company. Employees are empowered to make a difference—they are empowered to change.

Table 8.1. Toyota's Small-Group Improvements

Year	Number of Suggestions	Suggestions per Person	Adoption Percentage
1976	463,000	10.6	83%
1979	575,000	12.8	91%
1980	860,000	18.7	94%
1985	1,000,000+	24.0	95%
1989	2,000,000	47.0	96%

Source: Shigero Shingo, *Study of the Toyota Production System from an Industrial Engineering Standpoint* (Tokyo: Japanese Management Association, 1981), p. 114.

People integration requires training. Taking advantage of our employees' abilities requires education in how to find opportunities for change and implement them. Employee integration also requires the strengthening of the abilities of employees at all levels. Horizontal integration of the staff is not enough. Vertical integration between management and staff is equally important. Anyone in the company should feel free to talk to anyone else, no matter what level or job function. Only then can the abilities of the employees be utilized and effectively shared.

The role of the employee has been discussed in nearly every chapter of this book. The focus on employee integration in order to effectively take advantage of employees' abilities has been discussed since the days of Henry Ford and is still a critical issue today. People integration requires people, and people need time, not to learn, but to understand and trust the change process. People integration takes patience. However, without people integration, all other forms of integration are merely high-tech exercises.

The Overall Integrated Enterprise

Many of the tools for integrative change have already been discussed, and more will be explained in Chapter 11. The common themes throughout all the literature that discusses enterprise integration are:

Management commitment

Time (employee commitment to integration is slow)

Supportive structures and systems (e.g., teaming)

Internal measurements (e.g., benchmarking)

Integrative technologies (e.g., information systems)

World Class enterprise integration starts at the top with management commitment and reaches the bottom with teaming and empowerment. It eliminates walls and barriers between departments and functions, but it also realizes that the integration process, especially the employee aspects, takes time. Therefore, World Class enterprise integration is a long-term commitment to change.[3]

A DATA-INFORMATION STRATEGY

Always be sure you're right, then go ahead.

Davey Crockett

Are we an information society? The United States seems to think so. However, before we get too wrapped up in collecting data and disseminating information, we need to note that the Japanese use little or no computer power to schedule the production floors of their World Class competitive factories, whereas we in the United States use a great deal of computer power. That doesn't mean that data and information are bad; it means that our obsession with data collection is often unfocused. Collecting data because we love data, or generating information because of the prestige attached to presenting a computer report is a waste. It adds no value.

An effective World Class integrated information strategy has focus, as does any other functional area of the organization. The focus needs to be targeted on the goals of the organization.

Building an Information Target

In developing a measurable target for all levels of our enterprise, we need to match the target to the function. For example, a target of customer service is interpreted differently for the different areas of an organization. For the production department, customer service is measured by the number of production-related problems with sold products. The engineering department measures customer service on design-related problems that cause ineffective product performance. For the customer service department, the measure should be response time and follow-up satisfaction. The measures of performance need to be broken down to measure the teams responsible for the various aspects of the operation being evaluated. Of course, positive responses and compliments should also be recorded.

Bringing the information system on target means that the information system focuses on the area of performance we want to maximize. I worked with a company that had incorporated a very elaborate quality system. The slogan of the company focused on its high level of quality. The plaques were on the wall, the statistical process control systems were in place, and quality personnel had been trained. However, the quality problems still remained enormous. When I was asked for an opinion on what was wrong, I requested the paperwork that the employees had filled out. The employees were asked to fill out and report on their job start and stop times and the quantity of units produced. They were measured on efficiency, and they were rewarded (bonuses were paid) based on this efficiency measure. The question I posed to the organization was "Are the employees rewarded for quality?" I was given some blue-sky answer about pats on the back and plaques. But the bottom line was that the employees were being rewarded for performance based on quantity, not quality, and that's what the company got from them. They had forgotten the old saying:

> You get what you pay for.

Building an information target does not have to be difficult. Let me try to simplify it. For example, if we are trying to build cars and our goal is profitability, then we can analyze the contribution made by each of the plant's resources to the profitability of the car. We will get numbers like:

Labor: 8–10%

Materials: 50–60%

Machinery: 5–10%

Burden: 20–40%

From this example it should be obvious that the resource that contributes to the profitability of the car is the materials resource. The materials resource is our critical resource. Therefore, if we have a goal focused on profitability, we want to make sure the information system measures individual performance on materials efficiency, whether it's in purchasing, storing, or materials waste in the manufacturing process.

Cadillac, a recent winner of the Baldrige award, had numbers similar to those listed above. However, they revised their goals and shifted to a focus on customer satisfaction. They needed to reevaluate the contribution of their resources to this new goal. They needed to identify their new critical resource. They did this through an extensive customer survey process. For example, they asked customers what was more important in a car seat: the fabric (materials), the stitching (labor), the contouring (engineering), and so on. For Cadillac, the overwhelming new critical resource was engineering. They revised the information systems focus to reflect the new importance of this resource.

Information Tools

Numerous information tools are available to us. They can be divided into the following categories:

Types and processing of information

Information analysis and organization tools

Before we discuss each of these areas, let us define data and information:

- Data—the collection of numbers, figures, measurements, reports, etc.; what goes into the data processing system
- Information—processed data rearranged into a summarized report, chart, graph, or screen display; the output of the data processing system

Types and Processing of Information   Numerous methods exist for collecting data and disseminating the processed information. For collecting the data, we use qualitative methods, such as surveys, reports, and interviews, which relate success stories or problems. We also use quantitative methods such as statistical sampling, time reports, or units of production. Numerous devices are available for collecting the data, including computer keyboards, sensors, time clocks, and so on.

Once the data has been collected, there are various tools for processing it: spreadsheets, word processors, data base management systems, or manual reports. The data is summarized, sorted, and grouped. Then the output information is generated using summary or exception (displaying only the errors) processing. The output is in the form of reports or computer screen displays.

The types of information that are generated include reports on success or failure, or better yet tendencies toward success or failure, which help us anticipate situations before they happen. The information may be financial (e.g., exchange rates), or it may be technological or operational (e.g., inventory levels).

Next the information is made available to all areas of the organization through a variety of transfer processes. These processes include:

- E-mail—an electronic, international, information messaging system
- Fax—transmission of images over the telephone system
- Teleconferencing—a method of holding meetings in multiple locations using television-type images
- Electronic Data Interchange (EDI)—data directly transmitted between locations, as between vendors and customers for order processing

- Image Processing—source document images available on any computer terminal
- Networking—multiple computer access to the same data base without data transfer requirements
- Information Superhighway—a network tool that allows data and information of all forms to be processed and transmitted from anywhere to anywhere
- Integrative Technology—for example, Computer Integrated Manufacturing (CIM), is an information systems tool that integrates accounting, personnel, finance, marketing, production, engineering, robotics, inventory storage and retrieval, numerically controlled machines, and so on into a common data base

Like all operational environments, information systems should focus on:

Facilitating change

Increasing value added

Eliminating waste

The information processing system should do a self-check to see if it is, in fact, collecting data that focuses on goal-directed changes. If not, then it is generating waste. Not all data and information are "good" by their nature. Waste data and information are time consuming and resource consuming. One way to make sure that the data collection–information generation system is not generating waste is to involve the system users in the decision process. Ask the sources of the data if there are any problems in the data collection process, for example:

- Do you understand the purpose of the data collected?
- Do things happen that circumvent the accuracy of the data?
- Is there a better way (more timely, more accurate, more meaningful) to collect the data?

Similar questions could be asked of the people who receive the information, for example:

- Is the information presented to you in the form that you use it (sequence, timeliness)?
- Is there too much information?
- Is something missing?
- Should some pieces of information be consolidated?

As with all technologies, if the users (customers of the technology) aren't involved in the development of the technology, they are unlikely to have a stake in its use. In information systems technology, as in most changes, ownership is very important. If the users of the system have ownership of the system, they will tend to ensure its success.

Information Analysis and Organization Tools   Information systems should be a step in the path toward better integration. There are numerous tools available that help in integration, including:

The systems approach

Object-oriented programming

Software modularization

The Systems Approach   The systems approach is a tool used by many Deming and Baldrige award winners as well as by ISO 9000 to document and analyze a particular process. The systems approach is a tool whose usefulness is not limited to information systems. For example, if we were analyzing the invoice processing within our enterprise, we would take all the pieces of paper, all the phone calls, and all the paper transfer steps and would draw these steps on a wall, with little boxes and circles around them and lines connecting them to show the sequence of the flow. Then we would put times next to each box to indicate how long each step takes. We would continue this diagramming process until we had all the steps and all the pieces of paper diagrammed. Then we would look at this diagram and ask "Why do we do this?" or "How does this step help in achieving the goal of this process?" for each step in the process. We systematically, step by step challenge and redefine the process, eliminating waste and focusing on value added.

The systems approach has also been characterized as looking to the future rather than the past. We should focus on how things should be rather than focusing on how they are and trying to correct them. Future-oriented systems analysis is outlined in the following steps:

1. Focus on the key tasks.
2. Define the ideal system.
3. Concentrate on the process and the speed (time).
4. Assess ways of improvement toward the goal focus.
5. Build in simplicity.
6. Be sure every step is value-added (waste-eliminating).

Another systems tool is flowcharting, which defines the logical sequence for a process to occur. Flowcharting defines the decision-making process that occurs in any series of steps. Again, with flowcharting we are trying to logically identify the steps in a process and to identify and eliminate waste (unnecessary steps) in the process.

Object-Oriented Programming   Object-oriented programming is a new computer systems development tool that focuses on building information systems that are event- and goal-oriented. Programming is a series of events, not steps, that focus on the overall goal. For example, we might focus on systems development that will help us create a better-quality car in less time.

Software Modularization   Software modularization is a strategy that attempts to avoid duplication of effort. We build a software product that has building blocks, each of which can be rearranged into different systems to achieve different purposes. The Japanese have long been masters of this process, utilizing a modular software data bank where all software is available through a computer network and can be used by anyone on any machine.

Modular software avoids point solutions, that is, software that focuses on one specific solution and cannot find multiple uses. Modular software is generalized so that it can be cross-utilized.

In the United States, many forms of software are still incompatible. For example, small systems software, such as the PC, is not usable on medium-size systems, and medium-size products are

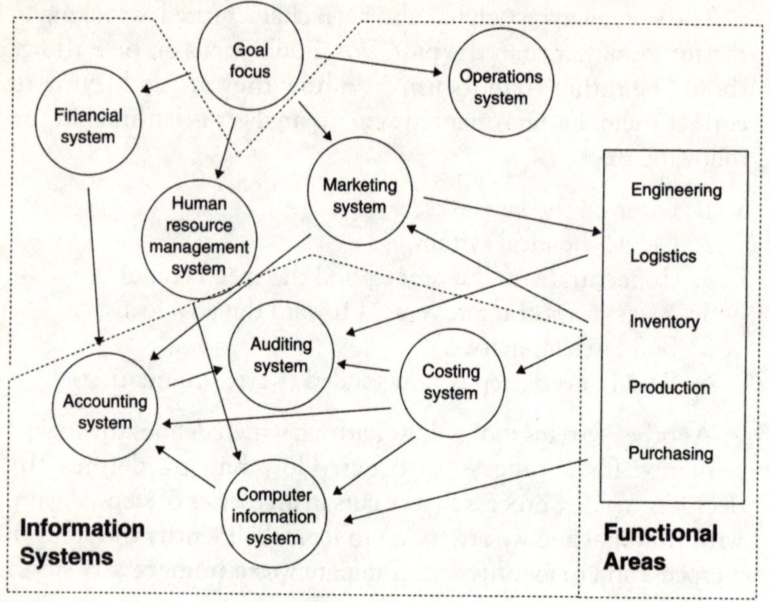

Figure 8.1   The Information Flow

not usable on large systems. The reverse is also true. Additionally, within similar size machines, the software is not transferable. Unfortunately, even within the same brand of equipment on the same size machine, the software is often not transferable.

Although a nationwide data bank of software across all sizes of machines might be nice, it really isn't feasible. However, software modularity within your organization *is* feasible and should be part of the information strategy for your enterprise.

The Integrated Information-Flow Diagram

Information integration can be very complex. However, as we have stated several times already, one of the keys to information integration is simplicity. In Figure 8.1, we see the information flow for an organization.* Note that systems such as the accounting system, auditing system, costing system, and computer information system are supportive information systems whose role is not to run the company but rather to supply information to the functional areas of the organization.

Figure 8.2 shows the feedback mechanisms that help management stay goal-focused. The feedback informs the various functional areas of the organization as to which elements are successfully goal-focused and which are generating waste.**

The information systems areas need to be reevaluated regularly to ensure that they are integrated and value-adding components

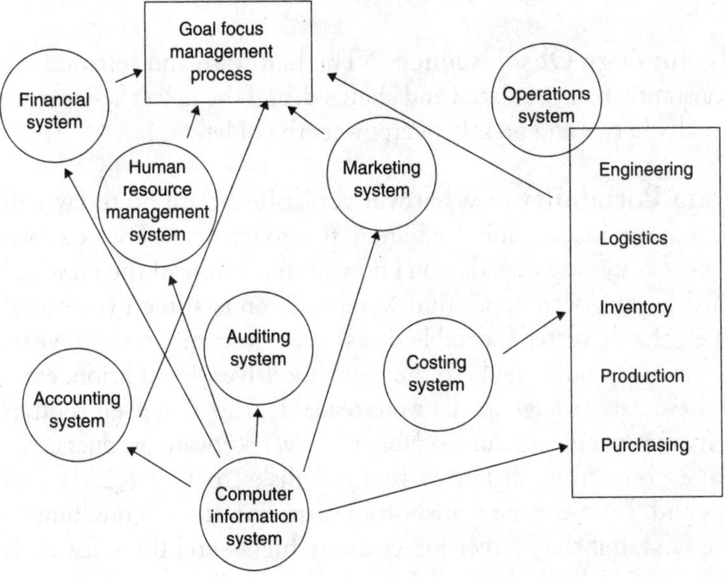

Figure 8.2   The Feedback Flow

---

*Each system is given guidance (goals) and feeds this guidance down into lower level systems.
**The feedback mechanisms supply an outward flow of information back to the higher information levels that can then respond and react.

of the organization. Much more detail is available on this integrated information flow process.[4]

The Short-Sightedness of Information Systems

Information systems are short-term systems. An investment in an information system should not be expected to last more than five years—and often it lasts less. There are several reasons for this, including:

Technology obsolescence

Data portability

Systems failure

Objective/goal-defeating systems

Technology Obsolescence   The hardware and software are constantly being updated and changed, and the newer systems are usually better and greatly overpowers the older.

Data Portability   Whatever you collect data on today will become an inaccessible medium in five to ten years. For example, how many computers do you know of that can read the punched cards or magnetic tapes that were used ten to fifteen years ago? Even the diskettes (portable disks) used on computers ten years ago are now unreadable to the new disk drives. In addition, even if these data storage media were readable, the data itself is often software-specific and unreadable to newer software products. We have gone from diskettes to hard disks to CD ROMs and beyond. Data can be transported from one storage medium to the next, but the conversion costs are high—and the software is often not convertible at all.

Systems Failure   Old systems technology, like old technology of any sort, is noncompetitive. To be competitive, we need to keep our software technology updated. This involves a continual, never-ending series of changes. As processes within the enterprise are updated, supportive systems need to updated as well.

Objective/Goal-Defeating Systems　　"Cost accounting systems are the enemy of efficient and productive production departments."[5] This statement focuses on the use of systems such as cost accounting, a system that has come to have its own agenda without regard for the needs of the production department. Systems of this type are goal-defeating. Another example is U.S. accounting systems, which list labor as a cost of operation (a negative, bad thing) and inventory as an asset (a positive, good thing). This classification is the opposite of what logic would dictate, and this type of thinking causes labor to be the first cost-cutting measure whenever cost cuts are required. To make matters worse, inventory carrying (financing) costs, which are often so high that they can easily destroy the profitability of a company, are buried in burden. This means that such costs are considered to be uncontrollable and are therefore ignored as a cost-reduction option. I have been in numerous situations in which inventory carrying costs are higher than labor costs. Accounting structures such as this are objective/goal-defeating systems. The United States is reevaluating its accounting-information systems, looking to redefine the measures that are used. The I-CAM project at Wright-Paterson Air Force Base in Dayton, Ohio, is working on a similar project.

Systems are in a constant state of flux. No system will last more than a few years without being updated. Even something as basic as a word processing package is constantly coming out with updated versions. Realizing this, we need to plan for a constant change environment in our information strategy. We need to focus on short-term, not long-term, systems development.

Software That Fits

The question often arises: should we purchase software, or should we develop it ourselves? Purchased software never fits exactly, but self-developed software takes forever. The answer to the question lies in your core competencies. Is software development one of your core competencies? If not, don't do it! Even if the purchased software doesn't fit perfectly, remember that it's only about a five-year solution, and then you'll need to purchase another software product that doesn't fit perfectly. That's still better than spending three of those five years developing your own software only to have it become obsolete two years later.

Several organizations offer software comparison services similar to that of *Consumer Reports*. For example, APICS offers a ratings service for production systems alternatives, and the Council of Logistics Management offers a software ratings and comparisons report for logistics software products (see Appendix 8.1). What you need to do is find the software ratings service for the type of software you are interested in, look over their features and functions list, and select about four or five products that seem to fit your needs. Order additional information from these organizations—possibly even demos. Test the software products with your own data to see if they work. You must use your own data. I have encountered situations in which a company purchased a software product only to discover that there weren't enough decimal places of accuracy or a large enough description field for chemical formulas. Only after testing the software in your environment, using a team of future users of the software to do the testing, are you ready to purchase and install the software.

Is There an Information Revolution?

There is definitely an information revolution! The time and volume of data necessary to be competitive require information accessibility. However, we need to pay attention to:

Integration

Focus

Simplicity

Modularity

Time

We also need to remember that the purpose of the system is to:

Facilitate change

Increase value added

Eliminate waste

Let me leave you with some additional reading on information systems development. Savage discusses a process for information systems restructuring, and Baker and Cleaves discuss improving information systems to achieve World Class status.[6]

A MEASUREMENT STRATEGY FOCUSED ON MOTIVATION

Never get so busy Making a Living that you forget to Make a Life.

Anonymous

Now that we've learned about World Class integrated information systems, we are ready to discuss how these systems should be used to measure and motivate performance. Measurement systems have a much higher purpose than supplying feedback to the accounting or costing system (see Figure 8.1). Measurement systems are the motivation systems of an enterprise. As we have already stated several times:

> Misdirected measurement systems
> generate misdirected results.

World Class measurement is motivationally directed measurement that is focused on the enterprise goals.

Properly Focused Measurement/Motivation Strategies

AT&T has focused its sights on the Malcolm Baldrige Award process. It has used the Baldrige criteria to develop goals and to focus its measurement system. So far, AT&T has won three Baldrige awards and one Deming award in the areas of both service and manufacturing, and they feel they are just getting started. Within the Baldrige criteria are defined areas of performance. Developing measurement systems within each organizations helps AT&T achieve the appropriate levels of performance. They started the process by initiating an internal Chairman's Quality Award (CQA) as a stepping stone to the Baldrige Award. They didn't want the goal-focused measurement process to seem unrealistic, so they took it one step at a time, using the CQA to initiate an internal movement toward the quality process and measuring the same categories as the Baldrige Award program. These categories are:

Leadership

Information and analysis

Strategic quality planning

Human resource development and management

Management of process quality

Quality and operational results

Customer focus and satisfaction

AT&T initiated specific measures at the business-unit and division level for each of the above categories, as well as three company-wide measures:

- People Value Added (PVA)—an index measuring employees' perceptions of leadership quality, overall job satisfaction, and diversity practices
- Customer Value Added (CVA)—an index measuring the satisfaction of AT&T's customers relative to that of their competitors' customers
- Economic Value Added (EVA)—a measure of financial value-added performance.[7]

Competitive measurement/motivation systems have been emphasized in literature in recent years. Cooper offers a fast way to decide whether your cost system is giving you bad information. An article by Eccles stresses that within the next five years every company will have to redesign how it measures its business performance. He notes that "one high-tech company has reorganized twenty-four times in the past four years to keep pace with the changes in its markets."[8] My book *The Plant Operations Handbook* has chapters on measurement systems that are appropriate for motivation. For additional information, review the discussion on management styles in Chapter 1.

> *Over the years, the design of performance measurement systems has focused primarily on financial and accounting information and led to the emphasis of efficiency criteria dealing primarily with direct labor. . . . If . . . firms intend to compete, the role and scope of performance criteria must change. . . . An increasing number of companies are responding to the competitive challenge and are acknowledging the need for more effective performance measurement systems.*
>
> Wisner and Fawcett

In Japan, there are numerous measures of performance, all directed at the goal. For example, vendors are measured on quality, quantity, timeliness, and sometimes cost. The best and worst vendors are listed on a board, and unanticipated rewards (bonuses) may be paid to the winners.

Measurement and motivation theory has a long history of discord. Some theorists believe that nonfinancial rewards are the best motivators, while others believe that only financial rewards motivate. Perhaps one of the first motivation theorists was Maslow; his hierarchy of needs theory states that individuals have different needs at different levels of success in their lives (see Figure 8.3). He suggests that the best motivator is dependent on the level of the employee and differs at different stages of his or her life.[9] This is a very people-oriented perspective on measurement and motivation.

> There is not one best motivator;
> it differs from person to person,
> and for any one person,
> the best motivator changes over time.

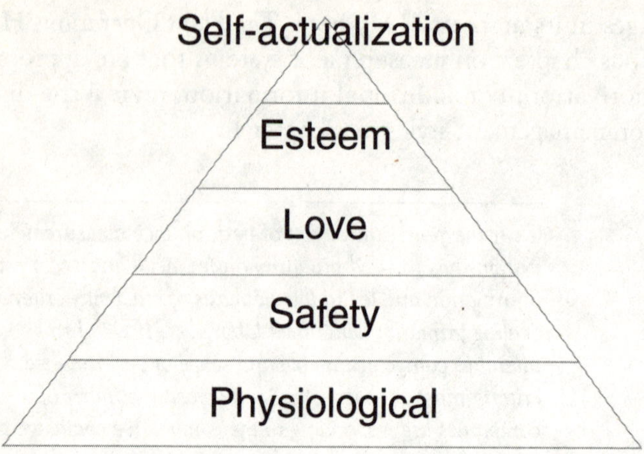

Figure 8.3　　Maslow's Hierarchy of Needs

Maslow's theories still enjoy respect today. However, we have added new motivators (buzzwords) that fit into the original model with names like:

Self-managed work teams

Full disclosure of all information to employees

Empowerment

The new employee power seems to be a motivator in itself. When employees are rewarded for the successes of their decisions, however, the motivation cycle seems to be complete. Some additional readings are listed for those who want more information about measurement and motivation.[10]

> The manager who motivates employees to work the hardest is the manager who works the hardest!

We need to measure. The tax accountant wants measures, the stockholders want measures, and management wants measures. However, by simply measuring for the sake of measuring and forgetting the motivational aspects of the measurement, we lose control of the direction in which the work force is moving. We want to motivate our enterprise to World Class excellence, and a strategy toward motivational measurement is an important step.

Types of Measures

The types of measures are too numerous for this book to discuss them all. Some examples are:

Statistical quality sampling

Job performance

Financial totals and ratios

Materials usage and inventory levels

Throughput

Costing

Productivity

Efficiency

Quality

We have already discussed how most of these measures focus on short-term, financial control rather than on motivators to improvement and change (see Chapter 3 on goals). We need long-term World Class measures, such as process measures, that motivate long-term improvements.[11]

The best measurement systems focus on results (quality output delivered to the customer), but several stages of measurement are necessary to check our progress toward this final measure. There are two categories of progress measurements:

1. Discrete measures—used for assessment
2. Continuous measures—used for control or improvement

When developing a measure, we need to realize that 85% of operating problems have common causes (extrinsic) that are related to the process (how things are done), not to the individual performing the step. Therefore, we need to focus more on measures that will improve the process and on measures that will motivate employees to look for improvement opportunities (continuous measures). The 15% of the problems that have special causes (intrinsic) cannot always be prevented, but we can reduce the effects of the variation caused by these special-case situations by again focusing on the process. Therefore, in order to maximize the improvement effort, we need to focus on continuous measures that look for process improvements.

> The best process is not a stable process,
>   but capable process,
> one that is capable of becoming better.

I want to highlight a few new measurement systems. The fact that new measurement techniques are available to us does not mean the old techniques are outdated. In fact, I prefer the old methods in many cases, because they focus on the desired motivation. I highlight these new methods because, although they can be helpful, they are not a cure-all and need to be used appropriately. The new measurements briefly discussed here are:

Activity-Based Costing

Activity-Based Management

Benchmarking

Activity-Based Costing (ABC)   Activity-Based Costing is a new costing approach that focuses on measuring the cost of all activities involved in a marketing, engineering, production, or shipping process, and so on. ABC is a move away from measuring only labor and materials costs and burying everything else in burden. ABC is an approach by which we measure all cost activities. Unfortunately, companies like IBM, the master of data collection, have backed off ABC because the data collections process is unnecessarily burdensome. The ABC strategy has shifted such that ABC is used to evaluate the contribution of resources toward the goal but, once the critical resource has been established, the data collection process is focused on the critical resource(s) only.[12]

Activity-Based Management (ABM)   ABM is similar to ABC in its focus on measuring all the activities the enterprise is engaged in. However, ABM focuses on understanding and attacking the drivers of the activity costs, whereas ABC focuses on the costs themselves. Like ABC, ABM should be used to identify the cost drivers but should not be used as an ongoing measurement tool.

Benchmarking   Benchmarking has two forms: internal and external. In external benchmarking, an organization compares its performance aspects with other organizations. As discussed earlier in this book, external benchmarking is valuable as long as your enterprise has a lot of room to grow. It is also valuable in helping you understand the competition. However, if you are on the verge of becoming World Class, there comes a point at which copying other companies is not valuable. The time comes to take the innovation step that leapfrogs you ahead of the competition.

Internal benchmarking is always helpful. Here we compare past performance with current performance and plan an appropriate future performance. Internal benchmarking can also be used as a cross-departmental comparison of performance. Benchmarking assistance is available from several sources. For example, APQC (see Appendix 5.2) has a Benchmarking Institute that has an extensive data base of comparative data. Canada and Mexico have similar organizations (see Appendix 6.1).

Let's look at two examples of considering criteria for change measurements. Motorola uses a specific set of three criteria for evaluating measurements. All activities must focus on:

Total customer satisfaction

Total cycle-time reduction

Total defects reduction per unit of work

Lowenthal focuses a chapter of his book on "Evaluating the Improvement." He lists six foundation criteria in developing a measurement system that evaluates change:[13]

Validity—the desired results

Completeness—thoroughness

Comparability

Inclusiveness—cover a wide range of activities

Timeliness

Cost-effectiveness

A World Class measurement strategy focuses on the goals of the enterprise and motivates employees at all levels to work toward those goals. World Class measurement tends not to be an individual, labor-efficiency-oriented measure. Rather, it tends to be a team measurement of quality output. The development of an effective World Class measurement/motivation strategy is a critical part of a shift toward World Class Management status.

SUMMARY

> It is better to
> shoot for the stars
> and miss
> than aim for the gutter
> and hit it

An operations manager was riding in a hot air balloon; because of intensive cloud cover, it had been days since he had seen the ground. Finally there was a break in the cloud cover, and he looked down and spotted an information systems manager on the ground. He yelled down, "Where am I?"

The information manager responded, "Three hundred feet up in the air heading north." Just then the balloon drifted into another cloud.

The operations manager thought to himself, "That's just the type of information I always get. The information was completely accurate but totally useless."

As with most things in life, there is no one best solution for integration, information, or measurement/motivation. The best solution for you is usually not found by simply copying someone else's solution. Also, the solution should be focused not on operational efficiency but on the goal, which in a World Class setting should be customer or employee satisfaction.

APPENDIX 8.1—SOME SOFTWARE ANALYSIS OPTIONS

American Production and Inventory Control Society
  (APICS)
500 West Annandale Road
Falls Church, VA 22046-4274
(703) 237-8344

Council of Logistics Management
2803 Butterfield Road
Oak Brook, IL 60521
(708) 574-0985

Value-Added Strategies

Happy is he who is able to learn the causes of things.

Virgil

Let me tell you about a little trip I'm taking. I got up this morning in Maui (I'm good at picking my conferences), planning to return home to the mainland a few days early. Last night, I learned that I needed to return home sooner than previously planned. I tried to call the airline to reschedule my flight. I called the 1-800 number of the airline, and after over twenty tries I finally got through. This was waste generation point #1, of which there will be many. I encounter less trouble than this trying to place calls in most developing countries. Anyway, I talked to the airline reservations people who had booked my flight, and they told me that I could change the flight schedule for a fee. Plenty of seats were available; however, since they actually flew the flight only from Honolulu to San Francisco, I would have to call the airline that handled the Maui to Honolulu leg of my journey myself and make the necessary flight changes.

Waste Generation Point #2: I proceeded to call the second airline and made the changes without difficulty. I thought I was on my way. Little did I realize that the fun was only beginning. I entered the world of lines known as the airport, and here is the process I encountered.

Waste Generation Point #3: I waited in line to have the luggage passed through a quarantine inspection, necessary for all checked luggage.

Waste Generation Point #4: At the check-in line in Maui, the check-in went fine, but the attendants refused to check my luggage all the way through to San Francisco because I didn't have the second ticket in hand. I flew to Honolulu.

Waste Generation Point #5: I waited in a long line to go through the security checkpoint.

Waste Generation Point #6: I waited in line to get on the plane. This line was exceptionally long, because the plane was loaded on a first-come, first-serve basis.

Waste Generation Point #7: After arrival in Honolulu, I waited for the luggage, which should have been checked through to San Francisco to begin with.

Waste Generation Point #8: I loaded the luggage onto a luggage cart and walked it from the in-state terminal over to the airline terminal for the flight to San Francisco. Upon arrival, I went to the airline counter to check the luggage (another line). After off-loading the luggage, I was told that I needed to reload the luggage and first go to another counter to get the tickets reissued.

Waste Generation Point #9: I waited in line and got the tickets reissued. They gave me my old tickets with some scribbling on them and told me to check the luggage. I was to return for my credit card after they had a chance to charge me for the cost of rescheduling the flight.

Waste Generation Point #10: I went back to the counter where my luggage was to be checked. After off-loading the luggage, I was told that I needed to reload the luggage onto the cart and get another agricultural clearance. The pink sticker I received in Maui didn't count in Honolulu. I needed a yellow sticker.

Waste Generation Point #11: I waited in line to get my yellow sticker.

Waste Generation Point #12: I finally checked my luggage, but not without another line.

Waste Generation Point #13: I waited in line to get back my credit card and then was sent to get my seating assignment.

Waste Generation Point #14: I stood in line to get my seating assignment.

Waste Generation Point #15: I was on my way—almost. Next I stood in another long line to go through the security check.

Waste Generation Point #16: Honolulu airport isn't that big, but for some reason the check-in counter is at the opposite corner of the airport from where the gate is. The walk was good exercise.

Waste Generation Point #17: I waited in line to get on the plane.

If it is as complicated to build a television as it was to get from Maui to San Francisco, the United States is in serious economic trouble. It would seem reasonable to expect that at Point #1 I should have been able to eliminate Points #2, 7, 8, 9, 10, 11, 12, 13, and 14. Some additional improvements, such as combining Points #3, 4, 5, and 6 and combining Points #15, 16, and 17 at each airport into one step, would also have been helpful. That would have reduced the process to three value-added points rather than 17 overlapping, waste-generating points.

This story is true; it really happened to me. I'm on the plane from Honolulu to San Francisco right now. And I'm traveling within the United States, not to some remote developed country where they don't know how to do things correctly (sarcasm).

ARE YOU VALUE-ADDED?

I was invited to a factory in Malaysia and asked to comment on a comparison between that factory and a competitor. Both factories had the same number of employees and the same amount of equipment. However, one factory generated about one-third the output of the other factory. The plant manager said, "I don't understand it. Our employees work every bit as hard as the employees of the other factory. Why is our output so low?"

After walking through the plant and making a few observations, I asked the plant manager to observe a few of the employees. I wasn't focusing on any employee in particular; I simply wanted the manager to observe the manufacturing process. I asked him to watch these employees and observe how much of their time was spent adding value to the product and how much was spent in waste. Waste includes:

Moving product

Positioning product

Walking from inventory to production

Preparing tooling

Filling out reports

The plant manager was amazed at how inefficient his employees were, but he soon realized that it wasn't his employees that were inefficient, it was the process that was inefficient. It doesn't matter how hard the employees work. If they are working on waste, the output of the plant won't increase.

Waste occurs in all the resource areas. Any time the process occurs, it affects resources. If it does not add value to the company, it is waste. Areas in which waste exists include:

Materials, such as inventory

Energy use

Machinery utilization

Marketing

Financing

Information systems

Accounting systems

Personnel

Manufacturing[1]

Invoicing

Purchasing

Decision making[2]

A World Class value-added strategy is a waste-elimination strategy. The literature is thick with individuals who have taught us the importance of adding value. One of the earliest writers on the subject was Frederick Taylor. More recently, the Japanese production philosophy JIT has focused on waste elimination. Other authors, such as Dertouzos, Lester, and Solow, have stressed this issue as well.[3]

The Principal objective of management is to secure "maximum prosperity" for the employer and the employee. . . . The close, intimate, personal cooperation between management and men [employees] is the essence of modern scientific or task management. . . . When the elements of scientific management are used without the true philosophy of management, the results could be disastrous.

Frederick Taylor

An alternative definition of QC would be, "Everyone doing what should be done, in an organized, systematic way.

Kaoru Ishikawa, father of the Japanese Company
Wide Quality Control (CWQC)[4]

Value-added strategies also apply to the process of management. Managers who are not focusing their activities on achieving the goals of the organization, focusing instead on fighting fires, are non–value-added managers. Review the discussion of World Class Manager characteristics in Chapter 1.

It has been argued that the United States is becoming a service-oriented society.[5] Unfortunately, this also means that we are giving away some of our value-added potential. It means that we are losing some of our industrial capability and along with it our technological implementation capability, an area in which the United States is already weak (see Chapter 7). Generating waste, for the nation, means an ever-decreasing balance of trade and an ever-increasing budget deficit. We need to focus on value-adding industries by strengthening our "know how" and our engineering capability, improving our innovativeness, and improving the productivity and quality of our output in every area.

I find adding value or eliminating waste an important strategy for life in general. If, for example, your personal goal is to have a successful, close, well-rounded family, then you need to establish a waste-elimination strategy. This strategy can involve eliminating items that deter you from the important areas that you want to add value in. For example, it may mean watching less TV and spending more time on family activities. The same advice applies whether your focus is on your career, your spouse, or some other area of your life.

> Talk is cheap,
> unless you're talking
> to a lawyer.[6]

FOCUSED WASTE ELIMINATION

A waste elimination strategy needs focus, just as all strategies do. The focus needs to be:

First, on the goal

Second, on the critical resource

Third, on supportive resources

The focus of a value-added strategy should be on the goal. For example, if the goal is customer satisfaction, customer service becomes the driver. The customer defines customer value added.

We need to be careful on the second and third points. Waste elimination in the supportive resources may add waste to the critical resource process. This was exemplified by the earlier example showing how improved labor efficiency often results in increased materials inefficiency, and vice versa. The priority for waste elimination should always be the critical resource.[7]

In addition to all the characteristics already discussed, waste elimination should include:

- Flexibility, responsiveness, the ability to convert functions or processes as needed

- Capital investment that supports value-added changes
- A focus on searching out positive changes
- Reducing the time-to-market
- Concentration on customers' expectations
- Thinking of the worker as a customer and involving workers in the improvement process
- High productivity in which technology is the servant of the process
- Efficiency in the operational measures of performance (e.g., quality, low inventories, and high throughput)
- Overall integration

AMATEK began its improvement process with a management seminar on total quality awareness. The top-management commitment, starting with the president, focused on being "the best you can be." AMATEK felt it had to change its fundamental way of managing in order to remain competitive in the future. It established the following set of goals:

Increase customer satisfaction

Improve operating value drivers

Increase employee satisfaction

AMATEK licensed the Westinghouse Technology Improvement Process and adapted this process for its own use. It developed a six-step methodology to improve process efficiency and thereby reduce cycle times, reengineering a complex manufacturing process. The seven steps are:

1. Commit to performance improvement.
2. Select and scope process.
3. Analyze current process.
4. Design new process.
5. Implement new process.
6. Manage process performance.
7. Return to step 1 and repeat the cycle.

AMATEK, after three years of total quality improvements, has reduced cycle times by 89% (from 22.5 days to 2.5 days), has reduced operating costs by 27%, and has shown a 280% increase in on-time deliveries (from 25% to 95%).[8]

VALUE-ADDED PROFITS

Suppose I am building a television, and in the TV I have a tuner and a power supply. It costs $10 to make each of these products. However, I can sell (or buy) the tuner on the open market for $15 and the power supply for $20. The power supply offers $10 of value-added profit, whereas the tuner offers only $5 of value-added profit. As part of my value-added strategy, I should build all the power supplies myself and have someone else produce the tuners (assuming I don't have enough capacity to build both). That way, I would maximize my value-added profits. This strategy has been understood by the Japanese for a long time. What you find is that the overseas Japanese plants tend to produce the low-value-added components while the Japanese produce the high-value-added profit items at home in their own factories.

In a World Class value-added profit strategy, we need a revised focus that centers on waste elimination and creation of value-added profits. We need to realize that time and competition erode value-added profits, because competition will drive the value-added profits down. Therefore, continuous value-added profits require continuous innovative changes. The function of the operations department, other than to create output, is to continually incorporate innovative, leading-edge, value-adding, profit-oriented change.

WORLD CLASS VALUE-ADDED STRATEGY

A World Class value-added strategy is focused on the three Cs:

- Customer—a focus on what the customer considers value-added; designing with the customer in mind and incorporating customer inputs; a customer-is-always-right, customer service orientation

- Competition—remaining competitive, which critically involves the employees and aspects of the internal organization
- Change—continuous, constant, positively directed changes in process and product

Building on this focus, the value-added emphasis next incorporates all the external influences, which need to be thought of as partners-in-profit. External influences include:

Vendors

Competitors

Government

Unions

Stockholders

Local community

These partners-in-profit incorporate issues such as:

Technology

Regulations

Environment

Globalization

World Class Management must work on building and continuously improving a company's value-added capabilities so that it can outperform the competition by establishing a value-added strategy along five measures:

- Speed—the ability to respond quickly to customer or market demands and to incorporate new ideas and technologies quickly into products and services
- Consistency—the ability to produce a product or service that unfailingly satisfies customers' expectations
- Acuity—the ability to see the competitive environment clearly and thus anticipate and respond to customers' evolving needs and wants
- Agility—the ability to adapt simultaneously to many different business environments

- Innovativeness—the ability to generate new ideas and combine existing elements to create new sources of value[9]

There is no true implementation of Total Quality or any other organization-wide improvement initiative without focus on both the customers and all the details involved in providing products and services to customers. This is true across all industries.

Mark D. Gavoor, Colgate-Palmolive Co.

Numerous publications add detail to the development of a value-added strategy.[10] The key principles of a value-added strategy are found scattered throughout this book.

Change the question from "How can productivity be increased?" to "What do we have to do to beat the competition?"

William Wassweiler[11]

SUMMARY

We believe that if we improve customer satisfaction, we could improve customer retention and market share and gain higher revenues. So we surveyed our customers. They told us that we needed to be better at resolving their problems, to become more consistent with our transportation service, and to reduce the cycle time on our responses to them. Our marketing and sales people needed to understand our customers' businesses.

Kent Sterett, Union Pacific Railroad

A value-added (waste-eliminating) strategy that focuses on customer satisfaction is an integral part of the drive toward World Class Management status. The elimination of waste starts with a commitment from the top to make sure all processes in the organization are value-added, including the job of the CEO.

CHAPTER 10

Training and Education

> *When you're through learning, you're through.*
>
> Vernon Law, pitcher, Pittsburgh Pirates

Let's expand your vision. Figure 10.1 shows ten circles (coins) forming a triangle. The triangle points upward. Moving only three circles, make the triangle point downward. The solution is given at the end of the chapter. After you have been trained how to do it, shifting directions becomes easy.

Give a man a fish
and you've given him a meal;
Teach a man to fish,
and you've fed him
for the rest of his life.

There are dozens of motivational speakers in the world. One common straw that they all tout is education. World Class Management involves positive, growth-oriented change, and change requires learning—learning what's wrong and learning how to do it better. A list of all the literature that focuses on learning would require a book all by itself. I include here just a few of my favorite quotes that stress what you've already heard many times:

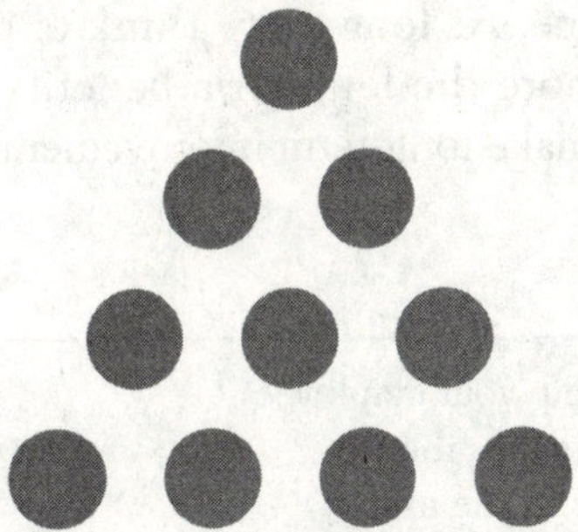

Figure 10.1   Ten Circles

- You can't change if you don't recognize the need for change.
- You can't change if you have no focus on what to change.
- You can't change if you don't identify what to change.
- You can't change if you don't know how to change.
- You can't change if you don't know what your alternatives for change are.
- You can't change if you are not empowered to implement change.

Nearly all the steps listed above require education and training. Education and training teach you and your employees how to change, focus the changes, and help you make value-added, goal-focused, innovative improvements.

The ability to think straight, some knowledge of the past, some vision of the future, some skill to do useful service, some urge to fit that service into the well-being of the community—these are the most vital things education must try to produce. If we can achieve them in the citizens of the land, then . . . we shall have brought to America the wisdom and the courage to match her destiny.

Virginia Gildersleeve

The most feared aspect of change is that it takes time. Managers think of training as lost production time rather than as value added to the labor resource. As long as we think of the short-term costs (time) and ignore the long-term benefits (a value-added employee who will make long-term improvements), we won't be World Class.

> The best way to help your employees
> is to give them a fishhook,
> rather than the fish.

CHARACTERISTICS OF WORLD CLASS TRAINING

A World Class organization is a learning organization. Using this theme, Steiger offers four components of change:[1]

1. Change has to have a group atmosphere.
2. Change must be part of the leadership methods.
3. The vehicle of change is education and reeducation.
4. The cornerstone of performance is measurement.

In an article by Tobin, a learning organization is described as one that lays the foundation for innovation, efficiency, and competitiveness. A learning organization has the following three characteristics:[2]

- An openness to new ideas
- A culture that encourages and facilitates learning and innovation
- Widespread understanding of the organization's overall goals and of how each person's work contributes to them

Learn to unlearn.

Benjamin Disraeli

According to Tobin's article, to create the learning organization a company must establish five foundations:

1. Visible leadership committed to change
2. Basic skills, including the mastering of a broad range of technical and nontechnical skills such as communications, teamwork, business skills, and self-motivation and improvement skills
3. Overcoming functional myopia (blinders) and focusing on the goals
4. Effective teamwork
5. Managers as resources, teachers, coaches, facilitators

An inadequate investment in Human Resource Development (HRD) is one of the major failures of U.S. businesses. We have thousands of years of experience available to us in our employee base, yet we barely and rarely tap into it. World Class Managers have learned how to tap into this experience base both by opening communication with it and by educating and training it in how to utilize this experience in order to make innovative changes within the organization. Top-down, authoritarian organizations miss a great opportunity for innovative change. Empowered organizations take advantage of this opportunity.

Learning organizations need trained trainers and educated educators. There is value in having those employees closest to the job or function be the ones who teach about it. However, they need to be taught how to teach so that the teaching process is a value-added process, not one that takes twice as long as necessary and accomplishes half as much as needed.

> *At Chrysler, we see the role of human resources [education and training] as twofold—to provide leadership and programs that contribute importantly to the direction and performance of the corporation, and to promote a participative work environment that results in enhanced employee job satisfaction and the production of quality goods and services.*
>
> Robert A. Lutz, President, Chrysler[3]

Learning, education, and training occur both in groups and through individual effort. Both should be encouraged. It isn't always necessary for an employee to sit in a classroom in order for him or her to be learning. The classroom adds synergy to the learning process and offers the student the opportunity for interaction through questions. However, the inquisitive employee may not have the classes available for what he or she wants to learn. Or perhaps employees want to delve into a subject deeper than the level offered by the classroom. They should be encouraged to learn, no matter what the setting.

> The more you know,
>   the more you know
>   you don't know.

In a classic article on learning organizations, Senge focuses on several key characteristics that World Class Managers (WCM) of such organizations must have:[4]

1. A WCM must teach "an accurate picture of current reality," which is just as important as "a compelling picture of a desired future."
2. A WCM must be a leader who takes on the roles of Designer, Teacher, and Steward of the big company ship that he or she is sailing.
3. A WCM requires a new set of skills in order to:
   Build a shared vision
   Build and test models
   Utilize systems thinking

He is educated who knows how to find out what he doesn't know.

George Simmel

One master example of a learning organization is Motorola, Inc., winner of the 1988 Malcolm Baldrige Award as an entire corporation. After winning the prize, Motorola went on to push its suppliers to become World Class by telling them that they had to be Baldrige Award–worthy if they were to continue to be suppliers for Motorola. One result of this threat was AT&T's winning of three Baldrige awards and the Deming Prize. I have had the benefit of working with Motorola on numerous occasions, doing training as far away as Malaysia, and have found their focus on education inspiring. The following information is from Robert W. Galvin, Chairman of the Board for Motorola.[5]

Motorola sees its driving thrust as one of constant renewal. Its management travels throughout the organization, offering seminars, speeches, and so on. Additionally, to strengthen the focus on education and to ensure that 100,000 employees have the skills necessary to achieve the company objective of 100% customer satisfaction, Motorola has set up its own training center at a cost of over $170 million. Motorola training focuses on:

- We train ourselves in awareness.
- We train ourselves in processes.
- We share experiences.
- We bring in the best teachers of the new ideas.
- We teach ourselves:
    How to better design for quality
    How to better design for manufacturability
    How to better analyze for quality results with such techniques as statistical process control
    How to improve our problem-solving skills
- We study the latest techniques in cycle-time management, because saving time can improve quality.
- We team the best people to employ these trained skills.

I want to point out . . . that these investments really are costless, as we have gained through greatly reduced manufacturing costs—over $250 million savings in 1987 [one year]—and are continuing to improve [training for the six-year period 1983 through 1988 cost about $220 million—including the building of the training center].

Robert W. Galvin, Chairman, Motorola, Inc.

CHANGE-ORIENTED ORGANIZATIONS

You can get anything in life that you want, if you help enough other people get what they want.

Robert Schuller, minister

Industrial organizations are formed in order to open the door to learning through courses, seminars, conferences, certification, books, magazines, and other literature. They also offer the opportunity for networking (meeting together and chit-chatting) and benchmarking (comparing yourself with others in your industry). Several have already been listed in this book, including QPMA, APQC, ASQC, and APICS. However, you need to identify the organizations of this type that can help you learn about the advances in your particular industry. Some additional Human Resource Management (HRM) organizations are listed in Appendix 10.1.

The proceedings of the APICS 34th International Conference offer invaluable discussions on education and its role in competitiveness.[6] And dozens of these types of conferences (with published proceedings) are held every year.

Developing a "World Class Manufacturing" (WCM) work force requires the accumulation of new skills while simultaneously "unlearning" old (bad) habits.

Michael R. DiPrima

In each stage of life, we do the best we can. We may look back and say "why?" but each stage was really a learning stage for where we are now. And now, we are learning for tomorrow.

SUMMARY

We must regain our leadership role through education.

Mike Ashapa

Education and training are so important to a World Class setting that motivates change that they require a chapter all to themselves, even if it is a short one. A World Class organization is a continually learning organization, one that continually searches for opportunities for self-improvement for every employee.

Not having a formal training program appears to be a guaranteed way to limit or even prevent success.

Henry Alex Hutchins, Applied Industrial Cybernetics

SOLUTION TO FIGURE 10.1 PROBLEM

Figure 10.2 shows how to change directions. Now that wasn't so hard, was it?

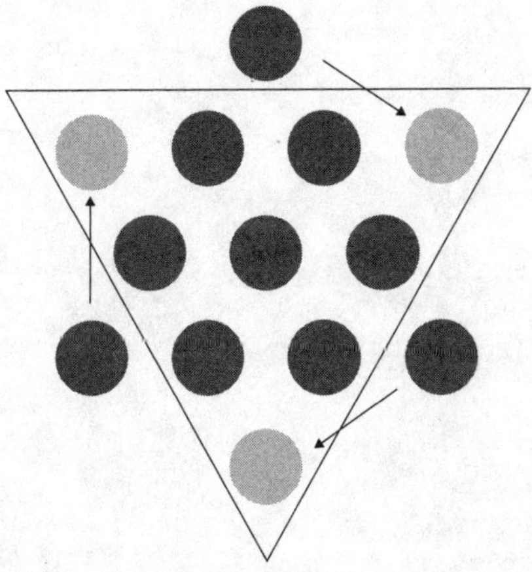

Figure 10.2   Ten-Circles Problem Solved

APPENDIX 10.1   HUMAN RESOURCE MANAGEMENT LEARNING ORGANIZATIONS

Center for the Effective Use of Human Resources
Human Resources Research Organization
66 Canal Center Plaza, Suite 400
Alexandria, VA 22314
(703) 549-3611

National Workforce Assistance Collaborative
National Alliance of Business
(202) 289-2984

PART THREE

World Class Management Tools

CHAPTER 11

Models for Change

> *The first signs of fundamental change rarely appear among one's customers. Usually they show up first among one's non-customers.*
>
> Peter Drucker

As I sit in the freezing snow of Provo, Utah, I think about positive, value-added change. Right now, a move to warmer Hawaii would be considered a very positive change, but I probably would never finish writing this book if I lived in Hawaii. However, I feel like putting the move to the test right now!

The business functions of an organization have, for a long time, focused on stability rather than change. For example, accounting, finance, personnel, the legal department, most upper management, and marketing would love nothing more than to enjoy steady, stable growth. Operations, traditionally, would love a perfectly balanced operation with just the right amount of inventory, just the right work force, and no problems. However, one competitive lesson we have learned is that stability breeds failure. If we try to stay where we are, we'll get run over. Just ask the American passenger railroads.

Operations has learned the new competitive lesson that the remaining functional areas are just waking up to:

> The only way to competitive success
> is through change management!

The function of the operational organization has changed from seeking stability to managing change—change in products and their components, change in demand, changes in resources and their availability, changes in operational technology, changes in competitive product makeup, changes in competition, and so on. And this lesson needs to be shared with the rest of the organization.

Continuous improvement (change) is critical in a global economy.[1] Changes should include:

Product innovation

Process innovation (what the Japanese are good at)

Technology innovation

Time-to-market innovation (Taiwan)

Marketing innovation

Uncontrolled and undirected change can be as disastrous as no change. We need to be able to stay ahead of the change process. We need to change ourselves faster than external forces can force us to change. We need to focus the change on a target. And we need to maintain our corporate integrity as we institute change.

To manage change, we need to incorporate into our business change models that facilitate the change process. Some of these change models, for example, Total Quality Management and Process Reengineering, are discussed in this chapter. The problem with the change models is that they are often thought of as just another fish story.

> Company and change models
> are like fish—
> after three days
> they stink.

Most change models contain some label of quality. "Quality" has become the flag behind which the battle for continuous change is most often fought. But quality doesn't fully define everything that is sought by the change process. Terms like Total Quality Management (TQM) and Quality Functional Deployment (QFD) seem to focus on quality; however, in reality, like all change models, they focus on positive, goal-directed changes in *all* the measurement areas—quality, productivity, efficiency, financial improvement, and so on. In this chapter, we discuss and compare several of the "trendy" change models (some aren't really change models, even though they get credit for being so). Before we discuss specific change models, let's first discuss the psychology behind change.

THE PSYCHOLOGY BEHIND CHANGE

A man was looking on the ground, brushing the grass aside. A curious bystander asked him, "What are you looking for?"

The man responded, "My keys."

The bystander offered, "Where did you drop them? I'll help you find them!"

The man said, "Over there," pointing to a place about ten feet away.

"Then why are you looking here?" queried the bystander.

"Because it's dark over there and I can't see. The light is much better over here!"

Are we looking for keys (changes) in areas where it's convenient, or are we looking in areas where we'll get the most benefit for our efforts? Often we take the easy way out when it comes to confronting change. Why do we avoid change? The psychology of change can be summarized in one word: *resistance*. Resistance to change should not be thought of as irrational. On the contrary, resistance to change is rational behavior, especially if the change directly affects our job function. Don't fear resistance; work with it. Remember from Chapter 1 that all change is not good change. Sometimes the way change is instigated makes the change bad. Sometimes the change fails, no matter how hard we try. But remember also that without change we are sure to fail, because we'll get run over. We need to manage our way around our resistance to change.

In Japan, rocks in a river signify resistance to change. Water flows smoothly down the river until it encounters the rocks, which resist this smoothness. The water must work its way around the rocks in order to successfully move farther on down the river. When change is implemented in companies, we also encounter rocks. Consultants have come up with a way to explain the source of the greatest resistance. They say (and quite rightly):

> The hardest rocks
> wear ties (or heels).

The strongest resistance to change comes from managers who are committed to their way of doing things. They learned to do it that way in school, or they've always done it that way and they don't understand why they need to change now. The line workers are accustomed to being jerked around. Changes coming from management are not anything new to them. However, I have seen organizations in which over half of management has quit because of a shift from an authoritarian to a participative management style.

Why does this resistance to change occur? The answer again is one word: *fear*. Fear of what? *The unknown!* Why is it unknown? *Lack of education and training!* Resistance to change should be anticipated and worked around by helping those who fight the change understand it and "buy into" it. If they feel ownership in the change, their resistance will greatly decrease.

Why aren't we trained and educated in the change process? Primarily because commitment and appropriate motivation are lacking. And the source of the necessary commitment and motivation is at the top. If we have the appropriate commitment and motivation from the top, does successful change necessarily follow? *No*, because we may not know what we are doing. We need tools like the change models discussed in this chapter to help us

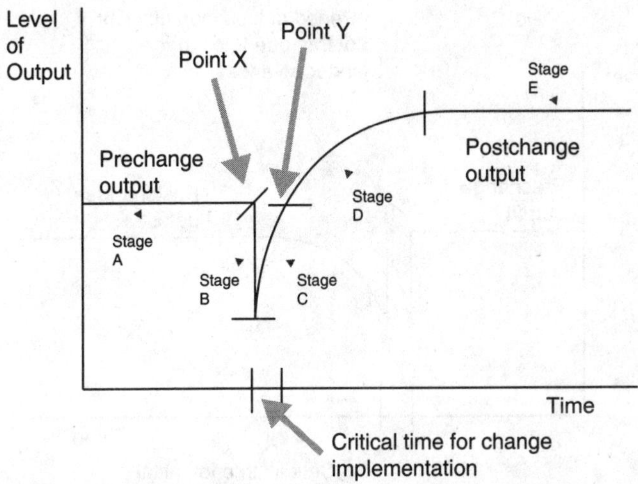

Figure 11.1   Change Function

implement change. But commitment from the top is a critical beginning. That commitment instills a desire for change throughout the organization. Next we need goals (Chapters 3 and 4) to give direction to the change process. Then we need training so that we know what to change, how to change it, and when to change it (Chapter 10). Understanding change begins with understanding the change process.

SOME GENERAL CHANGE MODELS

The change function shown in Figure 2.1 and expanded in Figure 6.2 is reprinted in Figure 11.1. At stage A, we are operating at a steady-state, stable level of operation. At stage B, change is implemented. The level of efficiency drops and a new learning curve kicks in, signified by stages C and D. Stage C is the most critical stage. If stage C takes too long (point X to point Y), the change may be dropped. This is what occurred with Florida Power and Light and what occurs in many JIT, TQM, or Process Reengineering implementations. Unfortunately, when a change process

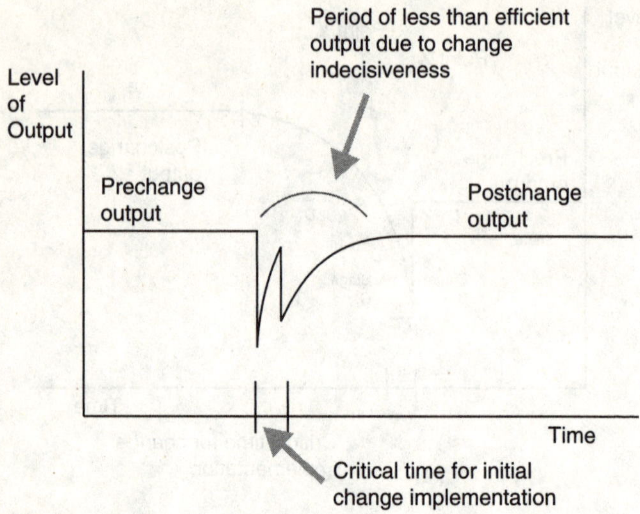

Figure 11.2   Backing Out of the Change

is dropped during stage C, the situation depicted in Figure 11.2 results. Most U.S. companies don't want stage C to last more than one year; with large changes, this short time span is impossible to achieve.

At stage D, we start to see a return on the change process; the final phase of the learning curve is kicking in. Finally, at stage E we have once again achieved stability, hopefully at a higher level of output.

Another model for change shows us as having to work our way through the phases of growth in a change process. These phases are:

- Phase I—We recognize the need for change, invest in new technology or processes, motivate innovation and experimentation, and encourage learning about new technologies for the sake of learning.
- Phase II—We learn how to adapt technology to areas beyond the initially sought-after results and keep the ideas flowing.

- Phase III—The organization goes through structural changes as process changes occur.
- Phase IV—The broad-based implementation of change occurs, affecting all aspects of the organization.[2]

The Japanese model for the continuous change process is called *kaizen*. It suggests that every process can and should be continually evaluated and continually improved. The primary focus of the improvements is waste elimination. For example:

Reducing process time

Reducing the amount of resources used

Improving product quality

Kaizen problem solving involves:

1. Observing the situation
2. Defining the changes that need to take place
3. Making the changes happen

One example of the implementation of the kaizen continuous improvement process is the Repair Division of the Marine Corps Logistics Base in Barstow, California. Utilizing the kaizen focus on continuous improvement, the division ran a pilot project and received results such as:

63% reduction in final assembly lead time

50% reduction in work-in-process inventory

83% reduction in the distance traveled by material

70% reduction in shop floor-space requirements[3]

The process and the system which controls it represent the real problem facing business today, not the people who work within the boundaries set for them by management. . . .
The improvement efforts and their supporting systems must be directed at the process and not the individual.

H. James Harrington[4]

The focus of any change model should be continuous improvement in the broad sense that includes both the Japanese incremental-step perspective and the U.S. breakthrough business-process-improvement-perspective. The need for change is rarely argued. What differs among the various change models is the speed of the change and the depth at which the change occurs. This is where the Japanese and the U.S. change methods bump heads. A comparison follows:

The U.S. change method:
- Fast change
- Fast return on investment
- Radical, dramatic change
- Deep, extensive changes reflecting the need to redefine the whole process
- Hunting for the one big change that will fix all problems
- **Process Reengineering,** characterized by rapid/radical changes and focuses on change implementation and high-tech solutions
- Delay in making any change because the change process is viewed as being so extensive, dramatic, and upsetting (The result is that there is more resistance to any change process.)
- Change ownership seen as belonging to some change "hero," who quite often is the CEO

The Japanese change method:
- Slow change
- Long-term return on investment
- Carefully planned out changes
- Thinking the change through carefully
- Planning before implementation
- Small-step changes
- **Total Quality Management,** which focuses on analysis and planning in the change process and technology-that-fits-the-situation solutions
- A less painful change process, because change involves small, undramatic steps (Therefore, there is much less "re-

sistance, and stepwise, small changes are continually occurring.)
- Shared change ownership

> Einstein was asked what he would do if he had 60 minutes left in which to save the world. His answer was that he would spend 55 minutes planning, and 5 minutes implementing.

Some methodologies have attempted, unsuccessfully, to combine the Japanese and U.S. approaches by suggesting the implementation of "radical changes without being radical." What they are hoping to do is implement big changes without upsetting the entire organization and encountering enormous resistance to the change process. But no one has come up with a good way to accomplish this (probably because no one really understands it), so the conflict between the two change approaches remains. Total Quality Management (TQM) continues to be viewed as "too slow" by the United States, and Process Reengineering (PR) continues to be viewed as "too destructive" by the Japanese.

Let us next consider the most prevalent models for change and discuss the procedures used in implementing these models. We will consider:

Quality Functional Deployment

Total Quality Management

Process Reengineering

Process Reengineering Variations

Benchmarking

ISO 9000

Award Processes

Some of these models simply supply us with focus areas of improvement. Others offer specific procedures for the change process. The models should not be thought of as exclusive in the sense that if you pick one you can't use any of the others. Rather, they should all be considered as stepping stones in the development of your own successful change program.

QUALITY FUNCTIONAL DEPLOYMENT (QFD)

Quality Functional Deployment (QFD) is the implementation of a continuous-improvement process focusing on the customer. It was developed at Mitsubishi's Kobe Shipyards and focuses on directing the efforts of all functional areas on a common goal. In Mitsubishi's case, the goal was "satisfying the needs of the customer." Several changes were instituted in order to accomplish this, such as increased horizontal communication within the company. One immediate result was a reduced time-to-market lead time for products.

QFD systematizes the product's attributes in a matrix diagram, called a house of quality, and highlights which attribute is the most important to a customer. This helps the teams throughout the organization focus on their goal (customer satisfaction) whenever they are making change decisions, for example, product development and improvement decisions.

QFD focuses on:

1. The customer
2. Systematizing the customer satisfaction process by developing a matrix for defining:
    a. Customer quality
    b. Product characteristics
    c. Process characteristics
    d. Process control characteristics
3. Empowered teaming
4. Extensive front-end analysis that involves fourteen steps in defining the "house of quality":
    a. Create and communicate a project objective.
    b. Establish the scope of the project.
    c. Obtain customer requirements.
    d. Categorize customer requirements.
    e. Prioritize customer requirements.

f.   Assess competitive position.

g.   Develop design requirements.

h.   Determine relationship between design requirements and customer requirements.

i.   Assess competitive position in terms of design requirements

j.   Calculate importance of design requirements.

k.   Establish target values for design.

l.   Determine correlations among design requirements.

m.   Finalize target values for design.

n.   Develop the other matrices.

Implementing and using QFD is not an easy process. A great deal of commitment throughout the company is required for the process to be successful. The results of effective implementation are well worth the effort. Reduced product development time, increased flexibility, increased customer satisfaction, and lower start-up costs are just a few of the benefits that can be expected through the use of QFD.

Gregg D. Stocker[5]

QFD has been widely recognized as an effective tool for focusing the product and the process on customer satisfaction. Much has been written on the subject.[6] As discussed earlier, QFD is a Japanese approach to focused change and therefore focuses on extensive analysis, utilizing the following philosophy:

> Make sure we are doing the right things
> before we worry about doing things right!

Detailed analysis through the matrices is time consuming, conceptual planning time is much extended by QFD. However, the overall design-to-market time should be cut because the design effort focuses on the most important areas.

Dave Henrickson

TOTAL QUALITY MANAGEMENT (TQM)

Simply put, TQM is a management approach to long-term customer satisfaction. TQM is based on the participation of all members of an organization in improving the processes, products, services and the culture they work in.

Karen Bemkowski[7]

As mentioned earlier, Total Quality Management (TQM) focuses on careful, thoughtful analysis. However, the analysis should be creative, innovative, and innoveering-oriented. The care comes in when it comes time to implement. We want to ensure that we are implementing positive, goal-focused changes before we move a muscle.

TQM is much broader than QFD. TQM is an enterprise-wide change model. Some people define TQM in general terms as simply making the "entire organization responsible for product or service quality." In many organizations, TQM encompasses everything and anything. However, there is also a specific, proceduralistic definition of TQM. Perhaps the best way to understand TQM is to look first at the process. Then we can consider its significance.

The TQM Process

TQM is not just a tool; it is an entire philosophy about how businesses should be run. The TQM philosophy is filled with ideas and attitudes, including:

Attitude of desiring and searching out change

Think culture—move from copying to innovating

Do the right things before you do things right

Focus on the goal

Measurement/motivation planning

Top-to-bottom corporate strategy

Company-wide involvement

Clear definition and implementation of quality

Education, training, and cross-training

Integration and coordination

Small, step-by-step improvements

In TQM, the philosophy behind change is that we become excited about changes. We look for the opportunity to change, because change should mean that we are becoming better. To be a TQM organization is to become an organization that wants to be the best and realizes that there is always room for improvement.

Success stories for TQM can be found in settings all over the world. TQM success is measured in terms of the successful implementation of change. Change can take the form of the implementation of new technology or the correction and improvement of old technology. Often, a successful TQM project results in the ability of employees to work together more effectively. The result is that the measurement of TQM success tends to be an internal success story, not always externally comparable.

Success in TQM can be found in large organizations such as PETRONAS, the national petroleum corporation of Malaysia. Because of its successes, TQM implementation is moving forward on a company-wide basis. TQM's systematic implementation of changes won the Deming Award, a Japanese quality award, for Florida Power and Light, a U.S. producer of electricity. TQM is receiving nationwide attention in Mexico through a sponsoring organization, Fundameca, the Mexican national productivity and quality improvement organization. Many other Latin American countries are also focusing national attention on TQM implementation, for example, Guatemala's "II Congreso Nacional Y I Cetroamericano De Calidad Total" meeting. Numerous success stories exist about specific individual companies such as the Solectron.[8]

In operationalizing TQM, several points are important:

The TQM coordinating team (quality council)

The three "P" teams—cross-functional teams

The TQM project implementation steps

Training programs

Measurement and feedback

Showcasing

Team building

Systematic Problem Solving (SPS)

TQM Coordinating Team   TQM implementations start with a coordinating team, often referred to as a quality council. This is a team composed of high-level corporate leaders from all the functional areas. It is appointed by the CEO and operates under his or her direction. The CEO takes an active part in directing the activities of the team. This quality council is responsible for organizing and measuring the performance of the other TQM teams within the organization. It oversees the installation, training, performance, and measurement of the other teams. The coordinating team focuses specifically on the corporate goal/vision and definition of quality.

Three "P" Teams   The quality council organizes three different types of teams, referred to as the cross-functional three "P" teams: process, product, and project teams. The *process teams* are ongoing, continuous-improvement teams set up at different levels of the organization that look for improvements in the organization's functioning processes. These teams should be composed of both "insiders" and "outsiders." The insiders know and understand existing functions and operations; the outsiders challenge the status quo.

The *product teams* are cross-functional but focus on a specific product, product line, or service. They are customer and vendor interface teams that are specifically oriented toward the development of new products and the improvement of existing products. Their life span coincides with the life span of the product they represent.

The *project teams* are limited-life teams set up to focus on a specific project, such as the construction of a new plant or a computer installation. These teams may be the result of a specific process or product that is being targeted, or they may be set up to research something the general management team is interested in developing or improving.

TQM Project Implementation Steps   The TQM project implementation steps are:

- Identify problems (opportunities).
- Prioritize these problems.
- Select the biggest bang-for-the-buck project.
- Develop an implementation plan.
- Use operations research and Management Information Systems (MIS) tools where appropriate.
- Develop guideposts and an appropriate measurement system.
- Carry out training.
- Implement the change.
- Install feedback, monitoring, control, and change mechanisms.
- After successful project implementation and ongoing status, repeat cycle.

The first function of the team is to identify its function and charter. If you are on one of the three "P" teams, your team's charter is laid out for you by the quality council. If you are on the quality council, the charter is laid out for you by the CEO and is aimed at the focused goals of the organization. After understanding its charter, the team will search for and identify problems that exist that prevent the organization from achieving this charter. The word *problems* has a negative connotation. Better wording would be "opportunities for improvements." We are not just trying to correct negative effects; we are looking for techniques or tools that will allow us to become better and possibly even best.

Next we take these problems (opportunities) and prioritize them based on their effect on the charter of the team (which should be focused on the goals of the organization). We do a type of ABC analysis (80-20 Rule or Parieto Principle) to determine which change would have the greatest effect. Then we select the biggest-bang-for-the-buck project and develop an implementation plan for this project. The implementation plan must contain guideposts based on a measurement system that points the team toward achieving its charter. The book *Breakthrough Thinking* does an excellent job of discussing opportunity identification techniques.[9]

Training of the implementers and users is critical, otherwise the planned project is doomed to failure. This training makes future users comfortable with the changes. It also offers a bit of ownership, since the planned users will feel comfortable with the changes.

The next step is implementation. Implementation should be a trivial process if all the planning and training steps have been performed carefully. Part of the implementation involves the installation of feedback, monitoring, and control mechanisms as laid out in the implementation plan. Careful monitoring allows corrective changes to be made whenever necessary.

After achieving successful project implementation and seeing that the ongoing status of the project is functioning correctly, the team repeats the implementation cycle, looking for more opportunities for change. If this process is carried out correctly, the list of change opportunities should become longer with each iterative cycle. Your team should now be open to newer and broader opportunities for change.

Training Programs   Training programs need to exist before and after project selection. Before project selection, the TQM team needs to understand what tools are available. This training involves an understanding of tools and techniques. Initial training could include programs in areas such as operations research/management science tools and techniques, motivational/philosophical training, semitechnical and technical education, the operation of the systems approach, and so on. Training programs that follow TQM team implementation should involve user training focused on the changes being implemented. These programs need to be defined (and often conducted) by the TQM team that has the best understanding of the change.

Measurement and Feedback   The issue of measurement and feedback has already been discussed several times. It is critical to recognize the motivational role of the measurement system and the importance of the proper implementation of an effective feedback (reporting) mechanism in ensuring the ongoing success of the implemented changes.

Showcasing   One of the best techniques for expanding implementation time is showcasing. We use the quality council to develop and implement a "sure-thing" TQM implementation project. What we are doing is attempting to demonstrate the successes of an organization-wide TQM implementation. In the United States, where quick, short-term benefits need to be demonstrated, showcasing becomes a critical part of the job of selling TQM.

Team Building   There are several types of teams required in a TQM environment, for example, the quality council and the three "P" teams. Understanding which teams need to be organized is just a small part of the problem of team construction. A much bigger problem is making sure the team is effective. Team training and team relationship building are necessary for effective interaction and for the synergy of the team (see Chapter 14 for a discussion about team building).

Systematic Problem Solving   One of the biggest downfalls of a TQM system, as far as the United States is concerned, is the implementation lead time of changes (how long it takes to implement the change). Often a decision is made to change, and then we start worrying about how to implement the change. Systematic Problem Solving (SPS) is a procedurization of the change process. No one perfect model exists for how this change procedurization should be set up. However, a few good examples are available. We will take a look at three of them: the SPS process used by Florida Power and Light when it won the Deming Award, the AT&T SPS process, and a generalized SPS model called the T-Model.

Systematic Problem Solving (SPS) at Florida Power and Light

Florida Power and Light (FP&L) referred to the SPS process they used when they won the Deming Award as their "Quality Improvement Story." It consists of a series of steps that is standardized and used to organize and document the change process. The steps are:

1. Team Information—Here they develop a Team Project Planning Worksheet that lists the team members, the meeting schedules, and an outline of activities in Gantt chart format. The Gantt chart lists each of the following "Quality Improvement Story" steps on a time line.

2. Reasons for Improvement—This step is a graphic, flow-charted look at why an improvement is desirable. FP&L analyzes which issues are being addressed and which are not in light of some goal they are trying to achieve. They follow the repeated "Why?" questioning process in order to determine the root problems.

3. Current Situation—Here FP&L applies Parieto principles to focus on the area that will maximize benefits with the least amount of effort. They graph performance history in order to get a better handle on the problem. They define targets and goals for the corrective action that is being planned.

4. Analysis—Here the primary tools are fish-bone (cause-and-effect) diagrams that analyze the possible reasons for the problems being considered. FP&L develops a Root Cause Verification Matrix in order to verify that they are truly working on the root causes of the problems.

5. Countermeasures—Here FP&L develops a Countermeasures Matrix and an Action Plan. This is the step at which the change takes place.

6. Results—FP&L uses Parieto diagrams and before-and-after graphs to substantiate that the changes are occurring and to monitor the performance of the implemented changes.

7. Standardization—This step establishes a documented procedure for the ongoing operation of the change using graphical and systems flow-charting tools.

8. Future Plans—This is a review of what was learned by the change process. It follows a philosophy of Plan–Do–Check–Act:

Plan is what you plan to do with regard to this change in the future. For example, are you going to look for even more improvements?

Do is what will be done next.

Check is a look at what the feedback mechanism will entail. What do you want to watch for?

Act is the next action to be taken by the team. For example, are we now going to look at the next-highest Parieto contributor to improvement?

Systematic Problem Solving (SPS) at AT&T

AT&T uses a methodology that includes tasks to be performed in four distinct stages:

- Ownership—team responsibility for the activities
- Assessment—clear definition of the process
- Opportunity selection—analysis of how process problems affect customer satisfaction and ranking of problems in order of opportunity for improvement
- Improvement—implementing and sustaining the change.

The ownership, assessment, and opportunity selection stages are considered management processes. Based on the overall four stages, grouped under management and improvement, AT&T developed a series of steps, called the Management and Improvement steps, that focus on the SPS process. These steps are:

1. Establish process management responsibilities.
2. Define process and identify customer requirements.
3. Define and establish measures.

4. Assess conformance to customer requirements.
5. Investigate process to identify improvement opportunities.
6. Rank improvement opportunities and set objectives.
7. Improve process quality.

Note that the AT&T process closely follows the Japanese model. More detailed information about this process is available through publications put out by AT&T.[10]

Quality excellence is the foundation for the management of our business and the keystone of our goal of customer satisfaction. It is therefore our policy to:

- *Consistently provide products and services that meet the quality expectations of our customers.*
- *Actively pursue ever-improving quality through programs that enable each employee to do his or her job right the first time.*

Robert E. Allen, Chairman and CEO, AT&T

The T-Model

The third Systematic Problem Solving model we are going to discuss is called the T-Model. This model is a systematized model for change with a philosophical as well as a procedural aspect that follows systems analysis principles. Philosophically, the T-Model looks for rapid, continuous-improvement, change implementation. Procedurally, it follows a series of basic rules, or steps. The basic rules of the T-Model are:

1. Define the area of change.
2. Define the purpose of the change. Don't ask why the change should be made, and don't perform an analysis of the change and its requirements. The purpose of the change needs to be defined first.
3. Evaluate the purpose. Does it eliminate waste and improve the value-added component of the product?
4. Define the constraints—environmental, customer, cultural, and so on.

5. Evaluate the techniques available for solving the problem.
6. Implement the change.
7. Set up mechanisms for monitoring, feedback, and data collection.
8. Take corrective action. Here we are reacting to the feedback. If the feedback is not what we want, then we return to step 2 above and rethink our corrective action.

The T-Model is more general than the Florida Power and Light example, because it is not applied to a specific situation. There are no specific tools assigned to each step. However, when the T-Model is applied to a specific example, such as the Florida Power and Light situation, it becomes more focused, detailing specific tools and procedures that should be used.[11]

The Good News About TQM

TQM was the first stage in realizing that we need to take "quality" (or the search for positive change) out of the quality department and make it a company-wide program. TQM is a strategy toward continuous, corporate-wide change. It is a philosophy, an operationalized process, and a fad. It becomes a fad if we expect quick results and become disenchanted when we are not "like the Japanese" after the first two months. TQM is a strategy to help us become leading-edge and World Class.

TQM differs from quality tools like TQC, SPC, or ILQC (see Chapter 5) in that it is not as directly focused on a specific procedure as these other systems. Rather, TQM is a continuous search for problems (opportunities) that eliminate waste and add value in all aspects of the organization, and it makes these improvements one small step (5–10% improvement) at a time.

In spite of its slowness, TQM has been extremely successful internationally and is receiving ever-increasing attention. References to TQM and its leadership abound.[12] TQM is a very specific process improvement step in a drive toward World Class status.

PROCESS REENGINEERING

Wisely, and slowly. They stumble that run fast.

William Shakespeare, *Romeo and Juliet*

Process Reengineering (PR) is rapid, radical change. It is not downsizing, which many companies are using it for, but rather work elimination. It is positive, growth-focused change that looks for opportunities to eliminate waste and improve value-added productivity, often through the implementation of technology such as image processing (see Chapter 8).

In 1994, $32 billion was invested in reengineering projects, two-thirds of which will fail. Why? Because the change process builds up a lot of resistance, thereby forcing its failure. Second, because PR is used as an excuse for downsizing, the downsizing result is often the elimination of critical employees who will be difficult to replace. The downsizing process is not carefully thought out, it is rushed through, and the results are disastrous.[13]

However, as with any tool, there are some extremely positive aspects to Process Reengineering that make it worthy of our attention. PR focuses on change implementation at the top of the corporate hierarchy. It generates a more top-down change culture, and it focuses on process-oriented changes.

PR's focus on the process emphasizes that the process, not the product, holds the secrets for the most dramatic improvements within an organization. PR focuses on an "all-or-nothing proposition that produces impressive results." PR is defined as:

> the fundamental rethinking and radical redesign of
> business processes to achieve dramatic improvements in
> critical, contemporary measures of performance, such
> as cost, quality, service, and speed[14]

The principles of reengineering include the following:

- Organize around outcomes, not tasks.
- Have those who use the output of the process perform the process.
- Subsume information-processing work into the real work that produces information.
- Treat geographically dispersed resources as though they were centralized.
- Link parallel activities instead of integrating their results.
- Put the decision point where the work is performed, and build control into the process.
- Capture information once and at the source.

The three Rs of reengineering are:

- Rethink—Is what you're doing focused on the customer?
- Redesign—What are you doing? Should you be doing it at all? Redesign how it can be done.
- Retool—Reevaluate the use of advanced technologies.

Some characteristics of process reengineering are:

Combining several jobs into one

Workers making the decisions (empowerment)

"Natural order" sequencing of job steps

Processes with multiple versions, depending on the need

Work performed where it makes the most sense

Reduction in checks and controls

Minimizing reconciliation

"Empowered" customer service representative

Hybrid centralized/decentralized organizations

As with TQM, the focus of the reengineering effort is the team. Departments are replaced by empowered process teams. Executives change their role from scorekeeper to leader. Organizational structures become flatter. Managers change from supervisors to coaches.

PR follows the following steps or phases in the change management process:

1. Mobilization:
    Develop a vision.
    Communicate the vision.
    Identify champions and process owners.
    Assemble the teams.
2. Diagnosis:
    Train and educate.
    Analyze current process.
    Select and scope the process.
    Understand the current customer.
    Model the process.
    Identify problems.
    Set targets for new designs.
3. Redesign:
    Create breakthrough design concepts.
    Redesign the entire system.
    Build a prototype.
    Utilize information technology.
4. Transition:
    Finalize transition design.
    Initiate implementation phase.
    Measure benefits.
    Utilize communication to avoid resistance.
    You cannot overcommunicate.

PR has many of the procedural characteristics of TQM; however, it is more philosophical than TQM. PR focuses on being competitive via the rapid and the radical, and it stresses the process as the key to successful change. Numerous books and articles discuss the philosophy of PR. The best is still the original by the gurus of Process Reengineering, Hammer and Champy. CASA/SME has put out an excellent booklet focusing on manufacturing processes that can be reengineered. *OR/MS Today* has published an excellent article that discusses first- and second-generation reengineering programs.[15]

PROCESS REENGINEERING VARIATIONS

Numerous variations have sprung up in an attempt to correct some of the problems of Process Reengineering. I will list several of them and offer brief information about each. I include references for additional information. The benefits of these variations have yet to be proved.

John Lipscomb has developed a program that focuses on reengineering improvements utilizing Quality Systems Deployment (QSD). QSD is a variation of QFD that focuses on customer-directed systems development. The contradiction is that reengineering is "rapid and radical" and QSD is systematic and carefully defined. This blending attempts to develop a change process that falls somewhere in between the two extremes and utilizes the benefits of each.[16]

Lowenthal stresses that the reengineering of the organization should focus on the core competencies and that the organization itself, not just the processes within the organization, needs reengineering. The enterprise needs to take advantage of its core competencies when it focuses its organization-wide business process improvements. Organizational Reengineering is defined as:

> the rudimentary rethinking and redesign of operating processes and organizational structure, focused on the organization's core competencies, to achieve dramatic improvements such as reduced cost, increased product and service quality, and increased market share and profitability[17]

Aetna is reengineering vital business functions across all its business units. The focus of these efforts is on the customer. It is replacing the traditional systems with new, refocused processes. Chairman and CEO Ronald E. Compton of Aetna stresses that there are several commandments inherent in any reengineering effort:

1. You have to give people a mission, a clear understanding of how to achieve that mission, and a road map for choosing the appropriate steps for action.

2. Either service the customer superbly or don't even try.
3. *Change is not something that happens. It's a way of life.* It's not a process, it's a value. It's not something you do, it engulfs you.
4. Technology is never really a problem. The problem is how to use technology effectively.
5. The wrong answer rarely kills you. What it does is waste time. *Further, time is a limited resource—the only absolutely limited one.*
6. The weak link in reengineering is will. Reengineering is a huge job, and it is agonizingly, heartbreakingly tough.
7. Once people catch on to reengineering, you can't hold them down. It's a lifetime venture.

Compton states that Aetna expects to save over $120 million annually from streamlining its processes.[18]

BENCHMARKING

Benchmarking is a comparative tool used to compare your current performance with your past performance, or with the performance of others. The use of Benchmarking varies with a company's stage of development. For example, in the early stages of corporate development, or if your company is low on the competitive ladder (highly non-competitive), then benchmarking with competitors or companies (external Benchmarking) who have better performance than you do is extremely valuable. Taking a look at how these companies organize, how they control quality, how they improve productivity, how they control inventory, etc., is quite valuable. Looking at their financial situation (profitability levels, asset ratios, equity ratios, and debt ratios) can help you find shortcomings in your own financial position.

If your company is high on the competitive ladder, or even leading edge, comparing yourself with your competitors is often not very useful. You want to innovate ahead of your competition, not copy them. Benchmarking your performance against yourself, either department to department, or current year to prior years, is more useful (internal Benchmarking).

The Appendix in Chapter 5 listed two organizations that are experts in the Benchmarking process. The APQC has a Benchmarking institute. And Jarrett-Thor International has valuable Benchmarking expertise.

ISO 9000

ISO 9000 is a model that is often advertised as a model for change and improvements. However, the ISO 9000 process tends to focus on stability. The ISO standard was developed by Europe in an attempt to standardize the quality of goods coming into Europe. For many companies, it seemed to be a trade barrier attempting to keep companies out of Europe. ISO 9000 focuses on quality in the internal process of the organization, ensuring that what was designed is what is actually built; it does not focus on the customer. Nevertheless, the ISO standard has become an international standard for quality and systems performance that many companies utilize.

ISO has come to define quality, not change. It is a set of standards for quality based on two main foundations:

- Management responsibility and commitment to quality, which should be expressed in a formal policy statement and implemented through appropriate measures
- A set of requirements that deal with each aspect of the company activity and organization that affects quality[19]

ISO can be used as a standard for improvement, and the ISO quality system requirements can become the focus of change systems. In this way, ISO criteria can be integrated into a change process. However, in and of itself ISO is not a change model, as is frequently believed.

AWARD PROCESSES

Award programs like the Baldrige, Deming, and Shingo prizes all have excellent standards from which to build change models.

Like the ISO criteria, these award-program criteria are an excellent foundation for developing a focus for your change program. For example, the Shingo Prize organization focuses on continuous improvement processes through total quality systems. The Deming Award focuses on demonstrated improvements resulting from a continuous improvement process. The Baldrige Award uses the following list of improvement criteria for award evaluation:

1. Leadership—senior management's success in creating and sustaining a quality culture
2. Information and Analysis—the effectiveness of the company's collection and analysis of information for quality improvement and planning
3. Strategic Quality Planning—the effectiveness of the integration of quality requirements into the company's business plans
4. Human Resource Utilization—the success of the company's efforts to utilize the full potential of the work force for quality
5. Quality Assurance of Products and Services—the effectiveness of the company's systems for assuring quality control of all operations
6. Quality Results—the company's results in quality achievement and quality improvement, demonstrated through quantitative measures
7. Customer Satisfaction—the effectiveness of the company's systems in determining customer requirements and demonstrated success in meeting them

Within these seven categories are 33 examination items and 133 subitems. Like the ISO process, the award process is not a change process, but it greatly assists an organization in establishing the criteria that should be incorporated into an effective change model. Going through the award process motivates the development of effective change procedures.[20]

WHICH CHANGE MODEL IS BEST

I'm always doing what I can't do yet in order to learn how to do it!

Vincent Van Gogh

There is no "best" change model. The best model for you is the one you build yourself that fits your organization and utilizes your goals and focus. However, some of the alternatives are better than others. A World Class change model should focus on effective, customer- and employee-oriented change management that offers competitive innoveering strategies. World Class change management is Total Quality Management or a modification of the Process Reengineering model that includes an additional focus on the analysis process. TQM offers the most structure and tends to be resisted least. Therefore, I tend to prefer it over the PR alternatives. However, I stress again that the best change model for you is the one you customize for yourself. Some literature has tried to solve this "best change model" problem.[21]

Once we understand that "what worked in American Industry for two hundred years won't work any more," we can begin to "Think Weird" and to challenge paradigms.

Robert A. Abair

CHANGE MODEL IMPLEMENTATION

Things do not change; we change.

Henry David Thoreau

A short but hard-working blacksmith had been watching the new lady school teacher in town very closely. Neither he nor the lady was married, and he felt that if he didn't get married soon he would be past his prime. One day, this school teacher came by his shop and asked him to do some repairs. He eagerly did the work, and when he was asked how much it cost he told her it would be free if she went out on a date with him. She eagerly agreed, since she found herself mildly attracted to him.

Near the end of their date, they were strolling through a grove of trees when the blacksmith asked if he could give her a kiss on the cheek. She eagerly agreed but told him, "Just one!"

The blacksmith had been hoping for just such an opportunity, so he had brought an anvil with him. He set the anvil on the ground next to her, stepped up on it, and gave her a kiss. Then he said, "Since the kissing is over (after all, she said just one), I guess I won't be needing this anvil anymore."

Implementing change cannot end with one kiss, even if the boss said "just one." Change is a continuous, ongoing, never-ending challenge that we need to take control of eagerly. This chapter has given us an anvil, and although it may be heavy we can't discard it. We should instead always look for ways to make it lighter (changing the change process can also be a positive change).

The keys to change model implementation, as we have stressed throughout the book, are:

1. Focus on a goal and develop a vision, mission, strategy, and operating plan for change built around this goal and the enterprise's core competencies.
2. Get the commitment for change from the top. This commitment includes a commitment to training and education. It also involves a commitment to empowerment, thereby placing the employees in charge of their own changes.
3. Select a change model and customize the model for your organization.
4. Develop change building blocks, implementing change without discarding old ideas but rather building on them.
5. Open your mind to breakthrough thinking (review the Nadler and Hibino books cited in note 9 of this chapter).

6. Utilize measurement to motivate change.
7. Develop a feedback mechanism to track and improve upon change performance.
8. Develop internal and external change contingencies (not all changes work out as planned). Internal change contingencies are contingencies against internally planned changes. External contingencies involve external (beyond your influence) changes.

None of these steps can be left out. Change implementation is important, but it has to be done right! Why? Because it directly affects your future!

> The first step to change
> is found in
> changing ourselves.

SUMMARY

All that is essential for the triumph of evil is for good men to do nothing.

Edmund Burke

World Class change is managed, focused change. A World Class Manager is one who takes advantage of change rather than letting change take advantage of him or her. To do nothing is to fail. However, to change is not necessarily to succeed. Change needs to have the characteristics discussed in this book. But remember:

> With no change
> you get
> no-where!

A World Class change-oriented manager is one who utilizes Quality Functional Deployment and Total Quality Management processes to define what changes are needed, to carefully plan the change implementation, to work around and with resistance, to develop commitment, and to make a difference. A World Class change manager is a manager who makes World Class changes.

CHAPTER 12

WCM Traits and Characteristics

You see, really and truly, apart from the things anyone can pick up [the dressing, the proper way of speaking, and so on], the difference between a lady and a flower girl is not how she behaves, but how she's treated. I shall always be a flower girl to Professor Higgins, because he always treats me as a flower girl, and always will; but I know I can be a lady because you always treat me as a lady, and always will.

Eliza Doolittle, *My Fair Lady*, George Bernard Shaw

This chapter is about you, the manager. To be a World Class Manager, you need to be a World Class Person, and you need to be able to find the World Class potential in everyone you deal with.

A World Class Manager doesn't have to offend someone else or make someone else look small in order to make himself or herself look good. A World Class Manager looks good because he or she is good! World Class Managers build up themselves by building up others.

I often get the reaction that management has nothing to do with your personal life. This reaction comes from individuals who approach management as a function in which you "keep a distance" from employees. World Class Management is "becoming one with your employees." A World Class Manager is involved with all the employees. He or she knows them by name, knows how many children they have, and even knows some of their personal struggles. A World Class Manager is a friend to the employees.

How do you become a friend to your employees? By being sincere and trustworthy. Terms such as *hypocrite*, *self-centered*, and *unethical* do not fit a World Class Manager. In this chapter, we highlight some appropriate World Class characteristics.

> The world's best reformers are those
> who begin on themselves.

The best definition of a World Class Manager that I have encountered is:

> A World Class Manager
>   is the type of manager
>   we would like to be
>   managed by.

THE WORLD CLASS PERSON

> *. . . if any man among you seemeth to be wise in this world, let him become a fool, that he may be wise.*
>
> 1 Cor. 3:18–19

To be a World Class Manager, you need to be a World Class Person. A World Class Person possesses an unshakable value system. He or she can be counted on to stick up for you when you need a friend. Some characteristics of a World Class Person are:

- Integrity:
    Ethical
    Honest

- Standards and Value System:
    Goal-focused
    Loving
    Humble
    Moral
    Obedient
- Society Value Added:
    Job enrichment
- Leader:
    Exemplary
    Enthusiastic
    Compromising
    Understanding
    Self-replacing
    Environmentally conscious
    Worker-safety conscious
    Open
    Sharing
    Fun-loving

Integrity   Integrity has many definitions; one I like is:

> Integrity is saying what you do,
> and doing what you say!

Integrity avoids the secretive and sneaky and is "up front" with everyone. Integrity is not trying to manipulate people by telling them "what they want to hear." It is caring more for your word than for the fine print of the contract. Integrity is feeling good about doing good. It's leaving a negotiation process with a clear conscience. As someone once said, "integrity is hard to define, but I sure recognize it when I see it!"

Integrity is having a value system that would make the Pope proud. I'm not asking you to be the Pope, but I am suggesting that we need to have people around us who respect us and trust us. We need to stand for a set pattern of values that are more important than our job or money. Only then can we have integrity.

> If you don't
>   believe in something,
>   you'll follow anything.

Earlier in this book I discussed nontrust systems, which are systems established in order to prevent fraud. I mentioned that the nontrust systems in most corporations, which involve computers, accounting, finance, and so on, are costing us more than the fraud they were set up to prevent would have cost. The biggest fraud that occurs nowadays is the result of the manipulation ("getting around the system") of the nontrust data collection systems that have been set up.[1] We would be better off in all ways, including financially, if we were to simply eliminate the nontrust baloney.

We need to realize that nontrust systems are developed by individuals who don't trust others because they know the kinds of things they would do if given half a chance. If we have integrity and demonstrate to others the value of integrity, we could save a fortune in time, complexity, and money by simply trusting people.

> Reputation is made by what you fall for.
> Character is made by what you stand for.

Being *ethical* is part of having integrity. Ethics primarily attacks manipulative business transactions in which you focus on being the winner. Being ethical suggests that the results of business transactions should be a win-win situation for all sides involved in the negotiation process.

Recently there has been a great deal of concern about the lack of ethics in U.S. business. For example, in an article in *New Accountant*, C. William Thomas suggests that younger managers are becoming less ethical and more manipulative. The article suggests that environmental costs and competitive demands are shifting our focus away from ethical business practices.[2] For example, we may install a chemical plant in India to avoid U.S. worker-safety regulations, or we may move a steel products factory to Mexico to avoid pollution regulations. Similarly, the Bok article suggests that our methods of training new managers, which focus on analytical processes, bring a blindness to the decision-making process and forget the ethical, people concerns of the decision process. We do what the numbers tell us to do rather than what our conscience tells us to do.[3]

We should view personal standards as the "bedrock" of ethical conduct, because all corporations or other entities are made up of people.

C. William Thomas

Being *honest* is part of integrity and ethics. However, I want to draw attention to this element because it's probably the most important. Honesty is the first step to integrity. All people feel that the world should be honest with them, even if they often "see the need" for a little dishonesty in their own lives.

Standards and Value System   Having standards and a value system sets the direction of your own life. Without it, no one, including you, knows where you stand, and no one stands with you. A standards and value system includes goals along with the other characteristics highlighted in this section.

A World Class Person's life is *goal-focused*, not just in business but in all areas. Personal goals should be long-range (10 years out), mid-range (2 to 5 years out), and short-range (within the next year) and should include:

Educational goals

Business goals

Social goals

Ethical/moral/religious goals

Family goals

Entertainment/vacation/travel goals
Physical goals

Personal success defines success in any other area. You can't be successful in business if your personal life is a mess. It will inevitably affect your business abilities as well. If you can't manage your family, how can you possibly expect to be World Class at managing your business? Your personal life and the life of your family are the foundation of a successful business career.

A goal-focused life is a life that has meaning. With a life that has meaning, you can find purpose in your job. Managers who lack meaning in their life work in order to keep their job and get a raise. Managers with meaning in their life work for the joy of it.

Life is like a jigsaw puzzle, but you don't have the picture in front of the box to know what it's supposed to look like. Sometimes you're not even sure if you have all the pieces.

Roger von Oech[4]

Being *loving* encompasses a whole list of attributes, including compassion, empathy, forgiveness, concern about others' feelings and opinions, and having a wise and understanding heart. Loving is caring about others, and, as the Bible says, love is having charity in your heart.

Humility is a difficult attribute to define, because if you think you're humble then you're not. Humility is realizing that we are all equally children of God and that He sees us all as equals, regardless of what luck life has dealt out to specific individuals. Humility is looking at an employee and realizing that he or she could probably do your job better than you do but you just happened to get there first.

Being *moral* is being the kind of person you want the boy who dates your daughter to be. Being moral is being a leader in your family, your community, and your church. It's standing up for your beliefs in dealing with issues that affect society, such as sex, family, alcohol, drugs, and religion. It's making a difference in the education process, especially as it affects your children.

Being *obedient* is being respectfully submissive. It's not being a puppy dog, nor is it being blind. It's expressing your opinion, sharing your ideas, and then supporting the decisions of your superiors even if you think they made the wrong decision. Being obedient means not undercutting your superiors' decisions—of course, I'm talking about judgmental differences, not ethical differences.

Society Value Added   The importance of being society value-added suggests that you should be more than self-interested. In most parts of the world, the betterment of society, not the individual, is what is worked for (see the section "What in the World is Ethical?"). An individual who does not contribute (add value) to society is considered a waste to society. I have been challenged in many countries by the statement "The thing that's gone wrong in the United States is that you are graduating more and more non–value-added individuals in your schools than ever before, and these non–value-added individuals contribute nothing to the economic and social growth of the United States." I'm not sure how to answer this challenge, but it does give us something to think about.

I have already observed that students in professional schools grow more and more preoccupied with the needs and problems of the clients they serve and less and less concerned with the impact of their profession on the larger society.

Derek C. Bok, President, Harvard University

Secondary to, but right in line with, being society value-added is your role in becoming increasingly more value-added. Often this is called *job enrichment*. It suggests that you are getting more than a paycheck out of your job (job retention). It suggests that you are becoming more valuable and that simultaneously your job is becoming more fun. Job enrichment suggests that you are broadening the role of your job, thereby making yourself a more valuable contributor to the goals of the organization (adding more value) while at the same time enriching yourself personally.

Leadership   The last major characteristic of a World Class Person who hopes to be a World Class Manager involves becoming a World Class leader. As we discussed in Chapter 1, a leader focuses on being an example rather than a cattle herder. A leader is a servant to employees, serving them as if they were important to him or her.

I was walking the local Provo mall early one morning for exercise (remember the snow outside), and I walked past a jewelry store. In the store were six employees—half asleep, totally bored, and completely tuned out—pretending to listen to a manager who seemed to be preaching a never-ending sermon. It struck me that the only person who was enjoying the browbeating was the manager. Everyone else was planning to go back to work and do things as they had always been done.

Most management involves very much a "do as I say, not as I do" philosophy. A leader has a "do as I do *and* as I say" philosophy, because both are the same. The leader is doing what he or she is saying. The leader manages by *example*. A leader with example offers direction. Such leaders focus on doing rather then telling, and whenever telling is necessary, they make sure to do what they tell.

A leader is also *enthusiastic*. A leader has goals and a vision.

A leader is *compromising* yet determined and decisive. Some things are worth fighting for, such as ethics, honesty, integrity, and morality, and some things are not worth fighting for, such as the procedure an employee uses in solving a problem. Employees, like children, don't do things the way you would like them done. But in many cases it's the end result you want, not the road traveled. So don't take away from the employee the fun in doing a job, which is figuring out how to do it. Let the employee have some fun, as long as the results are positive. Besides, you might be surprised to find out that the employee did the job in a better way than you. As a leader you need to be compromising yet determined and decisive, not wishy-washy. I often use a favorite saying of mine when someone becomes stressed over minor procedural differences:

> Don't sweat
>   the little things!

A leader is *understanding*. If you expect an employee's job to take precedence over a family crisis, you are only fooling yourself. The family crisis will affect the quality of the results, and you will lose the commitment of the employee to the job. However, if you take an employee's problem seriously and try to help, you will gain a friend for life. Often this takes patience, which brings me to another of my favorite sayings:

> We get too caught up
>   in the thick of
>   thin things.

A leader is *self-replacing*. Leaders prepare others to take their place. They realize that they can move up the ladder only if there is someone who can take their place. Also, the best leaders can disappear for a day or so and not be missed. Their presence is not as important to the operation of the business as is the confidence that has been instilled in the employees to proceed without them.

> All indispensable managers
>   end up in the same place—
>   the cemetery.

Leaders are *environmentally conscious* in the broad sense. They care about the pollution in the area in which they live, but they also care about the growth and development of the community. They care about the effect that labor-force changes and other aspects of their business will have on the community.[5]

Organizations must attempt to achieve harmony between managerial attitudes and behaviors in relation to environmental demands.

Thomas J. Zenisek

Leaders are *worker-safety conscious*, not because some government agency tells them to be so but because the employees are their friends and they don't want to see their friends at risk.

Leaders are *open* in all areas, sharing ideas, offering compliments, and meting out criticism. They don't have secret agendas, nor do they hide the truth. Openness breeds confidence. I'm not suggesting that you do what my friend did, telling a female employee that she had poor taste in dress styles. Openness is letting the employees know where they stand and identifying goals they are shooting for.

Sharing is caring. Share your life with your employees, and they will share their life with you. In the end, you should do more listening than talking. And you should ask more questions than you make statements. People don't want your opinions about how they should behave, nor do they want you to pass judgment. What they want is a listening, caring ear. Avoid phrases like:

You should have . . .

You could have . . .

Why didn't you . . .

One of my favorite phrases at work is *"Have fun!"* I use it so much that employees have given me T-shirts with this message written on them. Basically, I believe that you shouldn't be working if you can't have fun doing it. And if what you're doing isn't fun, then make it fun! Don't be dull and boring. Bring in donuts for everyone once in a while for no good reason at all. Sing a song out loud for no good reason at all. Play the *Lion King* sound track extra loud for no good reason at all—better yet, dance to it for no good reason at all. But be careful—having fun is contagious! Employees might actually enjoy working for you.

. . . men are that they might have joy.

2 Nephi 2:25, Book of Mormon

We have discussed the characteristics of a World Class person. When we look through the recent literature, we are overwhelmed by self-improvement books. They seem to be endless, and I have listed a few already. One excellent series that has become very popular is the group of books by Stephen R. Covey. In one of these books, *The 7 Habits of Highly Effective People*, Covey suggests characteristics that we can use to become World Class People (even though he doesn't use that terminology). He suggests that highly effective people tend to:

1. Be proactive—Have initiative; lead out in your life; choose, don't just react.
2. Begin with the end in mind—Understand your destination and show creativity.
3. Put first things first—Personal management and personal productivity are essential.
4. Think win-win—Realize the interdependence between you and others; develop interpersonal leadership.
5. Seek first to understand, then to be understood—Emphasize communication.
6. Synergize—Develop creative cooperation by valuing the differences.
7. Focus on renewal—Sharpen the saw; develop a spiral of upward growth; consistently grow.[6]

Covey stresses that highly effective people lead their lives according to principles and values that are universally valid. The ability to lead is an outgrowth of applying these principles to problem solving. In a follow-up book, *Principle-Centered Leadership*, Covey discusses the characteristics of a World

Class Manager who exhibits principle-centered leadership. Such leaders:

1. Are continually learning
2. Are service oriented—Life is a mission that includes helping others.
3. Radiate positive energy
4. Believe in other people
5. Lead balanced lives—They have a wide variety of interests.
6. See life as an adventure
7. Are synergistic—The interplay between parts produces more than the individual parts.
8. Exercise the four dimensions of being for self-renewal: physical, mental, emotional, and spiritual[7]

I had a friend who was searching for the perfect spouse tell me that the secret to finding the perfect marriage partner was to spend at least as much time being Mr. or Ms. Right as we spend searching for Mr. or Ms. Right. How can we find someone who is right for us if we're not right for anyone? Similarly, how can we find the perfect employee if we are a terrible employee or boss? We need to be World Class People in order to become World Class Managers.

> To make a difference,
>   we need to be different!

Of those to whom much is given, much is required. And when at some future date the high court of history sits in judgment on each of us—recording whether in our brief span of service we fulfilled our responsibilities to the state— our success or failure, in whatever office we may hold, will be measured by the answers to four questions—
were we truly men of courage . . .
were we truly men of judgment . . .
were we truly men of integrity . . .
were we truly men of dedication?

John F. Kennedy

FINDING THE WORLD CLASS
POTENTIAL IN EVERYONE

*One man practicing sportsmanship is far better than a
hundred teaching it.*

Knute Rockne

World Class Management is learning that the company doesn't
exist for you alone, but for the benefit of everyone. An excellent
analogy is foreign trade. Internationally, any time a trade barrier
is reduced, the cost of trade transactions goes down. Similarly,
whenever we reduce barriers between employees, we reduce the
cost of transactions between employees. The World Class Manager is open, honest, and willing to share. The WCM is not
obsessed with being protective of his or her ideas.

World Class Managers recognize that you cannot overcom-
municate when you are running a business. The more you share,
the better will be the tools available to your employees. WCMs
are team-oriented managers who take advantage of the synergistic effects of team interaction (see Chapter 14).

World Class Managers are World Class People who are confident enough in themselves to eagerly search out the potential in
the people around them. They trust themselves and the people
they deal with. They are not paranoid individuals who surround
themselves with nontrust systems in order to protect themselves
from their employees, customers, and vendors.

One approach to a marital relationship is to constantly follow
your spouse around (a nontrust system) so that he or she doesn't
talk to the wrong people, say the wrong things, or get any bad
ideas. The other approach is to build a two-way trust relationship in which both parties respect each other and trust each other
to avoid any behavior that would disrupt the trust relationship.
As World Class Managers, we need to build similar trust relationships with all our business associates.

World Class human relations, in which we search out the
potential in everyone, are built upon an effective, caring Human

Resources Management (HRM) system.[8] An effective, people-centered HRM program that incorporates the people-oriented characteristics we have discussed looks at what employees are becoming, rather than what they are right now. This type of system recognizes that a better person makes a better employee. In a recent article, Boyst listed several needs of a World Class HRM system:

Focus on continuous improvement.

Build a new workplace environment.

Rethink performance evaluations.

Focus on team building.

Establish job rotation and lifelong learning.

Rethink compensation.[9]

A husband, after complimenting his wife on a recent educational achievement, said to her, "I like you just the way you are becoming." Being World Class is finding the World Class potential in everyone with whom we interact.

This above all: to thine own self be true,
And it must follow, as the night the day,
Thou canst not then be false to any man.

William Shakespeare

WHAT IN THE WORLD IS ETHICAL?

. . . the wisdom of this world is foolishness with God.

1 Cor. 3:19

Does the United States define what is ethical for the entire world? We seem to have taken this as our role, since we place sanctions on countries that don't follow our ethical standards. For example, if a country has human rights offenses, we place an economic sanction on it, even though we had to fight a destructive internal war in order to eliminate slavery in our own country. If a country cuts down too many trees, we place sanctions on it, even though in the last couple of hundred years we have destroyed more of our own forests (by percentage) than any other country in the world. We tell other countries not to pollute, but we go into those countries and set up factories that are toxic and have high-risk health hazards. What is ethical? The answer differs from country to country, and the United States is not always right.

I am not saying that ethical standards are contradictory. I am saying that not all countries and peoples hold the same ethical values. For example, is it ethical for the United States to limit the economic growth of another country? If not, then why do we use economic sanctions to force certain behavior? Let us consider some other examples.

1. In the United States, we believe everything should be defined as black or white, good or bad. As discussed earlier, this is a very Christian perspective. A Hindu perspective would be that there is good and bad in everything and it is in the gray area in between that we live most of our life. This black-and-white versus gray perspective has a significant effect on how decisions are made. For example, the United States prefers to win, whereas other cultures prefer to compromise.

2. The United States focuses on a hurry-up, quick-results philosophy. Other countries, such as Japan, prefer the think-it-through-before-you-react approach to problem solving. Is intentionally moving too slow in a business transaction unethical?

3. Many countries see their government officials as tools for getting things done. Therefore, it is appropriate to hire them as consultants. In the United States, however, involving government officials as consultants is considered a conflict of interest or perhaps even bribery. Is it unethical to use government officials as agents in a business transaction?

4. The difference between the Christian rights-of-the-individual ethical system and the Asian rights-of-the-society ethical system has already been mentioned. For Asians, it is unethical to work in a profession that is non–value-added. Yet we

send many non–value-added, self-fulfilling people to Asian countries to engage in business transactions.

The list of ethical differences goes on and on. Rather than continue, I leave you with a book by Schuhmacher that you should consider reading. Although it is a little dated and somewhat controversial, it is still eye-opening reading.[10]

For what is a man profited, if he shall gain the whole world, and lose his own soul?

Matt. 16:26

BECOMING A WORLD CLASS MANAGER

Our scientific power has outrun our spiritual power. We have guided missiles and misguided men.

Martin Luther King, Jr.

As we have already discussed, a World Class Manager is an ethical manager. The topic of ethical management has received an enormous amount of recent attention. For example, *Time* devoted the May 25, 1987, issue to ethics, with the cover-page headline "What ever happened to Ethics?—Assaulted by sleaze, scandals, and hypocrisy, America searches for its moral bearings." The March 1994 issue of *New Accountant* addresses future graduates and young managers with the cover-page headline "Does Ethics Stand a Chance?—Are young managers less ethical?" In the search for World Class Ethical Managers, *Business Week*, on the cover of the August 1, 1994, issue, considers "Managing by Values—What is an ethical company?" Using Bob Haas, CEO of Levi Strauss, as their example, they attempt to demonstrate that ethics are back in style. Bob Haas focuses on "responsible commercial success" with programs such as paying the tuition for a contractor's underage workers in Bangladesh.

An article by Petrick and Manning offers steps to improving the organizational ethical climate:

- Improve the quality of the leader-follower exchange, which involves the establishment of a collaborative relationship where support is provided for ethical conduct.
- Reduce delays in the enforcement of organizational ethical guidelines.
- Improve personal ethical conduct by empowering individuals to analyze and resolve ethical conflicts on-site and by offering training that develops responsible, ethical decision-making skills.
- Leaders need to model the behavior they want to see in others.[11]

In today's global economy, the need to be internationally competitive in the work environment is an ongoing challenge for organizations. Part of that competitive edge is developing a reputation for superior productivity based on managing human resources with integrity.

Petrick and Manning

From this chapter, we have learned that the World Class Manager is a World Class Person first. Additionally, a World Class Manager:

- Adds value to society through his or her efforts—is environmentally conscious, employee-safety conscious, and looks to help employees develop their World Class abilities
- Focuses on eliminating waste and increasing value added
- Focuses on being productive rather than protective of ideas, opinions, and territory—doesn't let innovation get tied up in ego
- Gives employees time for self-evaluation (time to think), self-renewal, and self-improvement
- Cares about the personal aspects of employees' lives
- Focuses on breakthrough thinking—working smarter, not harder
- Understands and utilizes the change process to influence positive, goal-directed changes through leadership

---

All victory and glory is brought to pass unto you through your diligence.

Doctrine and Covenants 103:36

A World Class Manager is much more than tools and talent (these will be discussed in Chapter 13). A World Class Manager knows how to manage his or her life, knows how to lead his or her family, knows how to make a difference in the community, and knows how to lead employees. World Class Managers build in themselves and, through example, in their family, friends, employees, customers, peers, vendors, and anyone else they come into contact with:

Integrity

Standards and a value system

Society value added

Enthusiasm

Understanding

Environmental consciousness

And, most important of all, a World Class Manager has fun doing it!

The future will demand true leaders who can bring out the best in people.

Adolphson, DeVries, and Rinne[12]

SUMMARY

The highest reward for a man's toil is not what he gets for it but what he becomes by it.

John Ruskin

In an episode of *The Twilight Zone*, a stranger gives a woman a box. The woman is told that if she pushes a button on the box she will receive $2 million. At the same time, someone "she doesn't know and who doesn't know her" will die. After a period of soul searching, the woman decides to go ahead and push the button. The stranger returns, gives the woman the check, and asks for the box back. The woman wants to know what he is going to do with the box, and the stranger replies, "Take it to someone you don't know and who doesn't know you."

Are we so blind that $2 million would mean more to us than the life of another? Perhaps we need to do some soul searching of our own. Remember, in order to be World Class Managers we need to be World Class People.

Modern Man's seven diseases
 wealth without work
 pleasure without conscience
 knowledge without character
 commerce without morality
 science without humanity
 worship without sacrifice
 politics without principle, and
 rights without responsibility
   Mahatma Gandhi, 1948

> We can't put
> our faults behind us
>   until we face them.

CHAPTER 13

Personal Skills

> *The world cares very little about what a man or woman knows; it is what the man or woman is able to do that counts.*
>
> Booker T. Washington

Two women were walking through a forest when they happened to pass by a lake. A frog croaked up to them, "Help, I am a tall, handsome author, but an evil witch turned me into a frog! If one of you will give me a kiss, I can turn back into an author."

One of the women bent over to pick up the frog, and the other quickly spoke up, "You're not really going to kiss that frog, are you?"

The first woman, as she picked up the frog, said, "Of course not. A talking frog is worth a lot more than an author."

I've known many managers who have turned out to be frogs, but the frog can be turned into a World Class Manager (a leader) given the right tools to work with. Without the right tools, he or she may stay a frog forever. This chapter discusses some of the basic tools for World Class Management. This set of tools is by no means complete. Like everything else that this book discusses, it is continually changing.

This chapter discusses the personal skills of a WCM, such as oral, written, and verbal communication skills, personal characteristics, and computer literacy. The tools are discussed in two groups in order to show how they are related, but the groupings overlap considerably. The two groups are:

1. Categories of skills
2. Areas of skills

> When the time for
>   decision arrives,
>   the time for preparation
>   has passed.

CATEGORIES OF SKILLS

The perpetual obstacle to human advancement is custom.
John Stuart Mill

World Class Management skills fall into four major categories:

People skills

Creative skills

. Change-oriented skills

Basic tools of the trade

People Skills   The importance of people skills in World Class Management performance should be thoroughly ingrained into your belief system by now. I mention it again because it cannot be forgotten.

We have discussed people skills to a greater or lesser degree in every chapter of this book, with special emphasis placed on these skills in Chapters 2, 5, 9, 10, and 12. Teaming, a crucial people skill, is discussed in Chapter 14. The value of leading, as opposed to driving, with special emphasis on the power of example, was stressed in Chapters 2 and 12.

The Quality and Productivity Management Association (QPMA) (listed in Appendix 5.2) has established a set of nine leadership standards they feel leaders will need in the year 2000. These standards are:

1. Priorities and values that focus on:
    * organizational effectiveness
    * anticipating and exceeding customer expectations
    * giving employees a sense of purpose and pride

    Relationships should be guided by vision, core values, and critical goals.
2. Open and honest communication, external and internal to the organization
3. Agility in dealing with change
4. A pursuit of knowledge and learning for the leader and for everyone else in the organization
5. Innovation and creativity
6. Commitment and courage
7. Systematic approach to performance and problem solving by:
    * assessing what needs change
    * anticipating what should happen
    * organizing to get the change implemented
    * empowering those necessary
    * ensuring that the change gets done
8. Teamwork
9. Empowerment distributed throughout the organization

Creative Skills   World Class leaders need to foster creativity. In the books by von Oech cited in Chapters 1 and 2, the author emphasizes the need to forget the routine and open our minds to new and creative ways of thinking. He focuses on snapping your mental locks and opening yourself to new, creative ideas. Some of his suggestions from *A Whack on the Side of the Head* are:

* Look for the "second right answer."
* Don't be blinded by "what's logical."

- Break the routine and "don't follow the rules."
- Avoid the "practical," and look at situations through someone else's eyes.
- Get out of a world of specialists where "people know more and more about less and less."
- Avoid "going along with the crowd," and "be foolish" once in a while.

In *A Kick in the Seat of the Pants*, von Oech suggests that we need to role-play in order to be more creative. He suggests four roles:

1. Explorer—"Get off the beaten path."
2. Artist—Ask "what if" questions and look for hidden analogies.
3. Judge—Find "what's wrong" with the idea in order to work out the bugs.
4. Warrior—Fight for your idea, or it won't be implemented.

Every child is an artist, the problem is how to remain an artist after he grows up.

Picasso

Nadler and Hibino, cited earlier, are the authors of the books *Breakthrough Thinking* and *Creative Solution Finding*. They stress that conventional thinking is dead and that we need to search out methods of creativity.

Change-Oriented Skills   Our most critical, and also most abused, resource in life is *time*. Time makes change impossible to avoid. Therefore, a World Class Manager takes change by the horns and controls it, rather than allowing it to control the manager. We need to avoid being protective of the status quo. We need to influence and manage change by being a positive influencer and motivator of the change process. We need to position our organization for continuous success by motivating the change

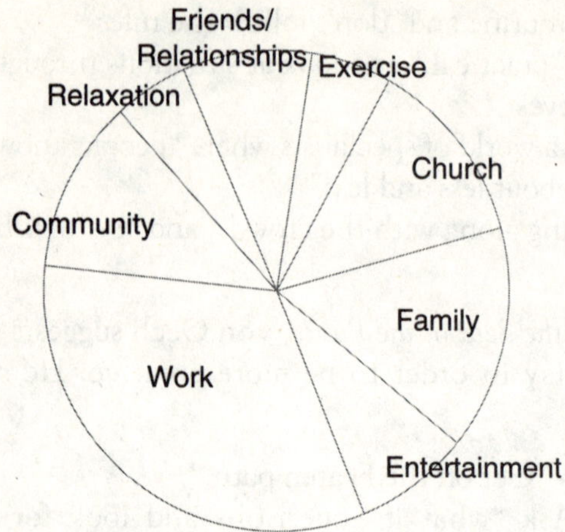

Figure 13.1   The Time Pie

process. Some of the business aspects of technology and time management were discussed in Chapter 7.[1]

Being World Class allows us to understand the time pie. The time pie shows that there is only a limited amount of time in our life; we need to define how we want to cut the pie (see Figure 13.1). The cuts of the pie define our priorities. Expecting the pie to become bigger is unrealistic. The only thing we can control is how we cut the pie. If we try to shove more into one piece of the pie, then the other pieces of the pie will become smaller.

I find it disappointing when people say, "I know I spend a lot of time at work and away from my family, but when I'm with them I spend 'quality' time with them." This statement is used as if quality somehow makes up for a lack of quantity. It's like having an employee come to you and say, "I'm only going to put in four hours today, but I'll make it quality time." We want the full eight hours out of our employees, just as our children want the quantity time, as well as quality time, out of us. We should focus on making our work time more "quality" time and less "quantity" time rather than hurting ourselves in areas where quantity time is needed.

> What counts is not the number of hours you put in, but how much you put in the hours.

To become World Class Managers, we need to develop change management skills that focus on managing our most critical resource—time. Becoming World Class requires us to motivate the change process within our enterprise.

Basic Tools of the Trade   The list of basic skills needed by a World Class Manager is enormous. However, I would like to emphasize a few here:

- Computer skills—you can't live without them anymore
- Measurement skills—an understanding of the measurement process and the reports that go along with it, for example balance sheets, profit and loss statements, market share, financial ratios, operational ratios, efficiency, productivity, and quality
- Communication skills—reading, writing, listening, speaking
- Creative problem solving and open-minded thinking

Fifty-one percent of being smart is knowing what you are dumb about.

Ann Landers

AREAS OF SKILLS

The world is full of willing people, some willing to work, the rest willing to let them.

Robert Frost

World Class Managers need to develop a set of skills that make them effective managers in each of four areas:

Individual performance skills

Job functional skills

Enterprise management skills

Beyond-the-enterprise skills

I will list several of the skills that are necessary in each of these four areas. An APICS (listed in Appendix 5.2) certification called the Certification in Resource Management (CIRM) focuses on the manager's ability to manage an enterprise's resources in these same four categories.

Individual Performance Skills

- Oral and written communication skills
- Listening and reading skills
- Ability to focus on the core problems
- Negotiation skills
- Computer literacy skills (e.g., utilizing a word processor, spreadsheet, or electronic mail)
- Teaming skills (e.g., team leadership, membership, and organization)—the ability to accomplish change through teaming

Job Functional Skills

- Understanding the business processes—how you and your job affect the total corporation
- Identifying and organizing the interactions that relate to business processes and activities
- Understanding the perspective of other functions
- The ability to recognize and integrate organizational functions

Enterprise Management Skills

- The skills necessary to search out the core competencies and develop a vision, a mission, a strategy, and critical success factors
- A Human Resource perspective
- An understanding of how the change process affects the enterprise
- The ability to develop corporate and division strategies
- An understanding of the tools necessary to make strategic and operational decisions, such as break-even analysis, make-buy decision analysis, return-on-investment analysis, and cost-benefit analysis
- The skills necessary to develop a focused measurement system
- The ability to develop a focused information, productivity, quality, training, and technology strategy

Beyond-the-Enterprise Skills

- An understanding of globalization and localization
- Legal, governmental, union, and environmental understanding
- An understanding of stakeholder influences, including employees, owners, customers, vendors, financial institutions, agents and dealers, and the local community
- An understanding of the time phasing of an enterprise, through start-up, growth, maturity, and decline
- An understanding of how the change process affects the world around the enterprise

Being a World Class Manager means being well-rounded in your skills. It means stepping back and looking at the big picture once in a while rather than getting wrapped up in the details. It suggests a focus on building effective change while still stressing the goals of the enterprise.

Straighten up your room first, then the world.

Jeff Jordon

SUMMARY

This chapter may be short, but it's important. I could spend pages discussing each skill listed. My aim was to identify the important skills. You can't be World Class if you're a frog and lack the skills that support World Class thinking!

> Past experience should be a guidepost,
> not a hitching post.

CHAPTER 14

Teamwork Skills

He has the right to criticize who has the heart to help.

Abraham Lincoln

A father and his son took daily walks through Central Park in New York City. Every day they would walk past a statue of General Sherman, who sat in full military gear upon his horse. As they walked past the statue, the father would tip his hat at it and say, "Hello, Sherman."

The son would imitate this gesture, making a mock salute and saying, "Hello, Sherman."

One day while walking past the statue, the father tipped his hat and the son made his salute. Then the son asked the father, "Who is that sitting on Sherman?"

Isn't that the way it is? Each of us has our own perspective on what we see, and we don't discover other people's perspectives unless we communicate with them. That's what teaming is all about: communicating with others so everyone can benefit from the synergy of ideas.

I was working on teaming problems at Applied Magnetics Malaysia (AMM) in Penang, Malaysia. The work force is composed of 60% Muslim, 30% Buddhist, and 10% Hindu. The management is American (Christian) plus a mixture of some of these other cultures. I was brought in to discuss multicultural team building. The resistance to open communication that existed in these cultures was enormous. Much time and patience were required to get the mixed-culture teams to work together and avoid culturally offensive occurrences. However, in the end, we ended up with teams of employees with such dramatically different ways of looking at life that many of the ideas generated were extremely innovative and often even revolutionary.

Within the United States, we have neither the cultural diversity nor the team relationship-building problems that exist in Malaysia. Despite this, I have found that the teams in the United States are seldom as effective as the teams in Malaysia. Why? The biggest reason seems to be that we in the United States are not willing to give team building the time it requires. We simply don't have the patience. Instead, we throw a bunch of people together and tell them to be creative without establishing the proper team dynamics. We create "groups" of people rather than "teams." This chapter discusses some of the aspects of team building, but by no means all. I want to stress immediately that effective team building takes time. People need to become used to one another before they can open up to a group, even in the United States. Without the proper time commitment, the other elements of team building won't be effective.

There are numerous teams in your life. The first, and most important, team is the quality circle of your life: your family. All the characteristics of effective teaming need to be present in your family if you expect it to perform well. If you can't get this primary quality circle to work well for you, you have little hope of the work circles in your life being effective.

To keep your marriage brimming
with love in a loving cup
Whenever you're wrong admit it
Whenever you're right shut up

Ogden Nash

Teaming is a shift of management styles away from the authoritarian (workplace communism) to the participative (workplace democracy) (see Chapter 1). There are many different forms of teams:

Quality circles

Management circles

Decision teams

Total quality management teams

Small-group improvement activities

The key element of all teams, no matter what they are called, is participative interaction among people.

> Being able
> to talk things out
> makes us better able
> to act them out.

We now discuss some of the other elements of teaming.

THE PURPOSE OF TEAMS

The purposes for establishing teams are many. A few of the most important are:

- To effect change, increase value added, and eliminate waste
- To build work-force cohesiveness
- To focus efforts
- To take advantage of synergistic perspectives
- To involve employees in the change process
- To build corporate-wide integration

To Effect Change, Increase Value Added, and Eliminate Waste   With teaming, we are attempting to implement different positive process improvements through people involvement. When people have ownership of the change, they are more committed to its success. For example, in Japan teaming means watching out for one another. Each employee sees himself or herself as an inspector searching for ways to improve the process. At Hitachi, teaming generates from forty to seventy-five value-added and waste-eliminating improvement suggestions per employee per year.

To Build Work-force Cohesiveness   When employees know and understand one another, they are much better at integrating. I've known people who have worked side by side for years and don't even know each other's names. Employees work better together if they know one another personally.

To Focus Efforts   Teams build a united focus. The team is given a charter with a goal, and team members work together toward that goal, each doing his or her part. Employees work together rather than going off in their own directions.

To Take Advantage of Synergistic Perspectives   As in the Applied Magnetics Malaysia example mentioned earlier, the synergy of a team effort results in more effective and creative solutions. The mixture of perspectives opens people's minds to new alternatives.

To Involve Employees in the Change Process   Teaming helps reduce the size of the no-man's-land that exists between management, who is making decisions, and the members of the work force, who are implementing the decisions. Teaming is a shift from the authoritarian to the participative, a shift from workplace communism to workplace democracy. Under authoritarian management, the role of management is to plan, lead, and control, and the employees do the work. Under participative management, management plans (defines the goals), but the team (including the manager) leads, controls, and performs.

The TRW-Thomasville Operations field case showed the following differences in the shift from authoritarian to participative management:

Authoritarian management:

- Set goals for subordinates; define the standards and the results that are expected.

- Give them the information they need to do the job.
- Train them how to do the job.
- Apply discipline to ensure conformity and to suppress conflict.
- Practice persuasive leadership.
- Develop and install new methods.
- Reward achievements and punish failures.

Participative, goal-oriented management:

- Employees participate in problem solving and goal setting.
- Give them access to the information they want.
- Create situations for optimum learning.
- Mediate conflict.
- Allow employees to set challenging goals.
- Teach improvement techniques.
- Enable employees to pursue and move into growth opportunities.
- Recognize achievements and help employees learn from failures.[1]

World Class companies involve people, making them a part of the solution rather than a part of the problem. . . . When Involvement strategies are effectively implemented, they absorb people, committing them to the company and its future.

Bell and Burnham[2]

To Build Corporate-wide Integration   Teaming builds sharing and focuses the entire organization on a common objective. Teams are composed of cross-functional team members, resulting in a corporate-wide integration. This integration is both horizontal and vertical: vertical in that many functional areas are mixed together into the same teams, and horizontal in that the manager is a team member right next to the employees and job titles are (hopefully) dropped.

One new method of performing this integration is through teamnets. Teamnets, which integrate the concept of teaming and networking, are networks of teams that cross all functional boundaries in order to focus on a common objective.[3]

Never look down on anyone unless you're helping him up.
Rev. Jesse Jackson

THE BENEFITS OF TEAMING

I was talking with a manager about his planning process, and he said to me, "You know what the problem with our planning process is? There are people who have left brains, and there are people who have right brains; well sometimes I feel like my planners fall into the middle category."

This confused me, so I asked him, "What's the middle category?"

He responded, "No brain!"

I felt confident that with this attitude he was not destined to get much cooperation from his planners in the future. This authoritarian, dominating, "I-know-it-all-and-everyone-else-is-dumb" attitude is what teaming attempts to get rid of. Teaming focuses on the abilities of the work force.

Reviewing the published literature, we find some specific benefits that managers cite as reasons for creating teams:

- Improvement in the quality of the decision process
- Improvement in the quality of the decisions
- An operations-oriented focus to the decision process
- Improved relationships overcoming personal differences
- Improved training
- Stronger employee commitment and more highly motivated employees
- A management perspective to the decision-making process for employees
- A greater awareness due to the interaction process

We have referred to Toyota's successes in team building in previous chapters. Toyota averages fifty improvement suggestions per employee per year (about one per week). It uses Quality Control circles (QC) as its quality improvement teams. The synergy of QC circles has created an environment in which suggestions can flow easily.

The puzzle to me . . . is that almost every manager in almost every organization supports teamwork. In fact, many feel it is essential. But very few organizations institute an organizationwide program to ensure team effectiveness. . . . Managers at all levels must learn to overcome the resistance to instituting a systematic team building concept.

William G. Dyer

STEPS TOWARD EFFECTIVE TEAMING

To understand the teaming process, we should first consider the *phases of team development:*

Forming—initial orientation

Storming—conflict and confusion

Norming—consolidation around tasks

Performing—effective teamwork performance[4]

Sadly, many teams are disbanded before achieving the fourth stage. Teams prior to the fourth stage are considered groups and have not evolved into a form that will take advantage of the synergistic benefits of teaming.

There are three *stages of teaming and employee involvement:*

1. Circle stage—Organizing a team to discuss quality problems (QC circles) is one of the first stages. Here the team is utilized for idea generation.[5]
2. Empowered stage—As we allocate authority and responsibility to the teams, we empower them to carry out their suggestions.
3. Fully functional stage—In the final stage, the teams set their own goals and direction, keeping them in line with

the goals of the enterprise. Consensus management in self-managed teams is fully integrated (e.g., the TQM teams discussed in Chapter 11).

In developing total work-force involvement, the team needs to be able to share and blend ideas from different backgrounds and come out with something bigger and better than each individual team member could have accomplished alone. This *team interaction* builds integration and requires two things in order to be effective:

1. First, the team members need to come from cross-functional areas to ensure that many differing perspectives are considered. It is important to include both insiders and outsiders. Insiders are team members who are directly involved in the area that the team is focusing on. Outsiders are individuals who do not have a direct interest in this area. The insiders know the technicalities behind the area of interest, while the outsiders can look at the situation with a broader perspective. Often the outsider is in a better position to question, "Why are we doing this at all?"

2. The second key consideration of team effectiveness is team-member interaction. The team members need to feel comfortable with one another. This may require social activities and time. Comfortable interaction won't occur the first time a team meets, and probably not the second, third, or fourth. But in order for team effectiveness to take place, comfortable interaction needs to occur eventually. Extra meetings might be necessary at first in order to build this level of comfort.

World class manufacturers have found that the best way to tap into and channel their peopleware power is through the collaborative, cooperative, synergistic effort of people working in groups (teams).

Charles G. Andrew[6]

Effectively organized teams need a *measurement system* that defines the team's performance. During the circle stage, the measurement still comes from management. However, in the fully functional stage, the team establishes its own goals and its own measures of performance.

Numerous tools have been suggested for establishing a measurement system. Activity-Based Costing is thought to be the most thorough, but it is also the most cumbersome and lacks focus.[7] Other tools, such as critical resource performance measurement, which is goal based, have been demonstrated to be much more focused and therefore more effective (see Chapter 3).

Effective teaming requires the establishment of an *environment of success*. The enterprise needs a top-to-bottom commitment to teaming and empowerment; otherwise, the effectiveness of teaming will be short-lived. The teaming process also requires a time commitment and a great deal of patience.[8]

No matter how well it is directed, the team will perform only as well as the individuals on it.

Andrew Grove, President, Intel

THE THREE FACES OF TEAMING

World Class Managers who utilize teams need to view their roles from three perspectives:

Team developer

Team leader

Team member

Team Developer The World Class Manager needs to understand how to define and establish a team. This task includes designating a purpose for the team (defining a team charter), selecting the appropriate members of the team, and recognizing that it takes time for the group to become an effective team.

Team definition also requires the outlining of the levels of responsibility and authority of the team (empowerment). Team empowerment is necessary because change is necessary.[9] Without empowerment, the interactive politics between the changer (management) and the changed (employees) will destroy effective change processes. Empowerment is more than authority—it is also responsibility (responsibility diffusion). The team is rewarded or penalized for its decisions. Therefore, the team becomes very committed to the change process.

Real-world examples of the benefits of empowerment include the following:

- General Electric increased productivity by 250% in empowered plants.
- Corning decreased defect rates from 1,800 parts per million to 9 parts per million.
- AT&T operator service has increased in quality by 12%.
- Senco S/A (Brazil) has shown inventory-cycle improvements of 300%.

An effective team should have internal and external members. The internal members are those "in the know" about the process being studied and should form the majority of the team members. For example, a product development team should include:

Engineering

Manufacturing

Marketing

Finance

Purchasing

Customers

An external member is someone who is not "in the know" about the process the team is analyzing. This individual should challenge the obvious, because he or she is not familiar with the obvious. This challenge generates a "rethink" attitude among the team member. External members of a product development team could be:

Inventory control clerks

Maintenance supervisors

Custodians

HRM personnel

Given a proper mix of team members, a synergy of ideas will be established. The quality of the decision process has been demonstrated to be higher when team members can openly discuss problems that are normally hidden in the data of an individual.

Team Leader	The team leader needs to focus on establishing trust among the team members. The different functions that have been integrated into the team hold a natural distrust for one another. This distrust prevents openness (the storming phase of team development). The team leader must assure team members that mutual understanding and respect can exist so that trust can develop. This requires controlling conflict so that disagreements don't get out of hand or become personal.

The team leader needs to make sure that all members of the team are heard from. Each represented functional area needs a chance to share its ideas in order for the hoped-for synergistic benefits to occur.

When the team arrives at the performing stage of team development, the team leader needs to back off from the leadership role and enter a note-taking, minute-taking mode. This allows ideas to flow freely.

Team leaders need to foster the synergy of the team by:

- Listening to and clarifying the presented suggestions
- Supporting all ideas—there are no dumb ideas
- Offering differing opinions and confronting problems openly, and encouraging others to do so
- Looking for the quality, value-added ideas
- Offering feedback on the teaming process by looking for and suggesting areas for improvement

Team Member	During the performing stage of team development, the manager should become a team member, sharing in but not dominating the creative process. Additionally, a manager may be asked to take on the role of team member on a team for which he or she is neither the developer nor the leader.

Whatever the role—developer, leader, or member—the World Class Manager needs to understand and perform each role effectively, acting as a team player, not an authoritarian figure.

THE REQUIREMENTS OF SUCCESSFUL TEAMS

Some of the requirements of successful teams are listed here in an attempt to consolidate many of the teaming ideas that have been scattered throughout this book. I will explain only those items that have not already been thoroughly discussed elsewhere. Successful teams require:

- Empowerment
- Problem identification and problem analysis skills training for all team members
- Team membership and participation training
- Time to evolve from grouping to teaming and to develop interpersonal relationships
- Elimination of job descriptions and titles within the team
- Team-motivated performance measures rather than individual performance measures
- Gainsharing—the employees share in the benefits of the improvements
- Management by team-established objectives
- Treating workers as customers
- Long-term change management focus
- Team cohesiveness through common goals and change ownership
- A defined problem resolution process such as the SPS process used in TQM (discussed in Chapter 11)
- A feedback and performance rating mechanism

A successful team is an excited team that recognizes both challenge and opportunity in the teaming process. A massive amount of literature on effective teaming is available. I have suggested just a few works that will add detail to our discussion.[10]

WORLD CLASS TEAMING

> *The way we run our department is by thinking of ourselves as a small business. . . . Before we went into teams, we were all functionalized. . . . Today the associates do everything. . . . We have far fewer people doing even more work.*
>
> Evelyn Carney, AMEX pioneer team member

Successful World Class Teaming is similar to the TQM teaming process discussed in Chapter 11. TQM teams are focused on and organized around a charter. They have a quality council that is the kingpin of all the teams. The quality council is a team that sets up teams, rather than having a manager set up teams, and these teams are established with a specific focus. Several types of teams are required in a TQM environment. They are referred to as the three "P" teams—project, product, and process. With their charter, the teams are empowered to implement change focused on increasing the value added and eliminating the waste.

Teaming does not make better managers; it makes better employees. A World Class Manager uses teaming to empower employees to be more effective. The manager becomes more effective by following all the principles described in this book, of which teaming or employee involvement is a critical element. Teaming does not replace good management, but World Class Management is difficult to attain without an effective, team-oriented organization.[11]

At the AMEX Investment and Insurance Services Group, Inc., a top-down view transformed the organization from a traditionally run insurance company into a company with a reputation for quality services and products. The process started in 1988 when President Sarah Nolan teamed a group of experienced employees with a charter to "set up a parallel business from scratch, throw out all the preconceived notions and discover new and better ways to run a financial services company."[12] This group was reintegrated into the main office in 1990. By mid-1991, 60% of the employees were involved in teams.

---

*I was looking at the attendance records for 1990, and they
had improved 27 percent over 1989. I think it's because
you feel such a strong responsibility to your team and your
customers.*

Pat Haskell, AMEX

Xerox felt the need for change, pushed by:

Global marketplace

Competition

Number of products and services

Complexity of products and services

Customer demands

It established a strategic imperative that would:

1. Unleash the power, creativity, and motivation of the
   people.
2. Place decision making closer to the customer.

Xerox started by setting a vision:

> Xerox, the document company, is the leader in
> the global document market, providing document
> services that enhance business productivity.

The new standard of productivity and the effort to bring decisions
closer to the customer established a focus on World Class productivity through Work Process Improvement. The primary tool
for accomplishing these improvements was employee empowerment. Xerox employees developed a TQM-type plan showing
where they are (current state), where they want to be (vision),
and how they're going to get there (transition plan). The transition began with the development of empowered work teams con-
sisting "of four to seven people who share responsibility and
accountability for providing their external and internal customers
with innovative products and services that satisfy their requirements." The empowered teams were allowed to define their own

work processes. They had the authority to make decisions on who they did work for and how they managed interpersonal relations. The manager, or team leader, took on the role of facilitator, communicator, integrator, mentor, teacher, coach, leader, monitor, and feedback provider. Xerox soon learned that empowerment increased not only customer satisfaction and productivity but also employee satisfaction.

Xerox found that the most difficult part of empowerment was not in orienting and training the employees but rather in getting management to let go of the decision-making authority. Managers were to be the enablers in the transformation process. They needed to communicate the vision of empowerment to the employees and, through their actions, help the empowered teams make their own decisions. This transformation is a gradual process, but it is well worth the time and effort if you can just get management to let go.[13]

World Class teaming is not a fad—it is the trend for the future. World Class Managers will understand and capitalize on the benefits of empowered teams.

They [the team] decided to use a "rotating coordinator." He or she is not in charge, but is responsible to coordinate the efforts of the team. The coordinator handles the distribution of the work and projects throughout the team, complaints and disagreements between team members, vacation schedules to some extent, and so on.

The teams are not yet at the point where they are hiring and firing, but we're moving in that direction.

Norma Bermudez, AMEX

SUMMARY

---

*When Thomas Edison was working on improving his first
electric light bulb, the story goes, he handed the finished bulb
to a young helper, who nervously carried it upstairs, step
by step. At the last possible moment, the boy dropped it—
requiring the whole team to work another twenty-four hours
to make a second bulb. When it was finished, Edison looked
around, then handed it to the same boy. The gesture probably changed the boy's life. Edison knew that more than a
bulb was at stake.*

James D. Newton

World Class teams are TQM empowered teams that act as agents
for change. World Class Managers, who are agents for change,
recognize the positive value of utilizing the brains, and not just
the brawn, of the work force.

---

*What you do for yourself may start you up in the world.
But from there on up, it's what you do for others.*

Burton Hillis

CHAPTER 15

The WCM in the Enterprise, Its Functions, and Their Integration

> *If a guest at the Boston Ritz-Carlton requests six hyper-allergenic pillows, the hotel's knowledge-based system will make sure she will have them waiting for her at any Ritz in the world.*
>
> Davis and Botkin[1]

This chapter is about the functions of the enterprise. I'm not talking about the starship *Enterprise*, but I do plan to "beam you up" so you can see the big picture of enterprise functions and how they are integrated. What we need, as World Class Managers, is a "beam me up" attitude toward all aspects of the company. We need to look at the big picture so we can see how all the pieces fit together.

> *Beam me up, Scotty!*
>
> Captain Kirk, Star Trek

This chapter does not attempt to discuss each aspect of the enterprise in detail. Rather, it attempts to show the interaction and integration of these aspects to help you appreciate the importance of thoroughly understanding the enterprise functions.

Chaos often breeds life when order breeds habit.
                                                    Henry (Brooks) Adams

---

ENTERPRISE FOCUS

To live is to change, and to be perfect is to change often.
                                                    John Henry Newman

---

When Dr. Robert Oppenheimer, supervisor of the creation of
the first atomic bomb, was asked by a congressional committee
whether there was any defense against the weapon, he quickly
responded, "Certainly."

"And that is . . . ?" inquired the committee.

Dr. Oppenheimer looked over the hushed, expectant audience
and subtly whispered, "Peace."

How often do we prepare ourselves for corporate warfare, and
how seldom do we look for peace? Is the purpose of the enterprise to fight a war, or is it to win the prize? Winning, for a competitive, World Class Manager, requires cooperation and
teamwork, not bloodshed.

The enterprise should focus on the key competitive strategy
areas:

The customer:

- Eternal—spouse and family
- Internal—fellow employees
- Immediate—the manufacturer you ship to
- Final—the end user of your product

Change

Value added and waste elimination

Trust—eliminate the intimidating nontrust systems

---

*Marriage should war incessantly with that monster that is
the ruin of everything. This is the monster of habit.*
                                                    Honoré de Balzac

---

Enterprise focus needs a target to shoot at. The focus of the World Class Enterprise should include:

Definition of the core competencies

Vision

Mission

Corporate and divisional strategy

Operating plan

Definition of the critical success factors

Measurement/motivation system

Empowered, team-based work force

Productivity and quality improvements

Global perspective

Technology policy

Training program

The enterprise focus needs to be shared and participated in. It should incorporate all the characteristics discussed in this book. An article on enterprise failure gave the following five factors as playing a major role in enterprise decline (defined as a slowdown in competitive momentum):

1. Entrapment and self-deception—a resistance to change, a comfortableness with the status quo, a self-justification that everything is going along as it should even when outsiders disagree
2. Hierarchical orientation—domination by the business bureaucracy over the basic competitive business drive
3. Cultural rigidity—tight administrative control that inhibits rapid, timely change
4. Desire for acceptance through conformity—a "don't rock the boat" attitude throughout the organization
5. Too much consensus and compromise—an unwillingness to "take the bull by the horns" and to risk making a decision for fear a mistake will then come back to haunt the organization[2]

The World Class Manager is one who has a focus on focusing the enterprise, and the World Class Manager's integrity and trustworthiness are critical elements in his or her effectiveness. Without a focused manager, it's impossible to build a successfully focused enterprise.[3] Now that we have a focus, let's look at the functions of the enterprise.

The preservation of the means of knowledge among the lowest ranks is of more importance to the public than all the property of all the rich men in the country.

John Adams

THE FUNCTIONS OF THE ENTERPRISE

It is impossible, in one short chapter, to discuss all the functions of an enterprise. I will highlight a few of the basic functions in order to demonstrate the need for functional enterprise integration. The functions of the enterprise include the business processes, the identification of appropriate business interactions, the understanding of all the perspectives of the different enterprise organizations, and the recognition of the integration mechanisms and how the integration should work.

A World Class Manager understands the abilities of individuals across all functional areas. The manager may not be able to do each job, but he or she will be familiar with how each function fits into the "big picture" (the "beam me up" attitude discussed earlier). Enterprise functional understanding includes:[4]

The business processes:

- Customer interaction
    Sales and marketing functions
    Customer support services
- Technology development
    Product design and development
    Process and industrial design and development
- Production processes
    Facilities planning
    Production

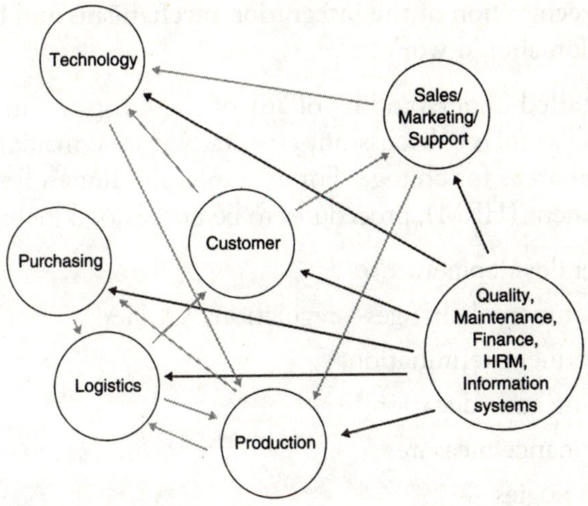

Figure 15.1   Business Interactions

- Logistics
    Purchasing and the receiving function
    Shipping and product distribution
    Internal product movement and inventory
- Support/information functions
    Quality Management
    Human Resources Management
    Finance and accounting
    Information systems
    Maintenance

The identification of appropriate business interactions:

- Who interacts with whom, and how (see Figure 15.1)

The understanding of all the perspectives of the different enterprise organizations:

- Continuous training and education

The recognition of the integration mechanisms and how the integration should work

A detailed understanding of any of these topics can require quite an extensive discussion, especially if we consider all the potential areas for change. For example, in Human Resources Management (HRM), procedures to be understood include:

Career development

Environmental changes—regulations, OSHA

Recruitment/termination

Training and education

Performance measures

Technologies

Concepts of HRM to be understood include:

Management by Objective (MBO)—individually, by team

Empowerment

Matrix management

Teaming

The CEO as a strategic guru is a thing of the past. CEOs must now focus on finding and motivating talent.

Bartlett and Ghoshal[5]

In a recent presentation, Boyst outlined the key HRM strategies for enterprise success. They are:

Continuous improvement

The new workplace environment

Rethinking performance evaluations

Team building

Planned job changes

Lifelong learning—cross-training

Compensation planning

The future consists of a perpetually changing environment and workplace. A company must maintain its competitive skills and so must the employee. . . . It is people that make things happen. . . . HRM will be one of the keys to the 1990's integrated management revolution.

William M. Boyst Jr., III[6]

Later in this chapter, we consider manufacturing as a detailed example of enterprise functions, improvements, and integration.

The human resources of an organization represent its most important, sustainable, competitive advantage. It is vital then, that our systems for managing our people help us maintain their commitment, their trust, enhance their development, and direct their effort toward outcomes of strategic importance to the organization.

Thomas C. Tuttle, Maryland Center for
Quality and Productivity (MCQP)[7]

ENTERPRISE INTEGRATION

Figure 15.1 shows an idealistic example of the business interactions. In it we see the customer as the center of all interactions, feeding the development of technology (product technology) and the sales and marketing functions. In response, the customer receives product delivered through the logistics system. Technology develops products and processes required to produce the products and delivers this information to production. Sales delivers projected customer demand to the production organization. Production utilizes the purchasing function to supply its raw materials, which are delivered by the logistics department.

The support functions integrate with all these operating departments. For example, HRM interacts with all the departments because every department has employees. Information systems (IS) collect and feed back all the appropriate information needs of the departments. Finance and accounting manage the costs and assets of the organization, and the quality function validates the products and processes throughout the organization.

Ideally, these functional circles do not exist in a World Class Enterprise. Rather, teams of employees are established to integrate all these functional processes. For example, a TQM product team would include technology, customer, sales/marketing, quality, production, logistics, and purchasing representatives along with some "external" representation (see Chapters 11 and 14).

Other models for World Class Enterprise integration exist. For example, Enterprise Resource Planning attempts to integrate the planning functions, from the business plan down through the production processes, with the financial and accounting functions.[8] The Integrated Information Flow model of enterprise integration looks at the integration process from an information perspective.[9] Some expansions of the Integrated Enterprise model as defined by APICS, discussed earlier, show how teaming, leadership, and motivation play important roles in the integration process.[10]

Another way to look at integration is through the measurement/motivation process.

> Companies that measure together
> motivate together.

Numerous areas of measurement can be integrated into an enterprise-wide perspective. For example:

- Measures of quality—e.g., reduced complaints
- Measures of operation costs—e.g., reduced inventory levels
- Measures of flexibility—e.g., reduced product cycle time
- Measures of reliability—e.g., equipment effectiveness
- Measures of innovation—e.g., time-to-market reductions
- Measures of productivity—e.g., improved output-to-input performance
- Measures of teaming and empowerment—e.g., increased suggestions per employee[11]

Perhaps one of the most important measures of integrated enterprise performance is the measure that validates that the enterprise has achieved the "we" status. It's one thing for management to think the enterprise is integrated, and it's entirely another thing for the employees to feel it is integrated. A "we" status measurement is taken simply by listening to the employees when they talk to each other, or to outsiders such as customers. Do they talk about "us" and "them" (referring to different management levels or functional areas in the company), or do they talk about "we" when referring to their place of employment? When an enterprise achieves the "we" status, it is well on its way to becoming World Class.

One last comment on integration touches on the constant upheaval of the structure of companies. It is best expressed by comparing it to the Japanese concept of integration and unity:

> Companies that
>   stay together
>   grow together.[12]

Companies that constantly redefine their structure build insecurity into the work force. This condition is especially visible during mergers and acquisitions. The employees become more concerned with keeping their jobs than with growth.

Write the vision, and make it plain upon tables, that he may run that readeth it.

Hab. 2:2

A MANUFACTURING EXAMPLE

As an example of the complexity of functional understanding, I will review the functional aspects of manufacturing (see the

Production circle in Figure 15.1). A World Class Manager would not be an expert at each aspect but would at least have some background on how they all function and how they are integrated into the "beam me up" perspective. Manufacturing functionality incorporates:

Facilities management:

- Objectives and strategic issues
  Cost effectiveness
  Employee safety
  Regulation compliance
  Managing internal and external interfaces
  Quality and productivity
  Change and value-added management
- Responsibilities
  Equipment maintenance procedures
  Preventive maintenance procedures
  Facilities maintenance procedures
  Subcontractor services
  Technological change implementation
- Measures
  Downtime
  Budgets
  Safety records

Process management:

- Objectives and strategic issues
  Developing and updating product processes
  Matching processes to available equipment
  New technology introduction
  Cost effectiveness
  Quality and productivity
  Change and value-added management
- Responsibilities
  Process design
  Costing
  Tooling and equipment

    Plant layout
    Material handling
    Testing
    Methods and standards
    Budget/cost management
    Technology introduction, for example:
        Just-in-Time (JIT)
        Computer Integrated Manufacturing (CIM)
        Computer-Aided Design/Computer-Aided
            Manufacturing (CAD/CAM)
        Total Quality Management (TQM)

- Measures
    Yield
    Scrap
    Cost
    Time-to-market
    Productivity
    Quality
    Change efficiency

Production management:

- Objectives and strategic issues
    Continuous improvement
    Meeting product specifications and schedules
    Efficient use of all resources
    Focus on the critical resource
    New technology introduction
    Cost effectiveness
    Quality and productivity
    Change and value-added management
- Responsibilities
    Resource selection
    Teaming
    Training
    Communication
    Continuous improvement
    Budget/cost management

      Technology introduction
      Total Quality Management (TQM)
- Measures
    - Time
    - Cost
    - Productivity
    - Quality
    - Change efficiency
    - Flexibility
    - Inventory levels

Integration management:

- Objectives and strategic issues
    - Between facilities management and process design:
        - Equipment
        - Facilities acquisition
        - Process considerations
    - Between process design and manufacturing:
        - Work force
        - Equipment
        - Timing
        - Production and process methods
    - Between facilities management and manufacturing maintenance:
        - Environmental
    - Continuous improvement
    - Safety planning
    - New technology introduction
    - Cost effectiveness
    - Quality and productivity
    - Change and value-added management
- Responsibilities
    - Integration methods selection
    - Information alternatives selection
    - Organizational structuring
    - Teaming

- Measures
    Throughput
    Cost
    Time
    Productivity
    Quality
    Change efficiency
    Flexibility

The term "World Class Manufacturing" has come to be identified with leading-edge manufacturing philosophies. The current bag of leading-edge philosophies includes:

- Strategic philosophies:

    Information sharing/integration

    International focus (global management)

    Long-term strategy

    Manager versus leader/facilitator

    Time-to-market strategies

    MRP II or JIT philosophies

    Simplification and focus

- Employee involvement philosophies:

    Teaming

    Empowerment

    Shorter organization charts

    Gainsharing

    Job security

    Cross-training and job rotation

- Improvement philosophies:

    Planning for Change

    Continuous Improvement

Total Quality Management (TQM)
Benchmarking
Risk and uncertainty assessments

- Quality philosophies:

Deming principles (or Juran or Crosby)
Total Quality Management
Total Quality Control
Quality Circles
In-line Quality Control
Statistical Process Control

- Production planning philosophies:

Just-in-Time production
Theory of constraints
Bottleneck allocation methodologies
Bill of Energy

- Computerization/automation philosophies:

Computer-Integrated Manufacturing (CIM)
Decision Support Systems (DSS)
Expert Systems (ES)
Artificial Intelligence (AI)
Computer-Aided Design/Computer-Aided Manufacturing
(CAD/CAM)[13]

Where there is no vision, the people perish.

Prov. 29:18

An additional focus of World Class manufacturing is on integration. The largest improvements in the manufacturing process are made by the white-collar employees (engineers, marketing/sales, purchasing, and scheduling). Senior management is often surprised that it is these employees, not the manufacturing floor, who are slowing down the output of the factory. It is important to make these individuals a part of the manufacturing team so that the team members can directly influence one another.[14]

The manufacturing example discussed in this section is not intended to scare you—it is intended to challenge you. To be World Class, you need to understand the enterprise and its functions. Some additional resources will help you outline and understand manufacturing's functions.[15] The Hayes and Wheelwright articles are somewhat dated but have become classics in manufacturing strategy. Similar resources are available for each functional area of an enterprise.

The Advanced Manufacturing Center of Schlumberger Technologies developed a five-year plan for achieving World Class Manufacturing status. The program required:

1. Total commitment and high-level involvement
2. All employees participating in a total team effort
3. Complete employee involvement and dedication
4. A mission statement committed to customer satisfaction
5. Continuous improvement through employee buy-ins to changes
6. A focus on supplier excellence[16]

NCR-Ithaca converted its plant from "an embarrassment to the pride of the company" through World Class Manufacturing strategies that focused on process improvements and teamwork. It now dominates 24% of the worldwide printer market. NCR-Ithaca instituted a change in management philosophy with an emphasis on quality as the responsibility of everyone in the organization. It focused on self-directed teaming and reduced management overhead from one supervisor for 24 employees to one supervisor for 100 employees. JIT and TQC production methodologies were instituted. Job flexibility was improved through cross-training, and operator flexibility was increased from two job skills per operator to eight job skills each. The results of these changes are impressive. Inventory on hand decreased from 111 days to 21 days (from 2,000 printers in process to 400).

Manufacturing cycle time went from 60 days to 8 days. Manufacturing floor space went from 45,000 square feet to 19,000 square feet. The successes go on and on. But most important, NCR-Ithaca sees its biggest challenges for competitiveness and change in its future.[17]

Education is a danger. . . . At best an education which produces useful coolies for us is admissible. Every educated person is a future enemy.

Martin Bormann, German Nazi leader

SUMMARY

Free curiosity is of more value than harsh discipline.

Saint Augustine

The business enterprise is an intricate, integrated entity, much like the starship *Enterprise*. Numerous systems pieces need to be understood in order for everything to work together effectively. No one system can become your god, whether it's the computer system, the production control system, the accounting system, or the data collection system. The system is yours to use, not yours to be controlled by. Believe it or not, if used correctly, systems management can be an enjoyable experience.

A World Class Manager understands the functions of the enterprise. He or she utilizes these functions in innovative ways in order to achieve the goals of the enterprise. A WCM uses the "beam me up" approach, looking for the big picture in all situations, and then utilizes his or her knowledge and experience to make changes happen.

Make it so!

Captain Picard, *Star Trek: The Next Generation*

CHAPTER 16

The WCM in the Environment

---

*Politicians are the same all over. They promise to build a
bridge even where there is no river.*

Nikita Khrushchev

All right, I can see it in your eyes. You want another puzzle or
you'll go crazy (or perhaps this will drive you crazy). Well, the
latest treat I have for you is to take sixteen matchsticks and
arrange them, as shown in Figure 16.1, in five equal-size squares.
By moving only two of the matches, rearrange the diagram so that
all sixteen matches are used but we are left with only four equal-
size squares. The four squares must be the same size as those in the
original diagram. (*Hint:* four squares will take sixteen matches
when there are no sides in common.) What I'm asking you to do
is simplify the diagram, take some of the complexity out of it. Can
you do it? Or do we enjoy complexity so much that we can't focus
on the simple? The solution is found at the end of the chapter.

A dog was carrying a bone in his mouth when he happened to
come to the edge of a river. He stopped to look down into the
slow-moving waters and saw his reflection. The dog was convinced that this second dog (his reflection) was carrying a bigger
bone than he was, so he dropped his bone to try to steal the larger
bone. As his bone drifted down the river, he realized that the

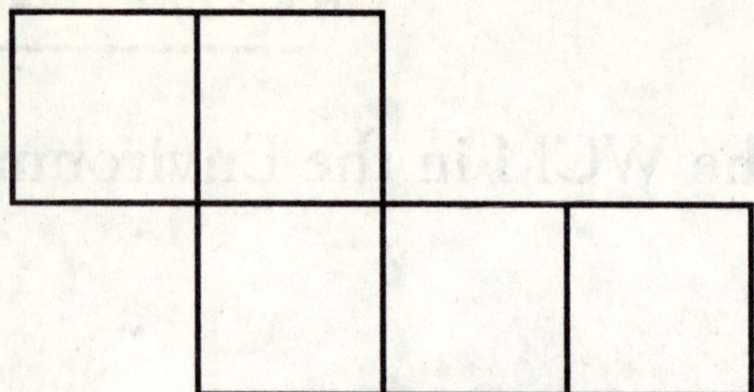

Figure 16.1   Sixteen Matches Make Five Squares

other dog had dropped his bone as well and now they were both left without any bone.

Do we ever chase mirages or reflections? One mirage is that the larger the computer you have, the better. Another is that the enterprise exists in an isolated shell, unaffected by the world around it. A World Class Enterprise does *not* exist in a shell; it exists in:

A community
A society
A country
A world

Nowhere is this more evident than in a global setting. The "shell" perspective on life is often held in the United States, but in most of the rest of the world, the enterprise is a critical element of the community. The enterprise is expected to "add value" to the society in which it is established and to the people in the community, not just to itself (see Chapter 6). We need to plan and think globally but act locally. We need to set up a global target but allow the local organization to utilize local processes for achieving those targets. And, in the end, we need to improve the environment in which our organization exists.

I use the term *environment* in the large sense. I am not just talking about pollution, I am also talking about stakeholders, as explained below.

The shoe that fits one person pinches another; there is no recipe for living that suits all cases.

Carl Jung

STAKEHOLDERS

I have long thought that the aging process could be slowed down if it had to work its way through Congress.

George Bush's writers

Upon being dismissed from his government job in the custom house, Nathaniel Hawthorne arrived home in deep despair. Hanging his head, he told his tale with all hopelessness to his wife, who didn't waste a minute before she set pen and ink on the table, lit the fireplace, and set him down. Putting her arms around his shoulders, she said, "Now you will be able to write your novel," which of course he did. This story is often used to demonstrate that from failure comes new opportunity—an important and valuable lesson. However, it also teaches a lesson of how an inspired leader (his wife) took a negative opportunity and turned it into a positive one. There is no question that Hawthorne's wife had a lot to do with the results, even though she put very little ink to paper. His wife was a stakeholder who took her commitment to her husband seriously.

Your life, as well as your business, has numerous stakeholders. They include:

- In life:

Spouse

Children

Relatives

Friends

Neighbors

Community

- In business:

Fellow employees

Suppliers

Customers

Community

Country

Communities and countries we interact with

Owners

It is your function as an individual (see Chapter 12) to add value to all the stakeholders in your life. It is your function as an enterprise to add value to all the stakeholders in your business community.

Globally (see Chapter 6), adding value might include involvement in schools, government, medical facilities, sports, and family, through subsidized recreational activities, housing, stores and so on. Adding value means improving the future of the children of your employees. Adding value includes improving the living standard of your employees and their families.

Tellabs feels that, for managers who are "striving for world class status, people involvement programs are the bull's-eye" of the target. Starting with a pilot project involving twelve employees, it soon expanded the project to three plants. It focused on building flexible people involvement and people systems. It focused on integrating performance management and compensation systems. Internally, Tellabs took seven job levels with fifty-two job titles and flattened them down to one level with one job title. The results: at the Lisle, Illinois, location, turnover has been reduced from 46% to 8%.[1]

ENVIRONMENTAL CONSIDERATIONS

A person who buries his head in the sand offers an engaging target.

Mabel A. Keenan

As I sit in my office in Provo, Utah, and look out my window, I see two things: the Rocky Mountains (barely) and haze. Haze is the PC (politically correct) term that is used in this valley for pollution. It is unfortunate that here, where we would expect to see beautiful scenery, we have some of the worst pollution in the United States. We often see only parts of the mountains, the parts that aren't "hazed" out. The Provo/Orem/Salt Lake community has been conditioned to endure this "haze" as something that is acceptable because it offers them jobs. The companies that generate the majority of the industrial "haze" spend a great deal of money trying to convince the public that it's the cars, not the companies, that create the haze. I wonder whether these advertising dollars could not have been better spent.

American factories are often moved from one part of the United States to another because the regulations in the new location aren't as tight. With the NAFTA agreement, this movement often includes Mexico or Canada. In the past, we have moved plants to India or Latin America to circumvent safety and pollution restrictions. This type of behavior is not World Class. It's cowardly. World Class behavior is ethical (see Chapter 12). World Class Managers make a difference in the lives of the stakeholders, not just a difference in the pocketbook.

The new buzzword for social consciousness in the environment is "green manufacturing." Following the principles of green manufacturing, the company designs and plans its plant to be appropriate to the environment. Pollution concerns are part of the planning process, not an afterthought implemented because of government force.

When we are considering technology improvements, we need to make sure that the cost of the technology is not higher than the benefit. This is part of Schuhmacher's message in his book *Small Is Beautiful* (cited in note 10, Chapter 12). It is like going from five squares to four in Figure 16.1—smaller is beautiful. One example of technology cost is the meltdown of the Chernobal Nuclear Power Facility. The energy generated through the entire existence of the facility was not worth the cost that the whole world has to pay for the disaster. I'm not opposed to nuclear energy, but we should consider whether the cost of "cheaper" nuclear energy is really worth it in the long run. If the price that we pay for nuclear-generated energy also included a cost element that took into account the breakdown and disposal of the waste products, would nuclear energy really be cheaper than other forms?

As another example, a World Class environmentally conscious enterprise should consider disposal costs of plutonium, plastics, glass, or any of the packaging and products it sells. I realize that this would destroy competitiveness, because your product would now have to be priced higher—or would it? Is lack of environmental consciousness a reason for lack of competitiveness, or is it just an excuse? An innovative technologist would be able to turn this "disadvantage" into a competitive advantage and still be considered "green." Some problems are easier to avoid than to solve. When the avoidance has detrimental effects on society, it is not World Class. This reminds me of the old saying:

> It's easier to be forgiven
> than to get permission!

Asking forgiveness may be easier, but is it ethical? Is it World Class?

I'm not going to spend a lot of time discussing the different kinds of pollution, such as air, water, noise, pornography, violence, and so on. I will simply say:

> If it isn't uplifting,
>   if it isn't adding value
>   (in the long run,
>   all things considered),
>   it isn't worth it!

Entertainment and television can be very value-added, or they can be very degrading. Disney is the master of value-added entertainment. You almost always come out of Disney movies feeling better than when you went in. Focus on adding value in your life. Similarly, focus on adding value in your business.

> What bothers me about TV
>   is that it tends to take
>   our minds off our minds.

As frustrating as it may seem at times, many good things are happening that improve our environment. Top executives from companies such as Dow, DuPont, AIG, Amoco, and Monsanto have gone on the road to discuss environmental stewardship, and they are spending their advertising dollars in support of the environmental agenda. They're developing waste management programs, recycling programs, pollution prevention programs, and environmentally conscious product-development programs.

Cynics claim that this behavior is simply an attempt to win sympathy and suggest that we should not support their hypocritical attempts at environmental consciousness. Frankly, I don't care. Anything that will improve my standard of living, and the standard of living of my children deserves my support. I'd rather support someone branded a hypocrite who is moving in the right direction than support nothing. This industrial support, hypocritical or not, is just the beginning. It's not even large enough to be called the tip of the iceberg. We have a long way to go, but at least we are starting to move in the right direction.[2]

SUMMARY

> *Corporation: an ingenious device for obtaining profit without individual responsibility.*
>
> Ambrose Bierce

The environment includes all the things around us, whether it's the air, the water, or the people (e.g., customers and employees). A World Class Enterprise needs to add value to, not detract from, all elements of its environment. There are numerous value-added components in all stages of industry. Some examples are:

- Technology development
- Technology implementation through engineering
- Product production
- Product accessibility and timeliness through logistics
- Retail accessibility and convenience
- Service-institution-appropriate services

The key to World Class environmental success in each of these value-added stages is the integrity of the individual World Class Manager in doing what is right, not just what is profitable.

> *The philosophers have only interpreted the world, in various ways; the point, however, is to change it.*
>
> Karl Marx

APPENDIX 16.1
CHANGING FIVE SQUARES TO FOUR

Figure 16.2 has the answer to Figure 16.1, showing which two matches to move. Did you find this problem challenging. If you can solve this one, you can probably solve more environmental problems than you're willing to admit. How are they related? Both types of problems require analytical thinking.

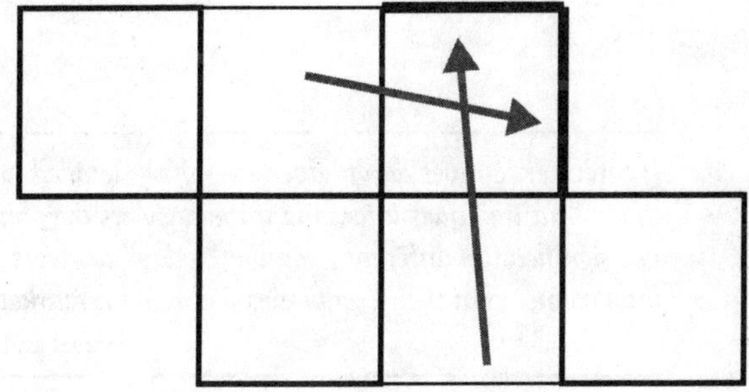

Figure 16.2   Sixteen Matches Make Four Squares

CHAPTER 17

The WCM Through Time

> *If senior executives don't have reasonably detailed answers to the "future" questions, and if the answers they have are not significantly different from the "today" answers, there is little chance that their companies will remain market leaders.*
>
> Hamel and Prahalad[1]

The Methodists were holding an annual conference at a college in Indiana. The presiding bishop was asking the group for an interpretation of current events when the president of the college volunteered, "I think we are in a very exciting age."

When asked to continue, the president said, "I believe we are coming into a time when we will see, for example, wonderful inventions. I believe men will fly through the air like birds."

Bishop Wright was visibly disturbed by this statement. He said, "This is heresy, this is blasphemy; I read in my Bible that flight is reserved for angels. We will not have such talk here in my area."

After the conference, Bishop Wright returned home to his two young sons, Orville and Wilbur.

This book is about World Class Change Management. Change is a direct result of time. As the bumper sticker says:

> Change happens.

Without time, everything would stay the same forever. With time comes change, and with change comes opportunity.

> Where you are in life
>   isn't nearly as important
>   as in what direction you're going.

The journey of a thousand miles begins with one step.

Lao-Tse

MANAGEMENT THEORY AND TIME

Some theories of business are so powerful that they last for a long time. But eventually every one of them becomes obsolete.

Peter Drucker

Things change. Change changes. Even the best way to manage change changes! This fact is evidenced by the series of management philosophies that has inundated management styles. Each philosophical stage held the key to competitiveness during a particular era. For example:

- Guilds—still very effective in Europe and many developing parts of the world
- Industrial Revolution—Henry Ford and assembly lines
- Scientific Management—Frederick Taylor, the father of time studies
- Humanistic (Human Relations) Management—Hawthorne Studies on human behavior
- Japanese Management—Edward Deming and inventory efficiency
- Productive Technology—automation replacing workers

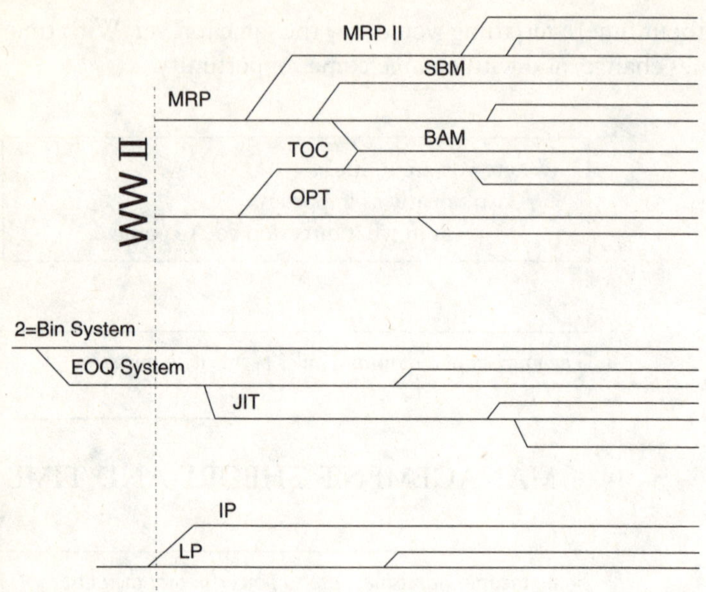

Figure 17.1   The Migration of Production Control Systems

- Information Technology—computers
- Change Management—change and time efficiency[2]

One of the most interesting ways to illustrate this change in management processes is through the changes that have occurred in production systems. Figure 17.1 shows how production control philosophies have migrated through a series of stages to the point where we now have an innumerable number of "right" ways to run a factory. Of course, no one right way will work for all factories; the correct way for any particular factory must be matched to the needs of that factory.

In Figure 17.1, the 2-Bin inventory control system is the earliest control system. Today it is still the most common system among small to mid-size manufacturers. Next Economic Order Quantity (EOQ) and Linear Programming (LP) were used for production control. After World War II (WW II), there was an explosion of production system technologies. Computers made

Material Requirements Planning (MRP) feasible and Integer Programming (IP) possible. Japan developed Just-in-Time (JIT) production out of the EOQ model, and Israel created Optimized Production Technology (OPT). Then, about ten years ago, Theory of Constraints (TOC) came out of OPT, and Manufacturing Resources Planning (MRP II) came out of the integration of MRP and the accounting functions. More recently, Schedule-Based Manufacturing (SBM) and Bottleneck Allocation Methodology (BAM) have been developed as improvements and refinements on some of the other production planning systems.

As a result, we have a multitude of management philosophies and production planning processes, all of which are still being used. Each is competitive when it is placed in an appropriate environment. Time has blessed us with an enormous bag of competitive tricks, and there will be more, rather than fewer, in the future. The only disadvantage of having all these alternatives is that we must understand them in order to use them properly.

One man's sunset is another man's dawn.

An American Tail—Fievel Goes West

THE TIME LINE OF THE ENTERPRISE

There is a well-known and often discussed corporate life cycle that is similar for both nations and products. This life cycle is diagrammed in Figure 17.2. The length of the cycle averages about 600 years for a nation. The United States is somewhere in the maturity stage and, some would argue, starting down the decline.

For companies, this cycle averages around 20 years; however, it is getting shorter all the time. For some companies, the cycle is only as long as the life of a specific product that they were established to produce. For the company, birth often revolves around some piece of technology or some entrepreneur's idea of a profitable business. After birth, the cycle shifts to start-up, at which time it is still run primarily by the entrepreneur. However, at some point the company becomes too large to be run by a sole

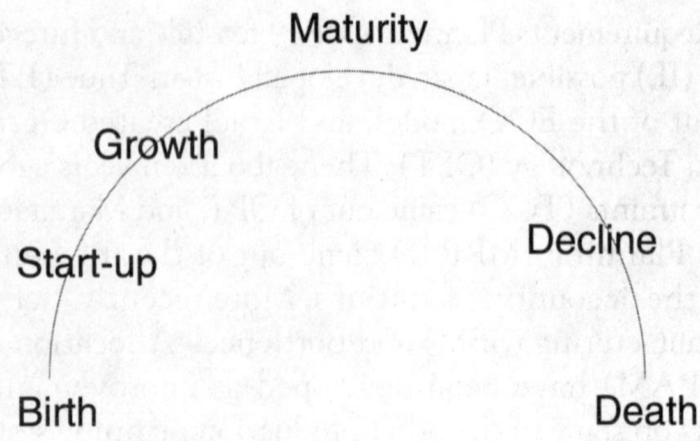

Figure 17.2   The Time Life Cycle

entrepreneur, and professional managers are brought in. For most businesses, this involves about thirty to fifty employees. With a professional management staff in place, the entrepreneur is often phased out of the picture, and the company jumps into its growth stage. Unfortunately, along with growth and a professional management staff comes the search for stability, which results in bureaucracy. We have now entered the maturing phase of the organization. With maturity often come complacency and resistance to change. Without change, the company starts to lose its vigor and drive, resulting in decline.

For products, the life cycle can be as short as just a few months, especially in the high-tech industries, or as long as hundreds of years. A company's life, or even a nation's life, can be tied to the life of a product. In the case of a nation, many nations have grown and died around a natural resource that is extracted; when the resource is depleted, prosperity ends and the nation is overthrown. In the case of a company, the company is established to produce a new piece of technology, and its existence revolves solely around the production of the product.

Fortunately, the time life cycle does not have to signal the end of the enterprise. In Figure 17.3, we see how repeated product life cycles can be utilized to maintain the growth that has been

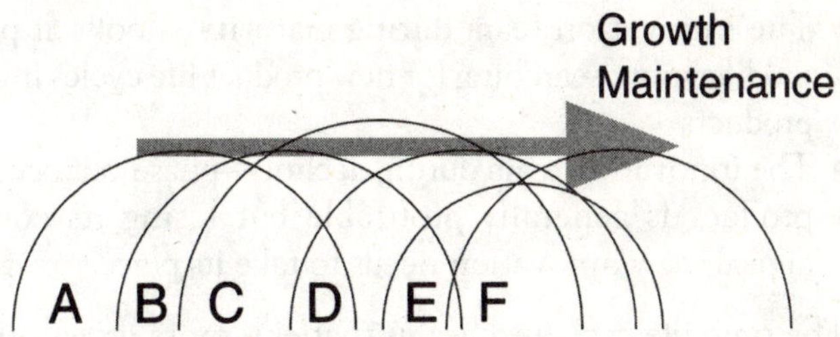

Figure 17.3 Growth Maintenance

established. Recently, because of the recession and competitive pressures, many companies such as IBM have found themselves in decline and have decided to downsize and regroup, searching for new products with new product life cycles on which to hang their growth maintenance. If they don't find successful new products, death is inevitable.

From Figure 17.2, we see that time and change will eventually lead to death unless, as in Figure 17.3, we innovate and reinnovate, change and change again, keeping ourselves on the top of the time life cycle, near maturity. In Figure 17.3, when curve A is in decline, curve B is in maturity, curve C is in growth, and curve D is in start-up. To be a growth maintenance company, we need products in each stage of the time life cycle at all times. We cannot focus our efforts on just one product. This state is accomplished with the following teams:

- The new product innovation team—focuses on identifying new product ideas
- The new product development team—focuses on making the product producible in a timely and profitable fashion
- The marketing team during the growth phase—focuses on market expansion
- The production team—focuses on adequately planning productive capacity
- The marketing team during maturity—focuses on market maintenance

- The innovation team during maturity—looks at product modification, searching for new product life cycles in the old products
- The innovation team during decline—phase-out occurs; the product is generally profitable but losing its consumer appeal; new innovation needs to take its place.

The time life cycle teaches us that enterprise growth maintenance is dependent on repeated change and repeated innovation. Stability leads to stagnation—a sure sign of enterprise death.

FUTURE COMPETITIVE POWER

People who say it cannot be done should not interrupt those who are doing it.

Anonymous

The strategy for competitive power in the future depends on who you're talking to. For manufacturing, which we have considered in earlier chapters, the competitive power of the future lies in:

Rapid product changes

Time-to-market efficiency

Product cycle-time reductions

Commitment to customer satisfaction

Employee empowerment and teaming

Stakeholder integration

Quality and productivity initiatives

Manufacturing is a critical value-added element, third in importance only to agriculture and pure technology development. Manufacturing controls the product development engineering function and the production function and is a key to customer satisfaction. Maintaining this value-added status offers a critical competitive edge for the future (see Chapter 9).

Boldrin claims that the competitive future of manufacturing lies in:

1. The efficiency of material flow
2. Cycle-time reductions
3. Employee empowerment

He cites the example of Hargrove, a manufacturer of gas fireplace logs, which reduced floor space by 80% and cut cycle time by 50% by reengineering and simplifying the production floor.[3]

Burton sees the future of manufacturing as requiring:

1. The full emergence of the global corporation
2. Virtually instantaneous operations (customer responsiveness combined with very short cycle times)
3. Total supply chain integration
4. Engineering and manufacturing integration
5. New age of quality
6. More rapid continuous improvement
7. A growth in strategic alliances
8. Flat, unstructured organizations[4]

In retailing, it has long been believed that the new competitive power base is the retailer. Customers trust the store more and more and the manufacturer less and less. We are seeing a confidence shift. Customers look to the retail establishment to guarantee the quality of the product. However, the competitive edge in retailing in the 1990s and beyond is not in marketing but rather in logistics. Accessibility and timing are the competitive strategies of the future. Future value-added growth comes in the form of giving customers what they need when they need it and in the form (product type) they want.

The integration of the logistics function with the other retail functions, often referred to as speed sourcing, has been identified by stores such as Target and WalMart as a critical success factor. Technological investment in this integration is a key to the speed-sourcing strategy for companies like JC Penney.

In retailing and other forms of service organizations, such as banking, customer service was forgotten for a long time because it was considered too costly. Marketing was considered to be more important. However, customer service is becoming fashionable again and is considered a strategic competitive edge. Stores such as Target and Nordstrom are refocusing on customer service. They are building service into product returnability and even into the way their stores are structured and laid out. Similarly, banks are improving their hours and accessibility.

Daniel J. Sweeney, Vice Chairman of the Retail Service Industry Group of Price Waterhouse, a retailing industry consultant, and a member of the National Advisory Council of Brigham Young University, gave a presentation during a 1995 meeting of the council and identified four future vectors for retailing and the service industries:

1. Globalization will affect 90% of all retailers. Retailing will be changed by the new emerging middle classes in developing countries, which tend to have a strong family focus. The model for effective retail globalization is IKEA of Sweden.
2. Optimization (for example, taking advantage of scale economies) is growing. WalMart is the grand master in this area.
3. Electronification (such as greatly improved home shopping and CD-ROM catalogs) is on the increase.
4. Personalization (for example, anticipation marketing) is making its mark.

The future is coming. The World Class Manager will be ready for it!

Don't worry about people stealing your ideas. If your ideas are any good, you'll have to ram them down people's throats.

Howard Aiken

HOW THE WCM CHANGES OVER TIME

I was trying to explain a management concept to a plant manager, and we were interrupted numerous times, which disrupted our train of thought. After what seemed like the fiftieth interruption, the manager looked at me in disgust and said, "At work I spend all my time listening to customers, managers, employees, and vendors. At home I spend all my time listening to my spouse, my children, the TV, radio, and movies. I just don't seem to have any time to listen to *reason!*"

What frightened me most about what the plant manager said is that I could sympathize with him. I occasionally have the same problem myself. We just don't have time to listen to "reason." The key word here is "time." I temporarily left the working world and joined academia just to have a little "time." I had spent so much of my time fighting fires that I had never had the chance to look for the source of the fire. Academia gave me the opportunity to be "beamed up" and to take a look at the big picture—and to get paid for it. The ironic part is that I had always believed that:

> If you know how to do a job, you do it;
> and if you don't know how to do it,
> you teach it!

I found out that you learn more about a job by teaching it than by doing it, especially when some feisty student questions your "we've always done it that way" philosophy. Now when I go out and "do it," I have a much clearer perspective on what I'm doing. Teaching gave me a chance to "listen to reason." Everyone should try teaching some time. Whether you teach your fellow employees, at the local junior college, or at a university, the challenge of being challenged is invaluable.

You can't become a World Class Manager unless you take time to listen to reason. Therefore, the keys to becoming a World Class Manager are:

1. Taking TIME
2. To LISTEN (training)
3. To REASON (ideas)
4. So you can change (become better)

After saying this, the first question I often hear is "Where do I begin? What do I change first?"

My answer is always "The point of least resistance." Many things need changing. The World Class Management test in Chapter 18 lists the areas of change. Identify those areas in which you need improvement. Prioritize the needed changes in the order in which they either:

1. Would give you the most fun
2. Need the most help
3. Would offer the biggest benefit to your future performance

You need to feel positive about your efforts, so first do those what will make you feel the most successful. Then go on to the next thing. You can't do everything at once, but you can get started, one small step at a time.

In his book *The Evolution of Management Theory* (cited in note 2 of this chapter), Roth proposes an organizational structure that includes six dimensions. This structure is the "multi-level, multidimensional, modular organization" of Gharajedaghi; it includes:

1. Output units—manufacturing and logistics
2. Input units—supplier or even competitor sourcing
3. Environmental units—government and stakeholder relationships
4. Planning/decision-making unit—the integrative unit where all other units are represented
5. Control unit—monitoring, feedback, data collection
6. Management unit—facilitating decisions[5]

Roth suggests that the key future issues of the organization are:

Organization size and design
Marketplace pressures
Socioeconomic doctrine
The changing role of stakeholders
Private-sector involvement

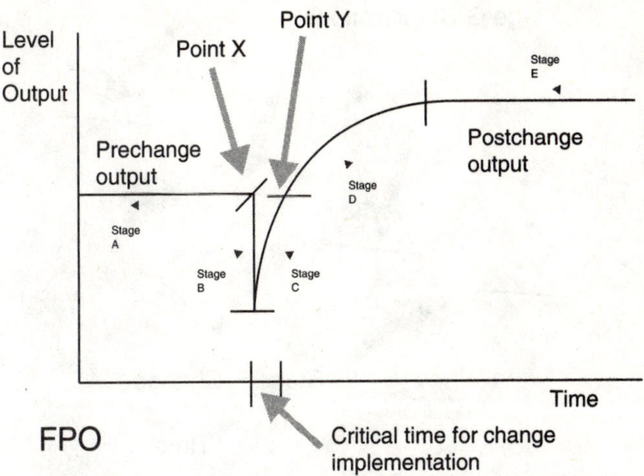

Figure 17.4 Change Function

An expert is someone called in at the last minute to share the blame.

Sam Ewing

CONTROLLING TIME

Figure 17.3 shows the need for constant innovation and change development. Figure 17.4 (taken from Figure 11.1) shows how change occurs. We need to integrate change over time by building transition bridges between the change phases. Figure 17.5 shows how these transition bridges occur in a company's growth path. Growth is not as smooth as Figure 17.2 would indicate. Rather, there are stages of growth in which we switch from change implementation (stages B and C in Figure 17.4 or stage F in Figure 17.5) to change stabilization (stages D and E in Figure 17.4 or stage G in Figure 17.5). Figure 17.5 shows that the change implementation process often has rough spots.

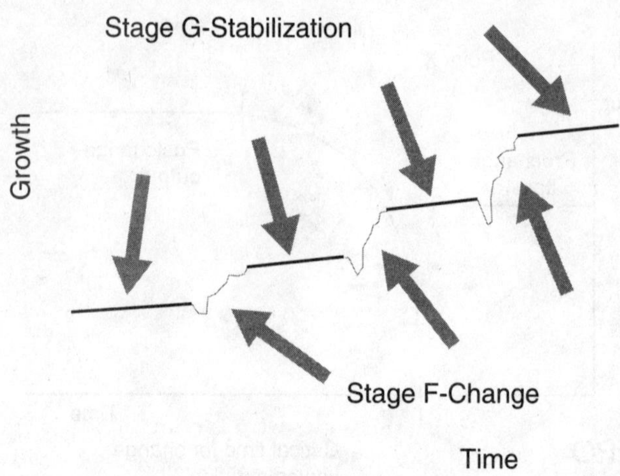

Figure 17.5   Growth Transitions

From these figures, we learn that change over time is not as comfortable as stability. In fact, we will often feel as if the change wasn't worth it (stage C of Figure 17.4 or the Florida Power and Light story), but without change we will die as an enterprise.

The tools for change are immeasurable, as we have seen throughout this book. Probably the best tool for World Class Change implementation is the TQM process outlined in Chapter 11. But we cannot forget that we need to change the individual (Chapters 12 and 13) before we can change the enterprise.

Why do parents spend the first year of a child's life trying to get the newborn to walk and talk, and then spend the next nineteen years telling the child to "be quiet and sit down"? Similarly, why are we excited about new ideas during the start-up phase of a company but leery of them during the growth and maturity stages? The attitude that motivates change should be constant and continuous. We shouldn't be like the grandfather who said:

> "The older I get, the better I was!"

If we work toward positive, goal-directed change as we go along, then we won't have to pretend we sought change after we have been forced into it.

Few people blame themselves until they have exhausted all other possibilities.

Francis Duffy

SUMMARY

A World Class Manager is a manager who is continually changing over time. A World Class Manager utilizes time to his or her advantage, understanding that time can either make an enterprise great or kill it. Stability cannot exist. Change will occur. The question is whether you will control it or it will control you as time goes on.

PART FOUR

Wrap-Up

CHAPTER 18

The World Class Management Test

The haves and the have-nots can often be traced back to the dids and the did-nots.

D. O. Flynn

As we near the end of this book, let's talk about another end—the end of your life. A friend of mine died not too long ago, and it made me think how I would like my obituary to read. This may not be the cheeriest exercise in the world, but try it anyway. Stop what you're doing, get a piece of paper, sit down, and write your obituary. How would you like to be remembered? What are the first things that you would like people to say about you as they try to come up with good things? Perhaps you would like them to say that you were always smiling or that you were fun to be around. Would you like them to say that you cared more about others than you cared about yourself, that you were selfless and kind? Would you like them to say that you were great with your family and that your spouse adored you? Would you like to have been considered a hero by your children? Would you like to be seen as having been a valuable contributor in your church or community? Would you like your employees and colleagues to say that they enjoyed working with you so much they hated to go home each day? Think about it! What would you like people to say about you at your funeral? Stop right now and write your obituary.

After you've written your masterpiece, read it through and ask yourself if it describes the way you really are. Do you stand in need of improvement? If you need improvement—and who doesn't—then why aren't you working toward improving?

The obituary you just wrote is your long-term goal. It's the eternal target you're trying to hit. If you're not there yet, you need to start planning a course of action that will get you there.

Being a World Class Manager isn't easy. No one promised that it would be. But it's worth it! And it's never too early to get started.

Know the difference between success and fame. Success is Mother Teresa. Fame is Madonna.

Erma Bombeck

HOW TO GET READY

Getting ready is the secret of success.

Henry Ford

My mother told me that I was getting a "pouch" in my midsection. I guess she meant that I was becoming overweight. In any case, a friend told me that if I went to the spa for a half hour each day I could easily solve my problem. So I decided to go. I went to the spa faithfully for two months, for about a half hour a day. It was painful watching all those people jogging, doing aerobics, riding bicycles, lifting weights, and swimming, but I was committed. I faithfully went every day and "watched" them. But when the two months were up I didn't notice any improvement in my "pouch," so I gave it up.

This spa story seems silly, but it's exactly what I see happening in management all the time. Managers will sit back and "watch" their employees struggle through the motions of implementing a new system. Then after two months the managers will give up on it because they decide that it isn't worth it, never asking the employees if they wanted it to begin with and never asking them if they wanted to stop after it had been running. Management wasn't committed to the change, and therefore, in management's eyes, it wasn't working.

Committing yourself to becoming World Class is much like committing yourself to any change. It all goes back to the bacon and eggs breakfast story: the chicken is involved in the breakfast, but the pig is committed to it.

Getting ready to become World Class means getting serious about changing. It means becoming an active participant in the change process—working out at the spa and not just sitting there "watching." It's working with your employees as they try to implement change, not just observing them. It's being committed to becoming World Class. It's doing something!

As we discussed briefly in Chapter 17, you can't change everything at once. The purpose of the World Class test that follows is to help you define the areas that need work. Once you have listed them, sequence them by priority. Then attack the list, one step at a time. Attempting to tackle everything at once will only frustrate you. Attacking the changes in order of priority will help you experience success at each step in the improvement process.

Now you're ready. Move forward with the test, and remember: you won't see any improvement (just like at the spa) if you're not committed to the change process.

I think society has changed tremendously in the last 25 years. Today everybody talks about their rights and privileges. Twenty-five years ago, everyone talked about their obligations and responsibilities.

Lou Holtz

THE TEST

I have categorized the WCM success factors in fourteen categories. These fourteen categories are by no means complete, but they are the most important areas of WCM change performance. They should set your direction for improvement, assisting you in problem identification and helping you focus your change process. They are summarized in Table 18.1.

1. Change Is Your Friend

- Do you expect your employees to "follow procedure"?
- Does it frustrate you if your customers change something about the products or services they expect?
- Do you use statements like "This is how we've always done it?", especially when talking to customers?
- Do you keep doing a job the way "it's always been done" even though you don't think it makes sense?

If you answered yes to these questions, you've failed part one of the test. A World Class Manager is bored by the mundane, the repetitive, the systematic. A World Class Manager enjoys identifying change and looks for opportunities for positive, goal-based change. And a World Class Manager enjoys the challenge of change. A WCM is a change manager, understanding resistance and fear and how to overcome them. A WCM understands the models for change, such as TQM and Process Reengineering (PR), and can systematize the change process with tools like Systematic Problem Solving (SPS).

Be aware that a halo has to fall only a few inches to be a noose.

Dan McKinnon

---

2. Taking Advantage of Time

- Do you feel overwhelmed by all the things you "have to do"?
- Are you dissatisfied with the amount of time it takes for your company to respond to a customer request?
- Are you uncomfortable with the products and services your company provides?

Table 18.1. The Success Factors of World Class Management

1. *Change is your friend*—A World Class Manager enjoys identifying change and looks for opportunities for positive, goal-based change. A World Class Manager enjoys the challenge of change.
2. *Taking advantage of time*—A World Class Manager focuses on doing the right things, prioritized according to the goals, rather than worrying about doing everything right.
3. *Innovation and creativity*—A World Class Manager prefers to innovate (innoveer) rather than duplicate (copycat), because he or she realizes that there isn't one best way.
4. *Defined goals*—A World Class Manager has goals in his or her personal life, family life, and professional life.
5. *Measurement oriented toward motivation*—World Class Managers utilize measurement systems as a motivator and keep a focus on the goals.
6. *Continuous education*—A World Class Manager promotes cross-training and a "big picture" understanding.
7. *Empowered teaming*—A World Class Manager takes advantage of people power.
8. *A people person*—World Class Managers are stakeholder-conscious, whether it involves the stakeholders in their personal life (spouse, family, friends) or those in their professional life (employees, peers, bosses, customers, suppliers).
9. *Self-improvement*—A World Class Manager is a Sunrise Manager, looking for opportunities for change. A WCM understands the importance of change in his or her personal life and wants to develop personal and professional skills that will make him or her a more valuable person both at home and at work.
10. *Focus on the family*—A World Class Manager puts first things first.
11. *Productivity and quality*—A World Class Manager has a clear definition of what productivity and quality means.
12. *Globalized but localized*—A World Class Global Manager focuses on centralized global strategy development with localized strategy implementation. A WCM sees the enterprise as a global entity, not as a domestic entity that occasionally has international transactions.
13. *Information and technology utilization*—A World Class Manager realizes that technological change involves risk but the long-run competitive benefits of technological improvement greatly outweigh many of the disadvantages.
14. *Integration*—A World Class Manager understands the benefits of and encourages integration, both horizontal and vertical.

Once again, yes answers constitute failure. A World Class Manager doesn't stress out about all the things that need doing. Most of them will go away by themselves. A World Class Manager focuses on doing the *right things*, which are prioritized based on the goals, rather than worrying about doing *everything right*. And one of the "right things" to do is to focus on customer and family responsiveness. The World Class Manager has patience to do the right things blended with the competitive urgency to keep things moving.

Patience accomplishes its objective, while hurry speeds its ruin.

Sa'di

---

3. Innovation and Creativity

- Do you believe that there is one best way to do a job?
- Do you prefer to follow a process that someone else is using "because it works for them" rather than develop your own way of solving the problem?
- Do you prefer telling your employees (or children) what to do rather than telling them to come up with their own way of doing it.

Once again, yes answers are bad! Enjoy the creativity suggested by authors such as Nadler and Hibino or von Oech. A World Class Manager prefers to innovate (innoveer) rather than duplicate (copycat), because he or she realizes that there isn't one best way. Even the best can be improved upon.

We can easily forgive a child who is afraid of the dark; the real tragedy in life is when men are afraid of the light.

Plato

---

4. Defined Goals

- Do you know what your or your company's core competencies are?

- Have you reviewed the business plan of your company, and do you understand how it relates to you?
- Do you have a written personal and corporate vision, mission, and strategy?
- Do you know what your target is?

I tricked you. This time no is the bad answer. A World Class Manager has goals in his or her personal life, family life, and professional life. A WCM knows what his or her employer expects, which should emphasize positive, goal-directed change focused on customers and employees.

5. Measurement Oriented Toward Motivation

- Do you motivate your personal performance and the performance of your employees using appropriate measures that are goal-directed?
- Are you personally motivated by goal-directed measures?
- Do you motivate your children to want to please you, rather than make them afraid of you?

Once again, no is the loser. World Class Managers utilize measurement systems as a motivator and keep a focus on the goals. A WCM understands the types of measures and establishes a measurement environment that motivates change in the critical resource relative to the overall goals.[1]

6. Continuous Education

Education makes people easy to lead, but difficult to drive; easy to govern, but impossible to enslave.

Lord Brougham

- Are you too busy to "read the instructions"?
- Do you want to know just enough to get the job done, and no more?
- Is the work your employees are doing "too valuable" to allow them time to share ideas or get cross-training?

- Do you feel that it's not necessary for your employees to have a "big picture" understanding of what's going on and that it's more important that they get their job done?

This time, yes is the bad answer. A World Class Manager promotes cross-training and a "big picture" understanding. Even training that on the surface seems irrelevant broadens one's perspective. For example, a World Class Manager should have a handle on the analytical tools that are available and should understand the terminology listed in Appendix 18.1.

Stay in college, get the knowledge.
And stay there until you're through.
If they can make penicillin out of moldy bread,
They can sure make something out of you!

Mohammed Ali

---

7. Empowered Teaming

- Do you believe that you understand your employees' job function better than they do?
- Do you believe that you have the best understanding of what improvements need to be made?
- Do you believe that paid employee discussion time is a waste of time and money?
- Do you feel that a team should produce some positive results within the first month of its existence or else be disbanded?
- Do you feel that teaming is good for other people, but you operate better as a "loner"?

This time, no is the right answer to the questions. A World Class Manager takes advantage of people power. A WCM is a Theory-Z, participative manager who is excited about developing the "circles" in his or her life. A WCM understands the three faces of teaming—developer, leader, and member—and is an active participant in each of these faces.

Many hands and hearts and minds generally contribute to anyone's notable achievements.

Walt Disney

---

8. A People Person

- Do you enjoy being around other people?
- Do you enjoy listening as much as you do talking?
- Do you "feel good" when you pay someone a compliment?
- Do you "feel bad" when you neglect someone (this includes spouse, family, employees, peers, and bosses)?
- Are you conscious of the stakeholders that are around you?
- Do you prefer leadership by example as the management style under which you and your employees are managed?
- Does it make you feel good (not envious) when someone does better than you at something?

This time yes is the right answer. A World Class Manager is stakeholder-conscious, whether it is the stakeholders in his or her personal life (spouse, family, friends) or those in his or her professional life (employees, peers, bosses, customers, suppliers). A WCM looks for opportunities for and gets excited about paying compliments but is also open and frank about expressing concerns. A WCM realizes that employee ownership of changes is important to the success of the change and therefore is willing to set aside his or her own pride and ownership for the success of the change.

Failure is an event, never a person.

William D. Brown

---

9. Self-Improvement

I hope that I shall always possess firmness and virtue enough to maintain what I consider the most enviable of all titles, the character of an honest man.

George Washington

- Do you feel that profitability is more important than a long-term relationship, whether it is with employees, customers, or family?

- Do you feel that once you give your word on something you'll stick to it "unless you feel the situation has changed"?
- Do you feel that you have no responsibility for or interest in the success of your employees?
- Do you feel that the success (financial or nonfinancial) of your peers (or spouse) gains you nothing directly?
- Do you feel that if you don't "toot your own horn" no one else will?
- Do you feel that learning about what other people do, even though you may never be doing it yourself, is a waste of time?
- Are you leery of what the future holds?

No is the right answer this time. A World Class Manager is a Sunrise Manager, looking for opportunities for change. A WCM understands the importance of change in his or her personal life and wants to develop personal and professional skills that will make him or her a more valuable person both at home and at work. A WCM believes in the long-term benefits of virtues such as integrity, trust, honesty, loyalty, morality, humility, and charity. A WCM is ethical!

Don't talk about yourself, it will be done when you leave.

Addison Mizner

---

10. Focus on the Family

- Is your family more important to you than your professional success?
- Is the success of your children in their schooling more important to you than your next raise or promotion?
- Do you come home from work and become an active participant of the home?
- Do you enjoy picking up a present or a card for your spouse on your way home from work?
- Do you listen to, rather than command or instruct, your family members?

This is a situation in which yes is the right answer. A World Class Manager puts first things first. Success in the home can make failure at work seem trivial, while failure in the home will drag failure into your work life as well. A WCM is a noncontrolling home participant. A WCM enjoys being at home and doesn't spend the entire time at home worrying about what he or she should be doing at work. A WCM will walk into the home after a long day and participate in home activities, not plop in front of the television, or go into a home office, disappearing from conscious existence as far as the family is concerned. A WCM is a World Class Person. A WCM should even bring presents home for family members every once in a while.

11. Productivity and Quality

- Do you know what your customer wants out of your products or services, and did you gain this knowledge by directly asking the customer what he or she wants?
- Do you understand and focus on value-added or total-factor productivity rather than on labor productivity?
- Does your company have a written and clear definition of what quality means to it?
- Are quality and productivity a part of the measurement/ motivation system of your enterprise, and do they measure performance at all levels of the organization, right down to the janitor?

The correct answer this time is yes. A World Class Manager has a clear definition of what productivity and quality mean. Productivity should focus on waste elimination or value added, and quality should focus on customer satisfaction. There are many different types and categories of value adding and customer satisfying, and a WCM understands and takes advantage of all of them in order to be World Class competitive.[2]

12. Globalized but Localized

- Does your enterprise have separate domestic and international divisions?

- Do your corporate vision, mission, and strategy focus on centralized, top-down, official declarations on "how things should be done"?
- Are repatriated expatriate managers (managers who return to the United States after an overseas assignment) treated like outsiders and shoved into some secondary, noncritical management role "until we can find a place for them"?
- Does the corporate office go through extensive effort to make sure the local offices know "what is expected of them" down to the most minute detail?

This time the right answer is no! A World Class Global Manager focuses on centralized global strategy development with localized strategy implementation. A WCM would see the enterprise as a global entity, not as a domestic entity that occasionally has international transactions. A WCM encourages localized leadership and ethical systems without sacrificing the corporate ethics.

13. Information and Technology Utilization

- Are you excited to learn about new technological developments?
- Are you convinced that the "old ways" still beat "newfangled ideas" all the time?
- Do you know how to search out new technology ideas?
- Are you discouraged because new technology changes faster than you can keep up with it, and therefore you avoid it?
- Do you encourage your employees to read about and learn about what's new?

I tried to trick you again. Just for variety, this time I mixed the answers. The correct answers are yes, no, yes, no, yes. Do you find this fun or frustrating? New technology is often both fun and frustrating. A World Class Manager realizes that technological change involves risk but that the long-run competitive benefits of technological improvements greatly outweigh many of the disadvantages.

14. Integration

- Do you enjoy working with other departments because it broadens your perspective?
- Do you understand how information flows throughout your organization, not just in your department?
- Do you encourage your employees to talk to people at all levels in any department without coming to you first?
- Do you feel free to talk to the CEO without a special appointment?

This time the answer should be yes in all cases. A World Class Manager understands the benefits of and encourages integration, both horizontal and vertical. He or she understands the flow of information and how it affects and motivates employees throughout the organization. A WCM avoids over-the-wall settings and encourages enterprise-wide integration.

WHAT TO DO FIRST

Second Kings:1–14 in the Old Testament relates the story of Naaman, the "captain of the host of the king of Syria," who was a powerful and influential man. However, "he was a leper." He went to the prophet Elisha to be cured of his leprosy and was told to wash in the Jordan River seven times and his "flesh shall come again." But "Naaman was wroth and went away." He expected to witness some great demonstration by the prophet or to be told to accomplish some fantastic deed, not told to do something so direct and simple. Eventually his servants convinced him to go down and be washed seven times; he did this and was cured.

The Naaman story is an excellent example of how we tend to look for the dramatic, the exciting, and the exceptional. We are often not satisfied with the beauty of the simple. This is also true when it comes to becoming World Class. We need to focus on the simple and the easy. When we look for what to change, we should change the easy things first and do those things that will give us the most sought-after results. We should not try to do everything, nor should we try to do the dramatic. We should focus on doing simple things that will give us the "biggest bang for the buck."

Table 18.1 lists what I believe are the fourteen success factors for World Class Managers. The Covey book *The Seven Habits of Highly Successful People* and the Miller/Schneck book *All I Need to Know About Manufacturing I Learned in Joe's Garage* also list characteristics that are needed in the World Class Manager. Whichever list you use, the most important thing is that you begin the change process immediately.

What should you do first? You should first commit yourself to changing and then begin the change process!

MEASURING YOUR PERFORMANCE

Even when you lack self confidence, keep in mind that if you want a woman to think you're a prince, you should treat her like a queen.

Marilyn vos Savant

I have a cousin who, when she was about three, came to her aunt to ask her for help in going to the bathroom. The aunt said; "Look at Joe, he's only two years old and he can go to the bathroom by himself."

The cousin responded; "Yes, but he's got a handle." (This story is unique because, believe it or not, it's true.)

In measuring your progress toward becoming World Class, keep the following in mind:

> To know if you are
>   getting better,
>   measure yourself
>   against yourself.

Don't measure yourself against someone else. Other people are on a different road using a different road map. Don't think they have a better handle on the situation than you do. The final objective may be the same, but they are coming from one direction and you are coming from another. Comparisons can be discouraging, frustrating, and highly misleading. What you need to do is make sure you are getting closer to the final destination (World Class status) by checking your map (goals and strategy) and monitoring your progress.

SUMMARY

Now that you have a list of things that need to be changed, prioritize them and start changing. First identify the areas in which you need improvement. As recommended in the last chapter, prioritize the needed changes in the order in which they either:

1. Would give you the most fun
2. Need the most help
3. Would offer the biggest benefit to your future performance

This list can then be used to sequence your changes. Pick the ones on top first. Doing first those things that will make you feel most successful will help you develop positive feelings about your efforts. Then go down the list. Remember that you can't do everything at once, but you can get started. Proceed one small step at a time—and have fun!

The process of moving toward World Class Management status shouldn't resemble the funeral for which you wrote your obituary; rather it should be a rebirth for the new, World Class you!

APPENDIX 18.1
BUSINESS TERMINOLOGY
FOR WORLD CLASS MANAGERS

This is a partial listing of business terminology with which a World Class Manager should be familiar. The terms on this list are all used in this book and focus only on the examples discussed. However, additional terminology is used in each of the specialized functional areas that exist in any business. As part of the educational process, a World Class Manager should be familiar with the terms on this list. The index at the back of the book will help you find where these terms are used in the book.

- Goals
    - Customer-based goals
    - Employee-based goals
    - Financial goals
    - Operational goals
    - Primary goals
    - Secondary goals
- Strategic planning
    - Aspirations statement
    - Business areas (BA)
    - Business plan
    - Business-unit strategy
    - Core competencies
    - Corporate strategy
    - Enterprise resource planning
    - Government
    - Growth maintenance
    - Joint ventures
    - Life cycle
    - Mission statement
    - Plan of operation
    - Strategic alliances
    - Strategy models
    - Stratification
    - Subsidiaries
    - Vision statement
- Measurement
    - Benchmarking
    - Efficiency
    - External quality
    - Motivation
    - Non–value-added
    - Performance

> Productivity
> Standard Industrial Classifications (SIC)
> Value added
> Waste elimination

- Change/innovation
  > Breakthrough thinking
  > Change manager
  > Change models
  > Change productivity
  > Continuous change
  > Motivating change
  > Recognizing change
- Change analysis processes
  > Flowcharting
  > Process Reengineering (PR)
  > Quality Council
  > Resistance
  > Showcasing
  > Systematic Problem Solving (SPS)
  > Systems approach
  > T-model
  > Total Quality Management (TQM)
- Time
  > Cycle time
  > Time-based competition
  > Time life cycle
  > Time pie
  > Time-to-market
  > Time-to-market technology
- Competition
  > Customers
  > Vendors
- Globalization
  > Culture
  > Developing country
  > Exchange rates
  > Internationalization

ISO 9000
Localization
Nationalism
Newly Industrialized Economies (NIE)
Politics
Religion
Tariff
Taxes
Trade barriers
Trade theory
Transnational
- Productivity/quality
    Cause and effect diagrams
    Company-Wide Quality Control (CWQC)
    Conformance
    Control charts
    Decision teams
    Deming Award (Japan)
    In-Line Quality Control (ILQC)
    Internal quality
    Labor dollar productivity
    Malcolm Baldrige National Quality Award
    NASA Award (U.S. government)
    Parieto charts
    Parieto principle
    Quality Functional Deployment (QFD)
    Quality Improvement Program (QIP)
    Quality levels
    Quality Systems Deployment (QSD)
    Scatter diagrams
    Shingo Prize (U.S. manufacturing)
    Statistical Process Control (SPC)
    Tool box
    Total factor productivity
    Total Quality Control (TQC)
    Value-added productivity
    Waste
    Zero Defects (ZD)

- Technology
    - Computer
    - Computer-aided design and manufacturing (CAD/CAM)
    - Computer-Integrated Manufacturing (CIM)
    - Facilities and equipment technology
    - Group technology
    - Process technology
    - Product technology
    - Pure research technology
    - Systems and procedures technology
    - Technology transfer
- Management
    - Activity-based management (ABM)
    - Authoritarian manager
    - Cash manager
    - Centralized
    - Circle
    - Commitment to Excellence (CTE)
    - Conflict Manager
    - Cool Manager
    - Crash Manager
    - Crisis Manager
    - Decentralized
    - Departmentalization
    - Diversification
    - Feedback
    - Focus
    - Focused management
    - Hierarchical organization
    - Integration
    - Leader
    - Leadership
    - Management by Objectives (MBO)
    - Networking
    - Over-the-wall
    - Participative Manager
    - Sunrise Manager

Design for Automated Assembly (DFAA)
Economic Order Quantity (EOQ)
Four stages of manufacturing
Green manufacturing
Integer Programming (IP)
Just-in-Time (JIT)
Kanban
Linear Programming (LP)
Manufacturing Resources Planning (MRP II)
Material Requirements Planning (MRP)
Optimized Production Technology (OPT)
Schedule-Based Manufacturing (SBM)
Theory of Constraints (TOC)

- Logistics
    Speed sourcing
- Information systems
    Artificial Intelligence (AI)
    Data
    Decision Support Systems (DSS)
    Electronic Data Interchange (EDI)
    Expert Systems (ES)
    Image processing
    Information
    Information flow
    Information management
    Information technology
    Object-oriented programming
- General
    ABC analysis
    Borderless company
    Borderless organization
    Communication
    Environment
    Management science
    Operations research
    Physical integration
    Subcontractors

CHAPTER 19

Winning Using WCM Strategies

> We may not know what the future holds,
> but we can hold on to the future!

It is time for us to quit playing copycat by trying to borrow some wonderful idea from Japan or a competitor. It is time for us to innovate ourselves ahead of our competition. It is time to change ourselves from the inside out and to manage that change so we can become World Class in our lives, our families, our enterprises, and our future. Let's bring the World Class Person that is within us out into the open. Let's become World Class People!

No matter how you look at World Class Management, the first and most important characteristic of a WCM is that a WCM will sit down right now and identify how he or she is going to change. Use the test in Chapter 18 to identify areas of change, prioritize the changes, and then boldly go where you've never gone before, one small step at a time. Use the building-block approach to make a difference. Remember:

> A big shot
>   is a little shot
>   who kept on shooting!

Get "beamed up" and see the big perspective of where you are, where you want to be (goals), and how you're going to get there. Be patient; never give up—never, never, never give up! Manage your changes, don't let changes manage you. Listen to what people (stakeholders) are saying, learn from them, and then innovate yourself ahead of your competition. Listen to other people.

It was pride that changed angels into devils; it is humility that makes men as angels.

St. Augustine

The five turnaround tips from Jack Smith, CEO of General Motors, are:

1. Establish a vision for the whole company.
2. Set clear expectations for performance at each level of the organization.
3. Construct realistic strategies that don't require rocket science.
4. Develop the capability to execute by reorganizing people and reallocating assets.
5. Focus everything—all assets, all decisions—on the customers. They are the ultimate arbiters of success or failure.[1]

One author claims that thirty-one major trends are shaping the future of American business. These trends include:

- Time control
- Home shopping growth
- The bifurcation of product markets
- Product and service quality becoming more important, if not everything
- Return of the family
- New employee benefits
- Public relations: tough times ahead for business

- The personal face of business
- Improvement of labor's image
- Growth of environmentalism
- The nation's mood: back to reality[2]

Riches are not from an abundance of worldly goods, but from the contented mind.

Mohammed

Learn from examples such as the following:

1. Ford, Sharonville, was scheduled for shutdown but was saved by utilizing Employee Involvement (EI), which required a letter of understanding with the United Auto Workers (UAW). Since the threatened 1986 shutdown, quality has improved by 53%.

2. L-S Electro-Galvanizing used laid off steelworkers and teaming to develop the organizational design of the company, including the administrative systems. The company effectively utilizes goal-based measurement/motivation systems, including profit sharing and gainsharing.

3. Albertson's focuses on quality and productivity improvement through training. It feels that the most important product is customer service.

4. Novell/Word Perfect has developed a model that it uses for continuous improvement. This model focuses on training at all levels of the organization.

He who merely knows right principles is not equal to him who lives them.

Confucius

---

5. Marriott International believes that associates are the key to success. It believes that if the hourly employees are taken care of, they in turn will take care of the customer. Marriott focuses

on the core expectations of the employees and attempts to gauge employee satisfaction, which is the prerequisite for quality service.

6. Boise Cascade believes that understanding and implementing the best strategies for the deployment and diffusion of quality initiatives are the key elements in successfully managing an enterprise transformation toward quality.

7. Wallace Co., a 1990 winner of the Malcolm Baldrige Award, developed sixteen strategic quality objectives and matrixed them against the seven Baldrige Award criteria. Managers used the Baldrige template to help them become World Class. The results include an increase in market share from 10.4% to 18%, an increase in on-time deliveries from 75% to 92%, and a 69% increase in sales volume.

The name of God is Truth.

Hindu proverb

---

8. Hewlett-Packard's statement of corporate objectives is that "the reason HP exists is to satisfy real customer needs."

9. Hollis L. Harris, president and chief operating officer of Delta Airlines, Inc., states that "we operate on the age-old adage that if you take care of the customer, the profits will take care of themselves."

10. Motorola, the company that everyone else is afraid to compare themselves to, was the first winner of the Malcolm Baldrige Award. It immediately required all its vendors to be Baldrige contenders. CEO George Fisher says, "I personally think the renewed focus on quality, cycle time, and customer satisfaction is far more important in the long run (to our global competitiveness)." Motorola emphasizes high goals and follow-through as the means to satisfying the customer. However, it does more than just state these goals; it makes sure that all the desired standards are implemented and that they are all focused on the objective of "Total Customer Satisfaction."[3]

---

*A man should first direct himself in the way he should go.
Only then should he instruct others.*

Buddha

What type of manager are you? You've read through a book that should have helped you decide where you are, where you're trying to go, and how you can get there. The question you need to answer is: Are you green and growing, or ripe and rotting? The key word in this phrase is *growing*. To be World Class is to grow (positive change). If you're growing both in your personal life and in your professional life, you're on your way to becoming World Class!

---

*In a world in which we are overwhelmed with a blizzard of
messages, we can easily lose sight of which messages are
really important. But, realistically there is only one message
that can never be ignored. It is the message of God, the
one message which gives meaning to all others. Read the
Bible and encourage others to do so. It's got a message for
each of us.*

William M. Ellinghous, President, AT&T

Chapter 1

1. For more information about Theory-X and Theory-Y managers, including some very interesting examples, read the book *The Human Side of the Enterprise*, by Douglas McGregor (New York: McGraw-Hill, 1985).
2. Theory-Z management is explained nicely, with examples, in the following book and article:

    Richard Tanner Pascale and Anthony G. Athos, *The Art of Japanese Management* (New York: Warner Books, 1982).

    Charles W. Joiner, Jr., "Making the 'Z' Concept Work," *Sloan Management Review*, Spring 1985, pp. 57–63.
3. Quality circles are a Japanese methodology for empowerment and teaming. For more information, see Chapters 5 and 14.
4. Many good articles discuss the role of leaders in a changing, growing organization, including the following.

    Peter M. Senge, "The Leader's New Work: Building Learning Organizations," *Sloan Management Review*, Fall 1990, pp. 7–23. This article focuses on the need for an organization to be "continuously learning" through leadership.

    John P. Kotter, "What Leaders Really Do," *Harvard Business Review*, May–June 1990, pp. 103–111. This article stresses that "good management controls complexity; effective leadership produces useful change." The article observes that "management controls people by pushing them in the right direction; leadership motivates them by satisfying basic human needs." This article offers three interesting leadership examples, and it is worth checking into just for the chance to read about the examples. They are American Express, Eastman Kodak, and Procter & Gamble.
5. Jack Welch's opinions about what makes a good manager (*business leader* is the term Jack prefers) are discussed in an interesting article:

Noel Tichy and Ram Charan, "Speed, Simplicity, Self-Confidence: An Interview With Jack Welch," *Harvard Business Review*, September–October 1989, pp. 112–120.

6. Root-cause identification is a theme of *Breakthrough Thinking*, a book that helps Total Quality Management (TQM) teams identify opportunities for improvements—changes! A follow-up book expands on this theme.

Gerald Nadler and Shozo Hibino, *Breakthrough Thinking* (Rocklin, Calif.: Prima Publishing & Communications, 1990).

Gerald Nadler, Shozo Hibino, and John Farrell, *Creative Solution Finding* (Rocklin, Calif.: Prima Publishing & Communications, 1995).

7. Total Quality is discussed in more detail in Chapters 4 and 10.

8. Later in this chapter, we discuss the Toyota production system as an example of continuous change and innovation. Toyota developed the Just-in-Time (JIT) production process, which uses a production control tool called the Kanban card. This card tracks and controls the quantity of products through the production process.

9. An interesting article on Tridon, if you are interested in more details, is "Workshop Report: Canadian Region—Building on the Past at Tridon-Oakdale," by Lea Tonkin, in *Target*, Summer 1990, pp. 34–37.

10. Some of you may catch this pun on the best-selling book *A Whack on the Side of the Head* by von Ouch. The book stresses creativity and open-mindedness in our thinking. See Roger von Oech, *A Whack on the Side of the Head* (New York: Warner Books, 1990).

11. The measurement and motivation of change are major topics of Chapter 8. Other organizations and authors have wrestled with this issue. One of the more interesting can be found in the work by Eli Goldratt and Bob Fox, who strongly support a Socratic process for the discovery, creation, and stimulation of change. They believe in the participatory development of change (a team process), and they believe that imposed change is ineffective change. Additionally, an incorrectly developed measurement system will block, rather than motivate, the change process. Some readings of interest include:

R. E. Fox, "Theory of Constraints," *NAA Conference Proceedings*, September 1987.

Eliyahu M. Goldratt and Jeff Cox, *The Goal* (Croton-on-Hudson, New York: North River Press, Inc., 1986).

Eliyahu M. Goldratt, *The Haystack Syndrome*, (Croton-on-Hudson, New York: North River Press, Inc., 1990).

Eliyahu M. Goldratt and Robert E. Fox, *The Race* (Croton-on-Hudson, New York: North River Press, Inc., 1986).

Eliyahu M. Goldratt, *What Is This Theory Called Theory of Constraints?* (Croton-on-Hudson, New York: North River Press, Inc., 1990).

Gerhard J. Plenert, "Bottleneck Scheduling for an Unlimited Number of Products," *Journal of Manufacturing Systems*, Vol. 9, No. 4, pp. 324–331.

Gerhard J. Plenert and Terry Lee, "Optimizing Theory of Constraints When New Product Alternatives Exist," *Production and Inventory Management Journal*, Third Quarter, 1993, Vol. 34, No. 3, pp. 51–57.

12. Articles discussing change and change management are endless. Here is a listing of a few of the better ones:

Robert H. Schaffer and Harvey A. Thomson, "Successful Change Programs Begin with Results," *Harvard Business Review*, January–February 1992, pp. 80–89. This article stresses that we should focus on results, not activities.

Rosabeth Moss Kanter, "Change: Where to Begin," *Harvard Business Review*, July–August 1991, pp. 8–9. This article encourages the following steps: (1) Begin with use-directed, action-oriented information; (2) be willing to build on platforms already in place; (3) encourage incremental experimentation that departs from tradition without totally destroying it.

Michael Beer, Russell A. Eisenstat, and Bert Spector, "Why Change Programs Don't Produce Change," *Harvard Business Review*, November–December 1990, pp. 158–166. This article focuses on the idea that "effective corporate renewal starts at the bottom, through informal efforts to solve problems."

13. Niccolo Machiavelli, *The Prince* (New York: Penguin Classics, 1984). If you want to read a really negative approach to business and government decision making, this book is for you.

14. See notes 6 and 10. Other works available on creativity include:

Judith A. Stimson, "Unleashing Creative Thinking for Change," *APICS 37th International Conference Proceedings*, October 30–November 4, 1994, APICS, Falls Church, Va., pp. 665–666.

Robert A. Abair, "'Dare to Change': Revolution vs. Evolution," *APICS 37th International Conference Proceedings*, October 30–November 4, 1994, APICS, Falls Church, Va., pp. 40–41.

15. Note 10 discusses Roger von Oech's book *A Whack on the Side of the Head*. Another good book by the same author is *A Kick in the Seat of the Pants* (New York: Harper & Row, 1986), which also focuses on building creativity in the reader.

16. Stephen R. Covey, *The 7 Habits of Highly Effective People* (New York: Simon & Schuster, 1989). Covey's book has been a worldwide best-seller. I've encountered it as far away as Malaysia. It can be found in any bookstore.

    Another excellent Covey book that discusses important issues related to the life-style and habits of a leader is Stephen R. Covey, *Principle-Centered Leadership* (New York: Summit Books, 1991).

17. There are two books in this vein:

    Tom Peters and Robert Waterman, *In Search of Excellence: Lessons from America's Best Run Companies* (New York: Harper & Row, 1985).

    Tom Peters and Nancy Austin, *A Passion for Excellence* (New York: Harper & Row, 1985).

18. This statement is a little idealistic. In reality, the Japanese work with single-digit batch sizes (one to nine units), whereas U.S. batch sizes can range in the hundreds of units. Only one item in each batch is worked on at a time; the rest of the batch is inventory. Therefore, a batch of 100 units creates a continuous, ongoing inventory of 99 units. Unfortunately, the batch is often not being worked on and is just idle inventory. This batch-size difference between the United States and Japan creates a tremendous difference in inventory levels.

19. Numerous books detail the Toyota JIT production philosophy. See:

    Shigeo Shingo, *Study of the Toyota Production System from the Industrial Engineering Viewpoint* (Tokyo: Japanese Management Association, 1981). Shingo has worked with Toyota and has an insider's viewpoint.

    Kenneth A. Wantuck, *Just in Time for America* (Milwaukee, Wis.: The Forum, Ltd., 1989).

20. More detail is available from Robert W. Hall, *Attaining Manufacturing Excellence* (Homewood, Ill.: Dow-Jones-Irwin, 1987).

21. This concept of innovating yourself out ahead rather than copying someone else is the theme of another one of my books:

    Gerhard Plenert, *International Management and Production: Survival Techniques for Corporate America* (Blue Ridge Summit, Pa., Tab Professional and Reference Books, 1990).

Chapter 2

1. The Malcolm Balridge National Quality Award (MBNQA) is the U.S. government's national award for quality.

2. A little of the history of FedEx and details of its quality program will be discussed more in later chapters.

3. FedEx offers a document called the *Quality Profile*, which outlines its various quality programs, including the GFTP and the SQI (Service Quality Indicators). For more information, contact Federal Express Corporation, Public Relations Department, 2005 Corporate Avenue, Memphis, TN 38132, (910) 395-3466.

4. The following books have excellent lessons for us in the area of goal setting (and numerous other principles discussed in this chapter). Covey's books focus on the characteristics of leadership, while von Oech's books focus on creativity, including discussions on the meaning of life.

   Stephen R. Covey, *Principle-Centered Leadership* (New York: Summit Books, 1991).

   Stephen R. Covey, *The 7 Habits of Highly Effective People* (New York: Simon & Schuster, 1989).

   Roger von Oech, *A Kick in the Seat of the Pants* (New York: Harper & Row, 1986).

   Roger von Oech, *A Whack on the Side of the Head* (New York: Warner Books, 1990).

5. This model comes from Timothy M. Mojonnier, "Top Management's Role in Fostering and Managing Positive Organizational Change," *APICS 37th International Conference Proceedings*, APICS, October 1994, pp. 49–51.

6. *Webster's New Dictionary* (New York: Russell, Gebbes & Grosset, 1990).

7. A detailed discussion of the aspirations statement can be found in Robert Howard, "Values Make the Company: An Interview with Robert Haas," *Harvard Business Review*, September–October 1990, pp. 133–144.

8. Another interesting example of the change process is found in Robert R. Bell and John M. Burnham, *Managing Productivity and Change* (Cincinnati, Ohio: South-Western Publishing Co., 1991), pp. 10–11.

9. For details on the ABS EI program, see the following interesting article:

Cash Powell, Jr., "Empowerment, the Stake in the Ground for ABS," *Target*, January/February 1992, pp. 7–17.
10. There are many good publications on effective World Class people relations. Some are:

William M. Boyst, Jr. III, "HRM—Key to the Integrated Management Revolution," *APICS 34th International Conference Proceedings*, APICS, Falls Church, Va., 1991, pp. 354–357.

Thomas F. Wallace, *World Class Manufacturing* (Essex Junction, VT: OMNEO, 1994). The section of the book that is of interest here is titled "Part III—People."

Gerhard Plenert, *International Management and Production: Survival Techniques for Corporate America* (Blue Ridge Summit, Pa.: Tab Professional and Reference Books, 1990).

Chapter 3

1. The traditional article in this area is C. K. Prahalad and Gary Hamel, "The Core Competence of the Corporation," *Harvard Business Review*, May–June 1990.
2. Some insight into the vision-creation process can be gained from the article "The Vision Thing," *The Economist*, November 9, 1991, p. 81.
3. More details about goal setting can be found in my book Gerhard Plenert, *The Plant Operations Handbook* (Homewood, Ill.: Business One Irwin, 1993).
4. Mapes wrote a fun article that discusses vision and mission statement creation:

James J. Mapes, "Foresight First," *Sky Magazine*, September 1991, pp. 96–105.
5. Alvin Toffler has written several interesting books about the future and change. The one that started it all off and is well worth your time reading is:

Alvin Toffler, *Future Shock* (New York: Random House Publishers, 1970).
6. Robert H. Schaffer and Harvey A. Thomson, "Successful Change Programs Begin with Results," *Harvard Business Review*, January–February 1992, pp. 80–89.

Chapter 4

1. The model is detailed in Robert W. Hall and Jinichiro Nakane, "Developing Flexibility for Excellence in Manufacturing: Sum-

mary Results of a Japanese-American Study," *Target*, Vol. 4, No. 2 (Summer 1988), p. 18.

2. Information about this model can be found in John B. Burnham, "Systematic Improvements in Physical Distribution or 'Why We Just Can't Do It Like We Used To?'," *APICS 34th International Conference Proceedings*, APICS, Falls Church, Va., October 1991, pp. 305–310.

3. The best article, if you're interested in more detail about this model, is Paul S. Adler, D. William McDonald, and Fred McDonald, "Strategic Management of Technical Functions," *Sloan Management Review*, Winter 1992, pp. 19–37.

4. This model comes from Timothy M. Mojonnier, "Top Management's Role in Fostering and Managing Positive Organizational Change," *APICS 37th International Conference Proceedings*, APICS, October 1994, pp. 49–51.

5. Michael Porter has long been known for his prominence in the strategy area. He has written two books that are classics in competitive strategy. He also has written an article that summarizes his thoughts on corporate strategy. All are worthy of your time if competitive strategy is of interest to you.

   Michael Porter, *Competitive Strategy* (Toronto: Free Press, 1980).

   Michael Porter, *Competitive Advantage* (Toronto: Free Press, 1985).

   Michael Porter, "From Competitive Advantage to Corporate Strategy," *Harvard Business Review*, May–June 1987, pp. 43–59.

6. This article has become a classic in manufacturing strategy development:

   Steven C. Wheelwright and Robert D. Hayes, "Competing Through Manufacturing," *Harvard Business Review*, January–February 1985, pp. 99–109.

7. If you're interested in additional information about the critical resource, an entire section on identifying and optimizing the critical resource can be found in Gerhard Plenert, *The Plant Operations Handbook* (Homewood, Ill.: Business One Irwin, 1993).

8. Michael E. Walters, "Manufacturing Excellence in the 1990s," *APICS 34th International Conference Proceedings*, APICS, October 1991, pp. 425–428.

9. Terence T. Burton, "Manufacturing in the 21st Century," *APICS 34th International Conference Proceedings*, APICS, October 1991, pp. 454–457.

10. Darryl Landvater, Steve Souza, and Thomas Wallace, "The ABCD Checklist for Manufacturing Excellence: An Integrated Strategic/Operational Measurement Tool," *APICS 34th International Conference Proceedings*, APICS, October 1991, pp. 458–459.

11. Renee M. Gregoire and Patrick J. Delaney, "Manufacturing Strategy: The Key to Competitive Advantage," *APICS 33rd International Conference Proceedings*, APICS, October 1990, pp. 9–13.

12. Wickham Skinner, "The Focused Factory," *Harvard Business Review*, May–June 1974, pp. 113–121.

13. For additional information, see:

    Terry Hill, *Manufacturing Strategy: Text and Cases* (Burr Ridge, Ill.: Irwin, 1994).

    David A. Garvin, *Operations Strategy* (Englewood Cliffs, N.J.: Prentice-Hall, 1992).

    Jagdish Sheth and Golpira Eshghi, *Global Operations Perspectives* (Cincinnati, Ohio: South Western Publishing Co., 1989). In this book, see the following articles:
    Steven C. Wheelright, "Restoring the Competitive Edge in U. S. Manufacturing," pp. 29–43.

    Kasra Ferdows, Jeffrey G. Miller, Jinichiro Nakane, and Thomas E. Vollman, "Evolving Global Manufacturing Strategies: Projections into the 1990's," pp. 44–55.

14. The Baldrige and Deming award criteria are available from numerous sources. Shingo Prize information is available from Shingo Prize for Excellence in Manufacturing, College of Business, Utah State University, Logan, UT 84322-3520, (801) 797-2279.

    Deming Prize information is thoroughly discussed in Cecelia S. Kilian, *The World of W. Edwards Deming* (Knoxville, Tenn: SPC Press, Inc., 1992).

    The Baldrige Award criteria are available from Malcolm Baldrige National Quality Award, National Institute of Standards and Technology, Route 270 and Quince Orchard Road, Administration Buliding, Room A537, Gaithersburg, MD 20899, (301) 975-2036.

    The NASA quality award seems to have died out because of extensive politics. Currently there is no NASA award, but it may be reinstated again in the future.

15. An article that may be helpful is Andrew D. Nicoll, "Integrating Logistics Strategies," *APICS 37th International Conference Proceedings*, APICS, October 1994, pp. 590–594.

16. The source for this list is John P. Kotter, L. A. Schlesinger, and V. Sathe, *Organization*, (Homewood, Ill.: Irwin, 1986), p. 360.

17. Two last references helpful in the development of corporate strategies are:

    Jeffrey N. Lowenthal, *Reengineering the Organization* (Milwaukee, Wis.: ASQC Quality Press, 1994), Chapters 1, 2, 4, and 6.

    Thomas F. Wallace, *World Class Manufacturing* (Essex Junction, Vt.: Oliver Wight Publications, 1994), Part I.

Chapter 5

1. Volumes of information are available on ISO certification. Every regional area has organizations that assist with the certification process. You need to contact your local certification representative to receive certification requirements for your area. They can be different, even though they attempt to be standardized. If you have trouble figuring out where to start in finding an ISO certifier, contact one of the quality organizations listed later in this chapter. Some helpful reading includes:

    Frank Voehl, Peter Jackson, and David Ashton, *ISO 9000—An Implementation Guide for Small to Mid-Sized Businesses* (Delray Beach, Fla.: St. Lucie Press, 1994).

    Jack Kanholm, *ISO 9000 Explained—65 Requirements Checklist and Compliance Guide* (Delray Beach, Fla.: St. Lucie Press, 1994).

    Suzanne E. Ewing and Glenna K. Russell, "Recipe for ISO 9000 Certification," *APICS 37th International Conference Proceedings*, APICS, October 1994, pp. 477–479.

    James Wilson Parisher, "Documentation for ISO 9000: What is the Right Balance?" *APICS 37th International Conference Proceedings*, APICS, October 1994, pp. 501–505.

    Ralph R. Kuhn, "How to Meet Europe's ISO 9000 Standard by 1992," *APICS 34th International Conference Proceedings*, APICS, October 1991, pp, 232–234.

2. My previous book contains a detailed discussion of how to calculate quality and productivity performance ratios:

    Gerhard Plenert, *The Plant Operations Handbook* (Homewood, Ill.: Business One Irwin, 1993).

    The cover story for the August 8, 1994, issue of *Business Week* is titled "Making Quality Pay—How Companies Are Rethinking the Management Buzzword of the 1980s." It has some excellent examples of the quality improvement process at work.

3. As with each of the World Class topics we are addressing, there is excellent reading material available on productivity improvements. A few good references are:

    Peter F. Drucker, "The New Productivity Challenge," *Harvard Business Review*, November–December 1991, pp. 69–79.

    Robert R. Bell and John M. Burnham, *Managing Productivity and Change* (Cincinnati, Ohio: South-Western Publishing Co., 1991).

    Andrew S. Grove, *High Output Management* (New York: Vintage Books, 1983).

4. National Productivity Board of Singapore, "Singapore, the Guiding Light of Productivity," *Productivity SA*, September/October 1994, pp. 11–13.

5. NAFTA has greatly reduced the transfer time requirements to Mexico. However, the example given here is still a good one because a significant transfer time to Mexico still exists, and the transfer time to Asia or South America, where many plants are being relocated to, is still very long.

6. Wickham Skinner, "The Productivity Paradox," *Harvard Business Review*, July–August 1986, pp. 55–59.

7. "Warner-Lambert Changes Focus and Comes Up a Big Winner," *Commitment Plus*, Quality and Productivity Management Association, May 1991, Vol. 6, No. 7.

8. Shigeo Shingo, *Study of the Toyota Production System from the Industrial Engineering Viewpoint* (Tokyo: Japanese Management Association, 1981).

    Shigeo Shingo, *Non-Stock Production and the Shingo System for Continuous Improvement* (Tokyo: Japan Management Association, 1988).

9. Numerous Deming articles and books exist, but most are difficult to read. Some of the better ones are:

    Howard S. Gitlow and Shelly J. Gitlow, *The Deming Guide to Quality and Competitive Position* (Englewood Cliffs, N.J.: Prentice-Hall, 1987).

    Mary Walton, *Fourteen Points and Seven Deadly Diseases from the Deming Management Method* (New York: Perigee Books, 1986).

    W. Edwards Deming, "Improvement of Quality and Productivity through Action by Management," *National Productivity Review*, Vol. 1, No. 1, Winter 1981–82, pp. 12–22.

10. One good source for Juran's models is J. M. Juran, *Juran's Quality Control Handbook*, ASQC, 1988.

11. Philip B. Crosby, *Quality Is Free*, (New York: McGraw-Hill, 1979).
     Philip B. Crosby, *Quality without Tears* (New York: McGraw-Hill, 1984).

Chapter 6

1. Three books from which I have drawn information for parts of this chapter, and which include excellent expansions of much of the material found in this chapter, are:
    John D. Daniels and Lee H. Radebaugh, *International Business—Environments and Operations* (Reading, Mass.: Addison-Wesley Publishing Company, 1994).
    Jagdish Sheth and Golpira Eshghi, *Global Operations Perspectives* (Cincinnati, Ohio: South-Western Publishing Co., 1989).
    Gerhard Plenert, *International Management and Production: Survival Techniques for Corporate America* (Blue Ridge Summit, Pa.: TAB Professional and Reference Books, 1990).
2. Kenichi Ohmae, "Managing in a Borderless World," *Harvard Business Review*, May–June 1989, pp. 152–161.
3. The Roper Organization, Inc., *The Public Pulse*, 1991, Vol. 2, No. 1, pp. 1–8.
4. Terence T. Burton, "Manufacturing in the 21st Century," *APICS 34th International Conference Proceedings*, APICS, October 1991, pp. 454–457.
5. John A. Quelch and Edward J. Hoff, "Customizing Global Marketing," *Harvard Business Review*, May–June 1986, pp. 59–68.
6. John T. Albin, "Competing in a Global Market," *APICS—The Performance Advantage*, January 1992, pp. 29–32.
7. For more detail on global relationships, see Robert B. Reich, "Who Is Them?" *Harvard Business Review*, March–April 1991, pp. 77–88.
8. Robert A. Howell and Stephen R. Soucy, "Determining the Real Costs of Doing Business in a Global Market," *National Productivity Review*, Spring 1991, pp. 157–165.
9. Donald F. Blumberg, "Improving Productivity in Service Operations on an International Basis," *National Productivity Review*, Spring 1991, pp. 167–179.
10. Gerhard Plenert, "Technology Transfer—A Developing Country Perspective," *IAMOT Newsletter*, September 1994, pp. 5–6.
11. E. F. Schumacher, *Small Is Beautiful: Economics As If People Mattered*, (New York: Harper Perennial, 1989).

12. Rajan Suri, Jerry L. Sanders, P. Chandrasekhar Rao, and Ashoka Mody, "Impact of Manufacturing Practices on the Global Bicycle Industry," *Manufacturing Review*, March 1993, pp. 14–24.

13. The Canadian statistics can be acquired from the Industry, Science and Technology Canada (see Appendix 6.1).

    The United States classifies all its industries by a Standard Industrial Classification (SIC) code. This coding scheme exists internationally; unfortunately, there are major discrepancies internationally as to what categories of products are allowed into each classification. Tables for the United States are available that show the average financial data for small, medium, and large firms within each SIC classification. One table is *Industrial Norms and Key Business Ratios*, put out by Dun and Bradstreet Information Services.

14. Peter C. Reid, *Well-Made in America* (New York: McGraw-Hill, 1990).

15. This is the major message of Gerhard Plenert, *International Management and Production: Survival Techniques for Corporate America* (Blue Ridge Summit, Pa.: TAB Professional and Reference Books, 1990).

16. Kenneth Chilton, "Changing Structures and Strategies: Survey of American Manufacturing Executives," Center for the Study of American Business, Washington University, St. Louis, Missouri, Working Paper 151, September 1993.

17. Bruce Kogut, "Designing Global Strategies: Comparative and Competitive Value-Added Chains," *Sloan Management Review*, Summer 1985, pp. 15–28.

18. Christopher A. Bartlett and Sumantra Ghoshal, "Managing Across Borders: New Strategic Requirements," *Sloan Management Review*, Summer 1987, pp. 7–17.

19. A detailed discussion of international ethical dilemmas can be found in the Daniels/Radebaugh book referenced in note 1 of this chapter. This book also contains a detailed discussion of trade theory and world financial transactions.

20. Nilly Landau, "Managing Exotic Risks," *International Business*, May 1994, pp. 62–66.

21. Dave Savona, "The Invisible Partner," *International Business*, November 1994, pp. 64–68.

22. Kenichi Ohmae, "The Global Logic of Strategic Alliances," *Harvard Business Review*, March–April 1989, pp. 143–154.

23. Gary Hamel, Yves L. Doz, and C. K. Prahalad, "Collaborate with Your Competitors—and Win," *Harvard Business Review*, January–February 1989, pp. 133–139.

24. Gerhard Plenert, "Plant Relocation: How Decisions Are Made Today", *Industry Forum*, March 1994, pp. 1–3.

    Gerhard Plenert, "Technology Transfer—A Developing Country Perspective," *IAMOT Newsletter*, September 1994, pp. 5–6.

25. George S. Yip, "Global Strategy . . . in a World of Nations?" *Sloan Management Review*, Fall 1989, pp. 29–41.

26. Rosabeth Moss Kanter, "Transcending Business Boundaries: 12,000 World Managers View Change," *Harvard Business Review*, May–June 1991, pp. 151–164.

    "The Boundaries of Business: Commentaries from the Experts," *Harvard Business Review*, July–August 1991, pp. 127–140.

27. Dave Savona, "World Commerce," *International Business*, August 1994, p. 42; September 1994, p. 38; and November 1994, p. 18.

28. Andru M. Peters, "The Pacific Rim Nations' Business Strategy for the Next 10 Years," *APICS 37th International Conference Proceedings*, November 1994, pp. 226–231.

    John T. Albin, "Competing in a Global Market," *APICS 37th International Conference Proceedings*, November 1994, pp. 244–248.

29. *International Management and Production and International Business—Environments and Operations* are cited in note 1 of this chapter.

    Jagdish Sheth and Golpira Eshghi, Global *Operations Perspectives*, (Cincinnati, Ohio: South-Western Publishing Co., 1989).

Chapter 7

1. Glenn Bodinson, "Time-based Competition Is the Competitive Advantage of the 1990s," *APICS—The Performance Advantage*, December 1991, pp. 27–31.

2. Artemis March, "Meeting Time and Cost Targets: The IBM Proprinter," *Target*, Special Issue 1991, pp. 18–24.

3. Dave Henrickson, "Product Design as a Team Sport," *Target*, Spring 1990, pp. 4–12.

4. Paul S. Adler, Henry E. Riggs, and Steven C. Wheelwright, "Product Development Know-How: Trading Tactics for Strategy," *Sloan Management Review*, Fall 1989, pp. 7–17.

5. Frederick Winslow Taylor, *The Principles of Scientific Management*, (New York: W. W. Norton and Company, 1967).

   Henry Ford, *Today and Tomorrow*, (Cambridge, Mass.: Productivity Press, 1988).

6. Bill Belt, Roger Brooks, and Rick Burris, "Management Technologies for World-Class Manufacturing," *APICS 37th International Conference Proceedings*, APICS, October 1994, pp. 143–147.

   Robert C. Camp, *Business Process Benchmarking*, (Homewood, Ill.: Irwin, 1994).

   Ashoka Mody, Rajan Suri, and Jerry Sanders, "Keeping Pace with Change: Organizational and Technological Imperatives," *World Development*, Vol. 20, No. 12 (1992), pp. 1797–1816.

7. Tony Seideman, "Multimedia Marketing," *International Business*, August 1994, pp. 26–28.

8. *International Business* had a special section in the September 1994 issue called "Information Technology Special Report." The technology study reported the following anticipated investments in technology:

	Decreases	Stay the Same	Increases
Information	1%	17%	82%
Manufacturing equipment	7%	31%	62%
Research	3%	34%	63%
Distribution	4%	39%	57%
Facilities	18%	40%	42%

9. Edward B. Roberts and Charles A. Berry, "Entering New Businesses: Selecting Strategies for Success," *Sloan Management Review*, Spring 1985, pp. 3–17.

   Steven C. Wheelwright, "A Rubber Mallet and a Two-by-Four: The Concept of Development Strategy," *Target*, Fall 1991, pp. 4–16.

10. William W. Lewis and Lawrence H. Linden, "A New Mission for Corporate Technology," *Sloan Management Review*, Summer 1990, pp. 57–67.

11. Tamara J. Erickson, John F. Magee, Philip A. Roussel, and Kamal N. Saad, "Managing Technology as a Business Strategy," *Sloan Management Review*, Spring 1990, pp. 73–78.

12. "Survey—Manufacturing Technology: On the Cutting Edge," *The Economist*, March 5, 1994, pp. 3–19.

13. Thomas E. Arenberg, "Engineering Productivity—JIT in the Product Delivery Function," *APICS 34th International Conference Proceedings*, APICS, October 1991, pp. 271–273.

 Joseph T. Vesey, "The New Competitors: They Think in Terms of 'Speed-to-Market'," *APICS 34th International Conference Proceedings*, APICS, October 1991, pp. 274–277.

14. Philip R. Thomas, Competitiveness Through Cycle Time: An Overview of CEOs, (New York: McGraw-Hill Publishing Company, 1990).

15. Tom Peters, "Time-Obsessed Competition," *Management Review*, September 1990, pp. 16–20.

Chapter 8

1. Michelle Monnin, Roger Miller, and Brian Schaenzer, "Are Your Goals and Measurements in Line with Your Time-Based Competition Philosophy?" *APICS 37th International Conference Proceedings*, APICS, October 1994, pp. E1–E3.

2. The following book has two excellent chapters, one on leadership (Chapter 9) and one on communications (Chapter 10):

 Robert R. Bell and John M. Burnham, *Managing Productivity and Change* (Cincinnati, Ohio: South-Western Publishing Co., 1991).

3. William A. Sandras, "Integration: Productivity Thrust of the 1990s," *APICS 34th International Conference Proceedings*, APICS, October 1991, pp. 400–402.

 Norman F. Barber, "Creating Organizational Integration," *APICS 33rd International Conference Proceedings*, APICS, October 1990, pp. 40–44.

4. My book *The Plant Operations Handbook* has several chapters that detail the information flow process. Sheth and Eshghi have a chapter (Chapter 7) on "Integration of Information Systems in Manufacturing," written by Arnoud De Meyer and Kasra Ferdows.

 Gerhard Plenert, *The Plant Operations Handbook* (Homewood, Ill.: Business One Irwin Publishing, 1993).

 Gerhard Plenert, "Total Integration of Accounting and Manufacturing Information," *APICS 34th International Conference Proceedings*, APICS, October 1991, pp. 366–367.

 Jagdish Sheth and Golpira Eshghi, *Global Operations Perspectives* (Cincinnati, Ohio: South-Western Publishing Co., 1989).

5. This is a statement regularly used by Goldratt. For more information about his philosophy, read his books or the books and articles by Bob Fox referenced in the notes for Chapter 1.

6. William G. Savage, "Implementing an Integrated System: Restructuring the Business, Not Just Automating It," *APICS 34th International Conference Proceedings*, APICS, October 1991, pp. 382–386.

    Tom Baker and Gerry Cleaves, "New Computer Solutions: World-Class Performance Through Improved Planning and Scheduling Integration," *APICS—The Performance Advantage*, October 1991, pp. 28–31.

7. This information was taken from a presentation in Guatemala by Lyle Tippetts, the Quality Director of the Caribbean/Latin America region of AT&T.

8. Robin Cooper, "You Need a New Cost System When . . . ," *Harvard Business Review*, January–February 1989, pp. 77–82.

    James D. Tarr, "Developing Performance Measurement Systems That Support Continuous Improvement Goals," *APICS 37th International Conference Proceedings*, APICS, October 1994, pp. 416–420.

    Michael G. Tincher, "World-Class Performance Measurements—How to Get Started," *APICS 37th International Conference Proceedings*, APICS, October 1994, pp. 424–428.

    Robert G. Eccles, "The Performance Measurement Manifesto," *Harvard Business Review*, January–February 1991, pp. 131–137.

    Joel D. Wisner and Stanley E. Fawcett, "Linking Firm Strategy to Operation Decisions Through Performance Measurement," *Production and Inventory Management Journal*, Third Quarter, 1991, pp. 5–11.

9. Abraham H. Maslow, "The Theory of Human Motivation," *Psychological Review* (1943), Vol. 50, pp. 370–396.

10. J. Thomas Brown, "Measuring Performance for Strategic Improvement," *APICS 34th International Conference Proceedings*, APICS, October 1991, pp. 107–112.

    Robert A. Abair, "Super Measurements: The Key to World-Class Manufacturing," *APICS 34th International Conference Proceedings*, APICS, October 1991, pp. 113–115.

    Holly E. Henson, "Performance Measurement in the New Manufacturing Environment," *APICS 34th International Conference Proceedings*, APICS, October 1991, pp. 126–128.

U.S. Department of Labor, *Road to High-Performance Workplaces: A Guide to Better Jobs and Better Business Results—1994*, U.S. Department of Labor, Office of the American Workplace, 1994.

11. The Maryland Center for Quality and Productivity, headed by Tom C. Tuttle, focuses on "strategic process measurement" as the way to quality results. The center has done an extensive amount of research in this area and has numerous publications. It is based at the University of Maryland, College of Business and Management, in College Park, Maryland.

12. *World Class Manufacturing* by Wallace has a chapter (Chapter VII) on World Class performance measurement. For example, the second article in this chapter is titled "Performance Measurements That Support World Class Manufacturing," by Thomas Vollmann. These articles discuss the fit of ABC into World Class measurement.

    Thomas F. Wallace, *World Class Manufacturing* (Essex Junction, Vt.: Omneo, an imprint of Oliver Wight Publications, Inc., 1994).

13. Jeffrey N. Lowenthal, *Reengineering the Organization: A Step by Step Approach to Corporate Revitalization* (Milwaukee, Wis.: ASQC Quality Press, 1994).

Chapter 9

1. Gerhard Plenert, "Successful Factory Management Systems," *Produktiviti*, Bil. 42. Jul/Ogos 1992, pp. 2–6.

2. E. Michael Shays, "Cleaning Up Waste in Decision Making—Breakthrough Thinking: A New Way of Attacking Problems Can Produce Startling Results," *Business Quarterly*, Vol. 56, No. 3, Winter 1992, pp. 43–45.

    Also see the Nadler and Hibino books on breakthrough thinking listed in the notes for Chapter 1.

3. Frederick Winslow Taylor, *The Principles of Scientific Management* (New York: W. W. Norton & Company, Inc., 1967).

    Michael L. Dertouzos, Richard K. Lester, and Robert M. Solow, *Made in America* (Cambridge, Mass.: MIT Press, 1991).

4. Kaoru Ishikawa, *Introduction to Quality Control* (Tokyo, Japan: 3A Corporation, 1990).

5. Gerhard Plenert, "Megatrend or Megadisaster," *OR/MS Today*, December 1994, pp. 24–26.

6. I saw this on a T-shirt in Maui.

7. For more details, see article I-6 by Darryl V. Landvater, titled "Resource Planning: For Manufacturing, Business, and the Enterprise," in Thomas F. Wallace, *World Class Manufacturing* (Essex Junction, Vt.: Omneo, an imprint of Oliver Wight Publications, Inc., 1994).

8. This information is from a presentation by Hay Wun Wain, Director of Total Quality Management for AMETEK, Inc., in November 1994.

9. G. Stalk, P. Evans, and L. E. Shulman, "Competing on Capabilities: The New Rules of Corporate Strategy," *Harvard Business Review*, March–April 1992, pp. 57–69.

10. For example, see Robert E. Olsen, "Developing a Manufacturing Strategy for the 1990s," *APICS 34th International Conference Proceedings*, APICS, October 1991, pp. 403–405.

11. William Wassweiler, "The Factory With a Future," *APICS—The Performance Advantage*, September 1991, pp. 26–28.

Chapter 10

1. Larry Dean Steiger, "The Learning Organization," *APICS 34th International Conference Proceedings*, APICS, October 1991, pp. 188–192.

2. Daniel R. Tobin, "Building a Learning Organization," Article III-1 in the Thomas F. Wallace, *World Class Manufacturing* (Essex Junction, Vt.: Omneo, an imprint of Oliver Wight Publications, Inc., 1994).

3. Robert A. Ulrich and A. Young, "A Shared Mindset," *Personnel Administrator*, March 1989, p. 45.

4. Peter M. Senge, "The Leader's New Work: Building Learning Organizations," *Sloan Management Review*, Fall 1990, pp. 7–23.

5. In "Education and Development in the Workplace," Chapter 13 in Bell and Burnham (see note 2, Chapter 8).

6. Patricia Lamfers, "Education: The Future of Our Competitiveness," *APICS 34th International Conference Proceedings*, APICS, October 1991, pp. 13–15.

   Michael R. DiPrima, "Education for the World Class Manufacturing/JIT Organization," *APICS 34th International Conference Proceedings*, APICS, October 1991, pp. 16–19.

   M. R. "Mike" Ashapa, "The State of Manufacturing Education in the United States," *APICS 34th International Conference Proceedings*, APICS, October 1991, pp. 27–29.

   Henry Alex Hutchins, "Measuring the Results of Training: A Case Study," *APICS 34th International Conference Proceedings*, APICS, October 1991, pp. 37–40.

Chapter 11

1. Bulent Kobu and Frank Greenwood, "Continuous Improvement in a Competitive Global Economy," *Production and Inventory Management*, Fourth Quarter 1991, pp. 58–63.

2. Cyrus F. Gibson and R. L. Nolan, "Managing the Four Stages of EDP Growth," *Harvard Business Review*, January–February 1974, p. 76.

3. Timothy N. Szendel and Walter Tighe, "Kaizen American-Style, Continuous Improvement in Action," *APICS 37th International Conference Proceedings*, APICS, October 1994, pp. 496–497.

4. H. James Harrington of Ernst & Young gave a presentation titled "Continuous Improvement or Breakthrough Dilemma" in Guatemala in November 1994 in which these comments were made.

5. Gregg D. Stocker, "Quality Functional Deployment: Listening to the Voice of the Customer," *APICS 34th International Conference Proceedings*, APICS, October 1991, pp. 258–262.

6. Another excellent article that, like the Stocker article, focuses on QFD procedures was written by Dave Henrickson, manager of the Western Region, Motorola Education and Training Center.

    Dave Henrickson, "Product Design as a Team Sport," *Target*, Spring 1990, pp. 4–12.

    Additionally, the Wallace book listed earlier has two sections worth looking at: I-3, "Linking Customer to Strategies via Quality Functional Deployment (QFD)," by Thomas F. Wallace, and II-6, "Quality Functional Deployment: Breakthrough Tool for Product Development," by William Barnard.

7. Karen Bemkowski, "The Quality Glossary," *Quality Progress*, February 1992, pp. 19–29.

8. P. Rama Ramalingam, "Making TQM Pay Off: The Solectron Experience," *APICS 37th International Conference Proceedings*, November 1994, pp. 472–476.

    Quang Bao and E. B. Baatz, "How Solectron Finally Got in Touch with Its Workers," *Electronic Business*, October 7, 1991.

    Linda Grant, "Six Companies That Are Winning the Race," *Los Angeles Times*, January 17, 1993.

    "Solectron Corp.," *Business America*, October 21, 1991.

9. Gerald Nadler and Shozo Hibino, *Breakthrough Thinking* (Rocklin, Calif.: Prima Publishing and Communications, 1990).

    Gerald Nadler, Shozo Hibino, and John Farrell, *Creative Solution Finding* (Rocklin, Calif.: Prima Publishing and Communications, 1995).

10. The following publications and additional information are available from AT&T's Customer Information Center, Order Entry Department, P.O. Box 19901, Indianapolis, IN 46219, 1-800-432-6600.

    AT&T Bell Laboratories, *AT&T's Total Quality Approach* (Publication Center of AT&T Bell Laboratories, 1992).

    AT&T Bell Laboratories, *AT&T Process Quality Management & Improvement Guidelines* (Publication Center of AT&T Bell Laboratories, 1989).

11. Gerhard Plenert and Shozo Hibino, "The T-Model: A Systematic Model for Change," *National Productivity Review*, Vol. 13, No. 4, Autumn 1994, pp. 543–549.

12. The organizations I have referenced in previous appendices are sources of publications and conference information that will help you implement a TQM environeeing. Additional readings include:

    Harry Costin, *Readings in Total Quality Management* (Fort Worth, Texas: The Dryden Press, 1994).

    Joel E. Ross, *Total Quality Management: Text, Cases, and Readings* (Delray Beach, Fla.: St. Lucie Press, 1993).

    Vincent K. Omachonu, *Principles of Total Quality* (Delray Beach, Fla.: St. Lucie Press, 1994).

    Articles of interest on TQM include two from the Wallace book listed earlier: IV-1, "Total Quality Management (TQM)," by Joseph Colletti, and IV-2, "Tools for Total Quality Management (TQM)," by Bill Montgomery.

13. Gerhard Plenert, "Process Re-Engineering: The Latest Fad Toward Failure," *APICS—The Performance Advantage*, June 1994, pp. 22–24.

14. M. Hammer and J. Champy, *Reengineering the Corporation* (New York: Harper Business, 1993).

15. M. Hammer and J. Champy, "The Promise of Reengineering," *Fortune*, May 3, 1993, pp. 94–97.

    M. Hammer, "Reengineering Work: Don't Automate, Obliterate," *Harvard Business Review*, July–August 1990, pp. 104–112.

    R. Jason, "How Reengineering Transforms Organizations to Satisfy Customers," *National Productivity Review*, Winter 1992, pp. 45–53.

    Peter Marks, *Process Reengineeering and the New Manufacturing Enterprise Wheel: 15 Processes for Competitive Advantage* (Dearborn, Mich.: CASA/SME Technical Forum, Society of Manufacturing Engineers, 1994).

Jerry L. Harbour, *The Process Reengineering Workbook: Practical Steps to Working Faster and Smarter Through Process Improvement* (White Plains, N.Y.: Quality Resources, 1994).

Harold L. Cypress, "Re-engineering," *OR/MS Today*, February 1994, pp. 18–29.

Ravi Ravikumar, "Business Process Reengineering—Making the Transition," *APICS 37th Annual International Conference Proceedings*, APICS, October 1994, pp. 17–21.

George Miller, "Reengineering: 40 U$seful Hints," *APICS 37th Annual International Conference Proceedings*, APICS, October 1994, pp. 22–26.

Steven A. Melnyk and William R. Wassweiler, "Business Process Reengineering: Understanding the Process, Responding to the Right Needs," *APICS 37th Annual International Conference Proceedings*, APICS, October 1994, pp. 115–120.

John E. Boyer, "Reengineering Office Processes," *APICS 37th Annual International Conference Proceedings*, APICS, October 1994, pp. 522–526.

Mark Stevens, "Reengineering the Manufacturing Company: 'New Fad or For Real'," *APICS 37th Annual International Conference Proceedings*, APICS, October 1994, pp. 527–530.

16. John R. Lipscomb, President of Lipscomb and Associates of White Lake, Michigan, has given presentations with the title "Reengineering Continuous Improvement Through Quality Systems Deployment."

17. Jeffrey N. Lowenthal, Reengineering the Organization: A Step-by-Step Approach to Corporate Revitalization (Milwaukee, Wis.: ASQC Quality Press, 1994).

18. Jeffrey N. Lowenthal, Senior Vice President and Managing Director of Performance Solutions International has made presentations with the title "Core Competencies and Organizational Reengineering."

19. The Wallace book cited earlier has an article by Robert L. Jones and Joseph R. Tunner titled "ISO 9000: The International Standard for Quality."

   ISO information can be obtained from any of the quality and productivity organizations mentioned in earlier chapters. The ISO organization, International Organization for Standardization, is located in Geneva, Switzerland.

20. The Wallace book cited earlier has an article titled "The Malcolm Baldrige National Quality Award Program," by Stephen George.

Malcolm Baldrige application information can be obtained from Malcolm Baldrige National Quality Award, National Institute of Standards and Technology, Gaithersburg, MD 20899, (301) 975-2036.

21. Dan J. Allen, "Work Reengineering and Total Quality Management: Synergy or Conflict," *APICS 37th International Conference Proceedings*, APICS, October 1994, pp. 506–507.

Robert A. Abair, "'Dare to Change': Revolution vs. Evolution," *APICS 37th International Conference Proceedings*, APICS, October 1994, pp. 40–41.

Chapter 12

1. Gerhard Plenert, "Don't Trust the Numbers," *Journal of Systems Management*, Vol. 40, No. 10, October 1989, pp. 34–37.

2. C. William Thomas, "Are Young Managers Less Ethical?" *New Accountant*, March 1991, pp. 3–10.

3. Derek C. Bok, "Social Responsibility in Future Worlds," *Computers and People*, September/October 1982, pp. 7–9.

4. Roger von Oech, *A Whack on the Side of the Head* (Stamford, CT: U.S. Games Systems, Inc., 1990), p. 51.

5. Thomas J. Zenisek, "Corporate Social Responsibility: A Conceptualization Based on Organizational Literature," *Academy of Management Review*, 1979, Vol. 4, No. 3, pp. 359–367.

Geary W. Sikich, "Environmental, Occupational, Health and Safety Regulations Threaten Many Corporations in the '90s: Reducing Environmental Vulnerability," *New Accountant*, March 1991, pp. 8–42.

6. Stephen R. Covey, *The 7 Habits of Highly Effective People* (New York: Simon and Schuster, 1989).

7. Stephen R. Covey, *Principle-Centered Leadership* (New York: Summit Books, 1991).

8. Joseph A. Petrick and Diana S. Furr, *Total Quality in Managing Human Resources* (Delray Beach, Fla.: St. Lucie Press, 1995).

9. William M. Boyst, "HRM—Key to the Integrated Management Revolution," *APICS 34th International Conference Proceedings*, APICS, October 1991, pp. 354–357.

10. E. F. Schuhmacher, *Small Is Beautiful*, (New York: Perennial Library, 1973).

11. Joseph A. Petrick and George E. Manning, "Ethics for Total Quality and Participation: Developing an Ethical Climate for Excellence," *Journal of Quality and Participation*, March 1990, pp. 84–90.

12. Don Adolphson, Matthew DeVries, and Heikki Rinne, "Rethinking Business: A Broader Sense of Responsibility," *Exchange*, Fall 1994, pp. 5–9.

Chapter 13

1. One additional book that focuses on time efficiency is Philip R. Thomas, *Time Warrior* (New York: McGraw-Hill Publishing Company, 1992).

Chapter 14

1. Robert R. Bell and Randall B. Duffy, "TRW-Thomasville Operations," field case, Tennessee Technological University, 1981.
2. Robert R. Bell and John M. Burnham, *Managing Productivity and Change* (Cincinnati, Ohio: South-Western Publishing Co., 1991), p. 13.
3. Jessica Lipnack and Jeffrey Stamps, "Crossing Boundaries with Teamnets."
4. Peter Mears and Frank Voehl, *Team Building* (Delray Beach, Fla.: St. Lucie Press, 1994), p. 11.
5. Some additional, valuable information on QC circles can be found in the Bell and Burnham book cited in note 2 of this chapter (pages 235ff.) and in the following article:

    Marilyn K. Hart, "Quality Control Training for Manufacturing," *Production and Inventory Management Journal*, Third Quarter 1991, pp. 35–40.
6. Charles G. Andrew, "Team Building: The Competitive Edge for the 90's," *APICS 34th International Conference Proceedings*, APICS, October 1991, pp. 406–410.
7. James R. Farmer, "Activity Based Accounting and Performance Measurement," *APICS 34th International Conference Proceedings*, APICS, October 1991, pp. 156–160.
8. Mel Nelson, "Team Building: Not the Way Daddy Taught Ya," *APICS 34th International Conference Proceedings*, APICS, October 1991, pp. 52–56.

    Gregory P. Shea and Richard A. Guzzo, "Group Effectiveness: What Really Matters?" *Sloan Management Review*, Spring 1987, pp. 25–31.
9. Blair R. Williams, "The Realities of Empowering Teams—A Case Study," *APICS 34th International Conference Proceedings*, APICS, October 1991, pp. 319–322.

Robert W. Hall "Empowerment: The 1990s Manufacturing Enterprise," APICS—*The Performance Advantage*, July 1991, pp. 26–58.

Also see "Making Employee Empowerment Work," by Steven R. Rayner, article III-2 of the Wallace book cited earlier.

10. See article III-3 in the Wallace book listed earlier, titled "Energizing Your Work-force with High Performance Teams," by Grace L. Pastiak.

The book by Mears and Voehl cited in note 4 of this chapter is very helpful.

St. Lucie Press in Delray Beach, Florida, has a whole series of books on "Teams" that is extremely helpful.

11. See "Work Improvement Programmes: Quality Control Circles Compared with Traditional Western Approaches," by Richard J. Schonberger, Chapter 8 in the Sheth and Exhghi book cited in References for Chapter 8.

12. *Commitment Plus*, Quality and Productivity Management Association, Vol. 6, No. 6, April 1991, pp. 1–4.

13. The Xerox information was taken from a presentation by Ted Allenbach, Human Resources, Xerox Corporation, in Guatemala in 1994 titled "Developing Quality Management and Self Managed Work Teams in a Service Organization."

Chapter 15

1. Stan Davis and Jim Botkin, "The Coming of Knowledge-Based Business," *Harvard Business Review*, September–October 1994, pp. 165–170.

2. Peter Lorange and Robert T. Nelson, "How to Recognize—and Avoid—Organizational Decline," *Sloan Management Review*, Spring 1987, pp. 41–48.

3. Edith Weiner, "Business in the 21st Century," *The Futurist*, March/April 1992, pp. 13–17.

4. The American Production and Inventory Control Society (APICS) (see Appendix 5.2) has developed an integrated enterprise manager certification program called CIRM (Certification in Resource Management) that includes similar components.

5. Christopher A. Bartlett and Sumantra Ghoshal, "Matrix Management: Not a Structure, a Frame of Mind," *Harvard Business Review*, July–August 1990, pp. 138–145.

6. William M. Boyst Jr., III, "HRM—Key to the Integrated Management Revolution," *APICS 34th International Conference Proceedings*, APICS, October 1991, pp. 354–357.

7. Taken from a presentation by Tom Tuttle titled "Reengineering Human Resources." The MCQP is located at the University of Maryland in College Park, Maryland.

8. Preston Blevins, "Enterprise Resource Planning (ERP)—An Executive Perspective," *APICS 37th International Conference Proceedings*, APICS, October 1994, pp. 138–142.

9. Gerhard Plenert, "An Overview of JIT," *International Journal of Advanced Manufacturing Technology*, 1993, Vol. 8, pp. 91–95.

   Gerhard Plenert, "Integration—Manufacturing's Hidden Buzzword of the 1990s," *International Productivity Journal*, 1991-III, Fall 1991, pp. 11–16.

   Gerhard Plenert, "Decision Support Systems in Manufacturing" *Malaysian Journal of Operations Research*, Vol. 1, No. 2, December 1992, pp. 37–43.

   Gerhard Plenert, "Manufacturing Management—A World Model," *Production Planning and Control*, 1992, Vol. 3, No. 1, pp. 93–98.

   Gerhard Plenert, "The Integration of Information Flow into an Expert System Using a Decision Support Systems Base," *4th International Conference on Systems Research Informatics and Cybernetics Proceedings*, August 1988.

   Gerhard Plenert, "Decision Support Systems," *Seventh International Congress of Cybernetics and Systems Proceedings*, September 1987, pp. 149–156.

10. Renee M. Gregorie and David M. Lehman, "Integrated Enterprise Management (IEM)," *APICS 37th International Conference Proceedings*, APICS, October 1994, pp. 155–159.

    Jay Proescher, "Leadership in the Integrated Enterprise," *APICS 37th International Conference Proceedings*, APICS, October 1994, pp. 181–184.

11. I recommend two books that deal extensively with performance measures:

    David W. Buker, Top Management's Guide to World Class Manufacturing, (Kansas City, Mo.: The Lowell Press, Inc., 1993).

    Gerhard J. Plenert, *The Plant Operations Handbook* (Homewood, Ill.: Business One Irwin, 1993).

12. Dave Savona, "America's Keiretsu," *International Business*, November 1994, pp. 46–63.

13. Details of these concepts can be found in Gerhard J. Plenert, *The Plant Operations Handbook* (Homewood, Ill.: Business One Irwin, 1993).

14. Ronald Nicol and Harold Sirkin, "Manufacturing Beyond the Factory Floor: The White Collar Factory," *Target*, Winter 1991, pp. 28–35.

15. As we mentioned earlier in this chapter, details about the functional processes in manufacturing can be found in the CIRM study aids put out by APICS. Some books listed earlier are also helpful:

Buker, *Top Management's Guide to World Class Manufacturing*; Wallace, *World Class Manufacturing*; Bell and Burnham, *Managing Productivity and Change*.

Here are a few more references that will help you:

Michael L. Dertouzos, Richard K. Lester, and Robert M. Solow, *Made In America: Regaining Productive Edge* (Cambridge, Mass.: The MIT Press, 1991).

William B. Miller and Vicki L. Schenk, *All I Need to Know About Manufacturing I Learned in Joe's Garage* (Walnut Creek, Calif.: Bayrock Press, 1993).

James P. Kelleher, "Total Quality Management in Production Planning and Control," *APICS 34th International Conference Proceedings*, October 1991, pp. 180–181.

Donald N. Frank, "Concurrent Engineering: A Building Block for TQM," *APICS 37th International Conference Proceedings*, October 1991, pp. 132–134.

Robert M. Grant, R. Kirshnan, Abraham B. Shani, and Ron Baer, "Appropriate Manufacturing Technology: A Strategic Approach," *Sloan Management Review*, Fall 1991, pp. 43–54.

Steven C. Wheelwright, and Robert H. Hayes, "Competing Through Manufacturing," *Harvard Business Review*, January–February 1985, pp. 99–109.

Robert H. Hayes and Steven C. Wheelwright, "Link Manufacturing Process and Product Life Cycles," *Harvard Business Review*, January–February 1979, pp. 133–140.

David F. Ross, "Aligning the Organization for World-Class Manufacturing," *Production and Inventory Management Journal*, Second Quarter 1991, pp. 22–26.

16. Thomas Beddingfield and Thomas Waechter, "Attaining World Class Manufacturing Status," *APICS 34th International Conference Proceedings*, October 1991, pp. 472–476.
17. Elaine J. Labach, "No Screws, No Glue, No Adjustments," *Target*, Winter 1989, pp. 23–30.

Chapter 16

1. Donna R. Neusch, "How Tellabs Took Aim at People Involvement," *Target*, Spring 1991, pp. 4–13.
2. Sana Siwolop and Amy Barrett, "Business and the Environment," *Financial World*, January 23, 1990, pp. 40–42.

Chapter 17

1. Gary Hamel and C. K. Prahalad, "Competing for the Future," *Harvard Business Review*, July–August 1994, pp. 122–128.
2. One book that I recommend that goes through this change of management styles is William Roth, *The Evolution of Management Theory* (Orefield, Pa.: Roth and Associates, 1993).
3. Bruce J. Boldrin, "Breaking the Time Barrier to Achieve World-Class Manufacturing," *APICS 37th International Conference Proceedings*, October 1994, pp. 662–664.
4. Terence T. Burton, "Manufacturing in the 21st Century," *APICS 34th International Conference Proceedings*, October 1991, pp. 454–457.
5. Jamshid Gharajedaghi, "Organizational Implications of Systems Thinking: Multidimensional Modular Design," *European Journal of Operations Research*, August 1984, pp. 155–166.

Chapter 18

1. L. O. "Larry" Smith, "Motivation! What Can I Do?" *APICS 34th International Conference Proceedings*, October 1991, pp. 379–381.
2. John S. W. Fargher, Jr., "Assessing Your Organization's Potential for Quality and Productivity Improvement," *APICS 34th International Conference Proceedings*, October 1991, pp. 375–378.

Chapter 19

1. Alex Taylor, "GM's $11,000,000,000 Turnaround," *Fortune*, October 17, 1994, pp. 54–74.

2. "31 Major Trends Shaping the Future of American Business," *The Public Pulse*, 1991, Vol. 2, pp. 1–8.

3. D. Keith Denton, "Lessons on Competitiveness: Motorola's Approach," *Production and Inventory Management Journal*, Third Quarter 1991, pp. 22–25.

   Sam Thomas, "Motorola's Six Steps to Six Sigma Quality," *APICS 34th International Conference Proceedings*, October 1991, pp. 166–169.

Chapter 1

Abair, Robert A. "'Dare to Change': Revolution vs. Evolution." *APICS 37th International Conference Proceedings* (October 30–November 4, 1994), 40–41.

Beer, Michael, Russell A. Eisenstat, and Bert Spector. "Why Change Programs Don't Produce Change." *Harvard Business Review* (November–December 1990): 158–166.

Covey, Stephen R. *Principle-Centered Leadership*. New York: Summit Books, 1991.

Covey, Stephen R. *The Seven Habits of Highly Effective People*. New York: Simon & Schuster, 1989.

Fox, R. E. "Theory of Constraints." *NAA Conference Proceedings*, September 1987.

Goldratt, Eliyahu M. *The Haystack Syndrome*. Croton-on-Hudson, N.Y.: North River Press Inc., 1990.

Goldratt, Eliyahu M. *What Is This Theory Called Theory of Constraints?* Croton-on-Hudson, N.Y.: North River Press Inc., 1990.

Goldratt, Eliyahu M., and Jeff Cox. *The Goal*. Croton-on-Hudson, N.Y.: North River Press Inc., 1986.

Goldratt, Eliyahu M., and Robert E. Fox. *The Race*. Croton-on-Hudson, N.Y.: North River Press Inc., 1986.

Hall, Robert W. *Attaining Manufacturing Excellence*. Homewood, Ill.: Dow-Jones-Irwin, 1987.

Joiner, Charles W., Jr. "Making the 'Z' Concept Work." *Sloan Management Review* (Spring 1985): 57–63.

Kanter, Rosabeth Moss. "Change: Where to Begin." *Harvard Business Review* (July–August 1991): 8–9.

Kotter, John P. "What Leaders Really Do." *Harvard Business Review* (May–June 1990): 103–111.

Machiavelli, Niccolo. *The Prince*. New York: Penguin Classics, 1984.

McGregor, Douglas. *The Human Side of the Enterprise*. New York: McGraw-Hill, 1985.

Nadler, Gerald, and Shozo Hibino. *Breakthrough Thinking*. Rocklin, Calif.: Prima Publishing & Communications, 1990.

Nadler, Gerald, Shozo Hibino, and John Farrell. *Creative Solution Finding*. Rocklin, Calif.: Prima Publishing & Communications, 1995.

Pascale, Richard Tanner, and Anthony G. Athos. *The Art of Japanese Management*. New York: Warner Books, 1982.

Peters, Tom and Nancy Austin. *A Passion for Excellence*. New York: Harper & Row, 1985.

Peters, Tom, and Robert Waterman. *In Search of Excellence: Lessons from America's Best Run Companies*, New York: Harper & Row, 1985.

Plenert, Gerhard J. "Bottleneck Scheduling for an Unlimited Number of Products." *Journal of Manufacturing Systems*, Vol. 9, No. 4: 324–331.

Plenert, Gerhard. *International Management and Production: Survival Techniques for Corporate America*. Blue Ridge Summit, Pa.: Tab Professional and Reference Books, 1990.

Plenert, Gerhard J., and Terry Lee. "Optimizing Theory of Constraints When New Product Alternatives Exist." *Production and Inventory Management Journal* (Third Quarter 1993), Vol. 34, No. 3: 51–57.

Schaffer, Robert H., and Harvey A. Thomson. "Successful Change Programs Begin with Results." *Harvard Business Review* (January–February 1992): 80–89.

Senge, Peter M. "The Leader's New Work: Building Learning Organizations." *Sloan Management Review* (Fall 1990): 7–23.

Shingo, Shigeo. *Study of the Toyota Production System from the Industrial Engineering Viewpoint*. Tokyo: Japanese Management Association, 1981.

Stimson, Judith A. "Unleashing Creative Thinking for Change." *APICS 37th International Conference Proceedings* (October 30–November 4, 1994): 665–666.

Tichy, Noel, and Ram Charan. "Speed, Simplicity, Self-Confidence: An Interview with Jack Welch." *Harvard Business Review* (September–October 1989): 112–120.

Tonkin, Lea. "Workshop Report: Canadian Region—Building on the Past at Tridon-Oakdale." *Target* (Summer 1990): 34–37.

von Oech, Roger. *A Kick in the Seat of the Pants*. New York: Harper & Row, 1986.

von Oech, Roger. *A Whack on the Side of the Head*. New York: Warner Books, 1990.

Wantuck, Kenneth A. *Just in Time for America*. Milwaukee, Wis.: The Forum, Ltd., 1989.

Chapter 2

Bell, Robert R., and John M. Burnham. *Managing Productivity and Change*. Cincinnati, Ohio: South-Western Publishing Co., 1991, pp. 10–11.

Boyst, William M., Jr. III. "HRM—Key to the Integrated Management Revolution." *APICS 34th International Conference Proceedings* (1991): 354–357.

Covey, Stephen R. *Principle-Centered Leadership*. New York: Summit Books, 1991.

Covey, Stephen R. *The Seven Habits of Highly Effective People*. New York: Simon & Schuster, 1989.

Howard, Robert. "Values Make the Company: An Interview with Robert Haas." *Harvard Business Review* (September–October 1990): 133–144.

Mojonnier, Timothy M. "Top Management's Role in Fostering and Managing Positive Organizational Change." *APICS 37th International Conference Proceedings* (October 1994): 49–51.

Nadler, Gerald, and Shozo Hibino. *Breakthrough Thinking*. Rocklin, Calif.: Prima Publishing & Communications, 1995.

Nadler, Gerald, Shozo Hibino, and John Farrell. *Creative Solution Finding*. Rocklin, Calif.: Prima Publishing & Communications, 1995.

Plenert, Gerhard. *International Management and Production: Survival Techniques for Corporate America*. Blue Ridge Summit, Pa.: Tab Professional and Reference Books, 1990.

Powell, Cash, Jr. "Empowerment, The Stake in the Ground for ABS." *Target* (January/February 1992): 7–17.

von Oech, Roger. *A Kick in the Seat of the Pants*. New York: Harper & Row, 1986.

von Oech, Roger. *A Whack on the Side of the Head*. New York: Warner Books, 1990.

Wallace, Thomas F. *World Class Manufacturing*. Essex Junction, Vt.: OMNEO, 1994.

Chapter 3

Mapes, James J. "Foresight First." *Sky Magazine* (September 1991): 96–105.

Plenert, Gerhard. *The Plant Operations Handbook*. Homewood, Ill.: Business One Irwin, 1993.

Prahalad, C. K., and Gary Hamel. "The Core Competence of the Corporation." *Harvard Business Review* (May–June 1990): 79–91.

Schaffer, Robert H., and Harvey A. Thomson. "Successful Change Programs Begin with Results." *Harvard Business Review* (January–February 1992): 80–89.

Toffler, Alvin. *Future Shock*. New York: Random House Publishers, 1970.

"The Vision Thing." *The Economist* (November 9, 1991): 81.

Chapter 4

Adler, Paul S., D. William McDonald, and Fred McDonald. "Strategic Management of Technical Functions." *Sloan Management Review* (Winter 1992): 19–37.

Burnham, John B. "Systematic Improvements in Physical Distribution or 'Why We Just Can't Do It Like We Used To?' " *APICS 34th International Conference Proceedings* (October 1991): 305–310.

Burton, Terence T. "Manufacturing in the 21st Century." *APICS 34th International Conference Proceedings* (October 1991): 454–457.

Garvin, David A. *Operations Strategy*. Englewood Cliffs, N.J.: Prentice Hall, 1992.

Gregoire, Renee M., and Patrick J. Delaney. "Manufacturing Strategy: The Key to Competitive Advantage." *APICS 33rd International Conference Proceedings* (October 1990): 9–13.

Hall, Robert W., and Jinichiro Nakane. "Developing Flexibility for Excellence in Manufacturing: Summary Results of a Japanese-American Study." *Target*, Vol. 4, No. 2 (Summer 1988): 18.

Hill, Terry. *Manufacturing Strategy: Text and Cases*. Burr Ridge, Ill.: Irwin, 1994.

Kilian, Cecelia S. *The World of W. Edwards Deming*. Knoxville, Tenn.: SPC Press, Inc., 1992.

Kotter, John P., L. A. Schlesinger, and V. Sathe. *Organization*. Homewood, Ill.: Irwin, 1986 (p. 360).

Landvater, Darryl, Steve Souza, and Thomas Wallace. "The ABCD Checklist for Manufacturing Excellence: An Integrated Strategic/Operational Measurement Tool." *APICS 34th International Conference Proceedings* (October 1991): 458–459.

Lowenthal, Jeffrey N. *Reengineering the Organization*. Milwaukee, Wis.: ASQC Quality Press, 1994 (Chapters 1, 2, 4, and 6).

Mojonnier, Timothy M. "Top Management's Role in Fostering and Managing Positive Organizational Change." *APICS 37th International Conference Proceedings* (October 1994): 49–51.

Nicoll, Andrew D. "Integrating Logistics Strategies." *APICS 37th International Conference Proceedings* (October 1994): 590–594.

Plenert, Gerhard. *The Plant Operations Handbook.* Homewood, Ill.: Business One Irwin, 1993.

Porter, Michael. *Competitive Advantage.* Toronto: Free Press, 1985.

Porter, Michael. "From Competitive Advantage to Corporate Strategy." *Harvard Business Review* (May–June 1987): 43–59.

Porter, Michael. *Competitive Strategy.* Toronto: Free Press, 1980.

Sheth, Jagdish, and Golpira Eshghi. *Global Operations Perspectives.* Cincinnati, Ohio: South-Western Publishing Co., 1989.

Skinner, Wickham. "The Focused Factory." *Harvard Business Review* (May–June 1974): 113–121.

Wallace, Thomas F. *World Class Manufacturing.* Essex Junction, Vt.: Oliver Wight Publications, 1994 (Part I).

Walters, Michael F. "Manufacturing Excellence in the 1990s." *APICS 34th International Conference Proceedings* (October 1991): 425–428.

Wheelwright, Steven C., and Robert D. Hayes. "Competing Through Manufacturing. *Harvard Business Review* (January–February 1985): 99–109.

Chapter 5

Bell, Robert R., and John M. Burnham. *Managing Productivity and Change.* Cincinnati, Ohio: South-Western Publishing Co., 1991.

Crosby, Philip B. *Quality Is Free.* New York: McGraw-Hill, 1979.

Crosby, Philip B. *Quality without Tears.* New York: McGraw-Hill, 1984.

Deming, W. Edwards. "Improvement of Quality and Productivity through Action by Management." *National Productivity Review*, Vol. 1, No. 1 (Winter 1981–82): 12–22.

Drucker, Peter F. "The New Productivity Challenge." *Harvard Business Review* (November–December 1991): 69–79.

Gitlow, Howard S., and Shelly J. Gitlow. *The Deming Guide to Quality and Competitive Position.* Englewood Cliffs, N.J.: Prentice-Hall, 1987.

Greising, David. "Making Quality Pay—How Companies Are Rethinking the Management Buzzword of the 1980's." *Business Week* (August 8, 1994): 54–59.

Grove, Andrew S. *High Output Management.* New York: Vintage Books, 1983.

Juran, J. M. *Juran's Quality Control Handbook*. ASQC, Milwaukee, Wis., 1988.

Kanholm, Jack. *ISO 9000 Explained—65 Requirements Checklist and Compliance Guide*. Delray Beach, Fla.: St. Lucie Press, 1994.

National Productivity Board of Singapore. "Singapore, The Guiding Light of Productivity." *Productivity SA.* (September/October 1994): 11–13.

Plenert, Gerhard. *The Plant Operations Handbook*. Homewood, Ill.: Business One Irwin, 1993.

QPMA. "Warner-Lambert Changes Focus and Comes Up a Big Winner." *Commitment Plus*. Quality and Productivity Management Association, Vol. 6, No. 7 (May 1991).

Shingo, Shigeo. *Non-Stock Production and the Shingo System for Continuous Improvement*. Tokyo: Japan Management Association, 1988.

Shingo, Shigeo. *Study of the Toyota Production System from the Industrial Engineering Viewpoint*. Tokyo: Japanese Management Association, 1981.

Skinner, Wickham. "The Productivity Paradox." *Harvard Business Review* (July–August 1986): 55–59.

Voehl, Frank, Peter Jackson, and David Ashton. *ISO 9000—An Implementation Guide for Small to Mid-Sized Businesses*. Delray Beach, Fla.: St. Lucie Press, 1994.

Walton, Mary. *Fourteen Points and Seven Deadly Diseases from the Deming Management Method*. New York: Perigee Books, 1986.

Chapter 6

Albin, John T. "Competing in a Global Market." *APICS—The Performance Advantage* (January 1992): 29–32.

Albin, John T. "Competing in a Global Market." *APICS 37th International Conference Proceedings* (November, 1994): 244–248.

Bartlett, Christopher A., and Sumantra Ghoshal. "Managing Across Borders: New Strategic Requirements." *Sloan Management Review* (Summer 1987): 7–17.

Blumberg, Donald F. "Improving Productivity in Service Operations on an International Basis. *National Productivity Review* (Spring 1991): 167–179.

"The Boundaries of Business: Commentaries from the Experts." *Harvard Business Review* (July–August 1991): 127–140.

Burton, Terence T. "Manufacturing in the 21st Century." *APICS 34th International Conference Proceedings* (October 1991): 454–457.

Chilton, Kenneth. "Changing Structures and Strategies: Survey of American Manufacturing Executives." St. Louis, Mo.: Center for the Study of American Business, Washington University, Working Paper 151 (September 1993).

Daniels, John D., and Lee H. Radebaugh. *International Business—Environments and Operations*. Reading, Mass.: Addison-Wesley Publishing Company, 1994.

Hamel, Gary, Yves L. Doz, and C. K. Prahalad. "Collaborate with Your Competitors—and Win." *Harvard Business Review* (January–February 1989): 133–139.

Howell, Robert A., and Stephen R. Soucy. "Determining the Real Costs of Doing Business in a Global Market." *National Productivity Review* (Spring 1991): 157–165.

Kanter, Rosabeth Moss. "Transcending Business Boundaries: 12,000 World Managers View Change." *Harvard Business Review* (May–June 1991): 151–164.

Kogut, Bruce. "Designing Global Strategies: Comparative and Competitive Value-Added Chains." *Sloan Management Review* (Summer 1995): 15–28.

Landau, Nilly. "Managing Exotic Risks." *International Business* (May 1994): 62–66.

Ohmae, Kenichi. "The Global Logic of Strategic Alliances." *Harvard Business Review* (March–April 1989): 143–154.

Ohmae, Kenichi. "Managing in a Borderless World." *Harvard Business Review* (May–June 1989): 152–161.

Peters, Andru M. "The Pacific Rim Nations' Business Strategy for the Next 10 Years." *APICS 37th International Conference Proceedings* (November 1994): 226–231.

Plenert, Gerhard, "The Development of a Production System in Mexico." *Interfaces*, Vol. 20, No. 3 (May–June 1990): 14–23.

Plenert, Gerhard. "International Industrial Management." *Organizational Development Journal*, Vol. 7, No. 1 (Spring 1989): 25–28.

Plenert, Gerhard. *International Management and Production: Survival Techniques for Corporate America*. Blue Ridge Summit, Pa.: TAB Professional and Reference Books, 1990.

Plenert, Gerhard. "Plant Relocation: How Decisions Are Made Today." *Industry Forum* (March 1994): 1–3.

Plenert, Gerhard. "Production Considerations for Developing Countries." *International Journal of Management* (December 1988): 358–364.

Plenert, Gerhard. "Productivity in a Developing Country Factory."
  APICS 37th International Conference Proceedings (November 1994):
  712–715.

Plenert, Gerhard. "Technology Transfer—A Developing Country Perspective." *IAMOT Newsletter* (September 1994): 5–6.

Quelch, John A., and Edward J. Hoff. "Customizing Global Marketing."
  Harvard Business Review (May–June 1986): 59–68.

Reich, Robert B. "Who Is Them?" *Harvard Business Review* (March–
  April 1991): 77–88.

Reid, Peter C. *Well-Made in America.* New York: McGraw-Hill, 1990.

Roper Organization, Inc. *The Public Pulse,* Vol. 2, No. 1 (1991): 1–8.

Savona, Dave. "The Invisible Partner." *International Business* (November 1994): 64–68.

Savona, Dave. "World Commerce." *International Business* (August
  1994): 42.

Savona, Dave. "World Commerce." *International Business* (September
  1994): 38.

Savona, Dave. "World Commerce." *International Business* (November
  1994): 18.

Schumacher, E. F. *Small Is Beautiful: Economics as if People Mattered.*
  New York: Harper Perennial, 1989.

Sheth, Jagdish, and Golpira Eshghi. *Global Operations Perspectives.*
  Cincinnati, Ohio: South-Western Publishing Co., 1989.

Stoddard, Jan, and Ramona Memmott. "Going Global by Working
  Together." *APICS 37th International Conference Proceedings* (November 1994): 709–711.

Suri, Rajan, Jerry L. Sanders, P. Chandrasekhar Rao, and Ashoka Mody.
  "Impact of Manufacturing Practices on the Global Bicycle Industry." *Manufacturing Review* (March 1993): 14–24.

Yip, George S. "Global Strategy . . . In a World of Nations?" *Sloan Management Review* (Fall 1989): 29–41.

Chapter 7

Adler, Paul S., Henry E. Riggs, and Steven C. Wheelwright. "Product
  Development Know-How: Trading Tactics for Strategy." *Sloan Management Review* (Fall 1989): 7–17.

Arenberg, Thomas E. "Engineering Productivity—JIT in the Product
  Delivery Function." *APICS 34th International Conference Proceedings*
  (October 1991): 271–273.

Bell, Robert R., and John M. Burnham. *Managing Productivity and Change.* Cincinnati, Ohio: South-Western Publishing Co., 1991 (p. 49).

Belt, Bill, Roger Brooks, and Rick Burris. "Management Technologies for World-Class Manufacturing." *APICS 37th International Conference Proceedings* (October 1994): 143–147.

Betz, Frederick. *Strategic Technology Management.* New York: McGraw-Hill Engineering and Technology Management Series, 1993.

Bodinson, Glenn. "Time-based Competition Is the Competitive Advantage of the 1990s." *APICS—The Performance Advantage* (December 1991): 27–31.

Camp, Robert C. *Business Process Benchmarking.* Homewood, Ill.: Irwin, 1994.

Erickson, Tamara J., John F. Magee, Philip A. Roussel, and Kamal N. Saad. "Managing Technology as a Business Strategy." *Sloan Management Review* (Spring 1990): 73–78.

Ford, Henry. *Today and Tomorrow.* Cambridge, Mass.: Productivity Press, 1988.

Henrickson, Dave. "Product Design as a Team Sport." *Target* (Spring 1990): 4–12.

Lewis, William W., and Lawrence H. Linden. "A New Mission for Corporate Technology." *Sloan Management Review* (Summer 1990): 57–67.

March, Artemis. "Meeting Time and Cost Targets: The IBM Proprinter." *Target* (Special 1991): 18–24.

Mody, Ashoka, Rajan Suri, and Jerry Sanders. "Keeping Pace With Change: Organizational and Technological Imperatives." *World Development,* Vol. 20, No. 12 (1992): 1797–1816.

Peters, Tom. "Time-Obsessed Competition." *Management Review* (September 1990): 16–20.

Plenert, Gerhard. "Advanced Technology and Integrated Systems." *Logistik 92 Conference Proceedings* (June 1992), Singapore.

Plenert, Gerhard. "'Free' PM Technology." *PMI (Project Management Institute) Seminar/Symposium Proceedings* (October 1987): 433–435.

Plenert, Gerhard. "Getting the Best of Technology Transfer." *Production and Inventory Management Review,* Vol. 5, No. 3 (March 1985): 58–59.

Plenert, Gerhard. "Production Technology Transfer: A US-Japan Example." *1992 International Symposium on Pacific Asian Business Proceedings* (January, 1992): 114–116.

Roberts, Edward B., and Charles A. Berry. "Entering New Businesses: Selecting Strategies for Success." *Sloan Management Review* (Spring 1985): 3–17.

Seideman, Tony. "Multimedia Marketing." *International Business* (August 1994): 26–28.

"Survey—Manufacturing Technology: On the Cutting Edge." *The Economist* (March 5, 1994): 3–19.

Taylor, Frederick Winslow. *The Principles of Scientific Management*. New York: W. W. Norton and Company, 1967.

Thomas, Philip R. *Competitiveness Through Cycle Time: An Overview of CEOs*. New York: McGraw-Hill Publishing Co., 1990.

Vesey, Joseph T. "The New Competitors: They Think in Terms of 'Speed-to-Market'." *APICS 34th International Conference Proceedings* (October 1991): 274–277.

Wallace, Thomas F. *World Class Manufacturing*. Essex Junction, Vt.: Oliver Wight Publications, Inc., 1994.

Wheelwright, Steven C. "A Rubber Mallet and a Two-by-Four: The Concept of Development Strategy." *Target* (Fall 1991): 4–16.

Chapter 8

Abair, Robert A. "Super Measurements: The Key to World-Class Manufacturing." *APICS 34th International Conference Proceedings* (October 1991): 113–115.

Baker, Tom, and Gerry Cleaves. "New Computer Solutions: World-Class Performance Through Improved Planning and Scheduling Integration." *APICS—The Performance Advantage* (October 1991): 28–31.

Barber, Norman F. "Creating Organizational Integration." *APICS 33rd International Conference Proceedings* (October 1990): 40–44.

Bell, Robert R., and John M. Burnham. *Managing Productivity and Change*. Cincinnati, Ohio: South-Western Publishing Co., 1991.

Boyst, William M. Jr. III. "HRM—Key to the Integrated Management Revolution." *APICS 34th International Conference Proceedings* (October 1991): 107–112.

Brown, J. Thomas. "Measuring Performance for Strategic Improvement." *APICS 34th International Conference Proceedings* (October 1991): 107–112.

Cooper, Robin. "You Need a New Cost System When . . ." *Harvard Business Review* (January–February 1989): 77–82.

Eccles, Robert G. "The Performance Measurement Manifesto." *Harvard Business Review* (January–February 1991): 131–137.

Henson, Holly E. "Performance Measurement in the New Manufacturing Environment." *APICS 34th International Conference Proceedings* (October 1991): 126–128.

Lowenthal, Jeffrey N. *Reengineering the Organization: A Step by Step Approach to Corporate Revitalization.* Milwaukee: Wis.: ASQC Quality Press, 1994.

Maslow, Abraham H. "The Theory of Human Motivation." *Psychological Review*, Vol. 50 (1943): 370–396.

Monnin, Michelle, Roger Miller, and Brian Schaenzer. "Are Your Goals and Measurements in Line with Your Time-Based Competition Philosophy?" *APICS 37th International Conference Proceedings* (October 1994): E1–E3.

Plenert, Gerhard, "Expanding the Value-Added Cost Component." Advanced Manufacturing Technology (October 1989): 86–94.

Plenert, Gerhard. "Integration—Manufacturing's Hidden Buzzword of the 1990s." *International Productivity Journal* 1991-III (Fall 1991): 11–16.

Plenert, Gerhard. *The Plant Operations Handbook.* Homewood, Ill.: Business One Irwin Publishing, 1993.

Plenert, Gerhard. "Solving Indefinable Problems With Backward Utopian Iteration." With R. W. Kaiser. *Kybernetes*, Vol. 19, No. 4 (1990): 59–62.

Plenert, Gerhard. "Total Integration of Accounting and Manufacturing Information." *APICS 34th International Conference Proceedings* (October 1991): 366–367.

Sandras, William A. "Integration: Productivity Thrust of the 1990s." *APICS 34th International Conference Proceedings* (October 1991): 400–402.

Savage, William G. "Implementing an Integrated System: Restructuring the Business Not Just Automating It." *APICS 34th International Conference Proceedings* (October 1991): 382–386.

Sheth, Jagdish, and Golpira Eshghi. *Global Operations Perspectives.* Cincinnati, Ohio: South-Western Publishing Co., 1989.

Tarr, James D. "Developing Performance Measurement Systems That Support Continuous Improvement Goals." *APICS 37th International Conference Proceedings* (October 1994): 416–420.

Tincher, Michael G. "World-Class Performance Measurements—How to Get Started." *APICS 37th International Conference Proceedings* (October 1994): 424–428.

Uhlemann, William R. "Management Integration for Your Focused Factories." *APICS 34th International Conference Proceedings* (October 1991): 207–210.

U.S. Department of Labor. *Road to High-Performance Workplaces: A Guide to Better Jobs and Better Business Results—1994.* U.S. Department of Labor—Office of the American Workplace, 1994.

Wallace, Thomas F. *World Class Manufacturing.* Essex Junction, Vt.: Omneo, An Imprint of Oliver Wight Publications, Inc., 1994.

Wisner, Joel D., and Stanley E. Fawcett. "Linking Firm Strategy to Operation Decisions Through Performance Measurement." *Production and Inventory Management Journal* (Third Quarter 1991): 5–11.

Chapter 9

Dertouzos, Michael L., Richard K. Lester, and Robert M. Solow. *Made in America,* Cambridge, Mass.: The MIT Press, 1991.

Ishikawa, Kaoru. *Introduction to Quality Control.* Tokyo: 3A Corporation, 1990.

Olsen, Robert E. "Developing a Manufacturing Strategy for the 1990s." *APICS 34th International Conference Proceedings* (October 1991): 403–405.

Plenert, Gerhard. "Megatrend or Megadisaster." *OR/MS Today* (December 1994): 24–26.

Plenert, Gerhard. "Successful Factory Management Systems." *Produktiviti,* Bil. 42 (Jul/Ogos 1992): 2–6.

Shays, E. Michael. "Cleaning Up Waste in Decision Making—Breakthrough Thinking: A New Way of Attacking Problems Can Produce Startling Results." *Business Quarterly,* Vol. 56, No. 3 (Winter 1992): 43–45.

Stalk, G., P. Evans, and L. E. Shulman. "Competing on Capabilities: The New Rules of Corporate Strategy." *Harvard Business Review* (March–April 1992): 57–69.

Taylor, Frederick Winslow. *The Principles of Scientific Management.* New York: W. W. Norton & Company, Inc., 1967.

Wassweiler, William. "The Factory With a Future." *APICS—The Performance Advantage* (September 1991): 26–28.

Chapter 10

Ashapa, M. R. "Mike." "The State of Manufacturing Education in the United States." *APICS 34th International Conference Proceedings* (October 1991): 27–29.

DiPrima, Michael R. "Education for the World Class Manufacturing/ JIT Organization." *APICS 34th International Conference Proceedings* (October 1991): 16–19.

Hutchins, Henry Alex. "Measuring the Results of Training: A Case Study." *APICS 34th International Conference Proceedings* (October 1991): 37–40.

Lamfers, Patricia. "Education: The Future of Our Competitiveness." *APICS 34th International Conference Proceedings.* (October 1991): 13–15.

Senge, Peter M. "The Leader's New Work: Building Learning Organizations." *Sloan Management Review* (Fall 1990): 7–23.

Steiger, Larry Dean. "The Learning Organization." *APICS 34th International Conference Proceedings* (October 1991): 188–192.

Ulrich, Robert A., and A. Young. "A Shared Mindset." *Personnel Administrator* (March 1989): 45.

Chapter 11

Abair, Robert A. " 'Dare to Change': Revolution vs. Evolution." *APICS 37th International Conference Proceedings* (October 1994): 40–41.

Allen, Dan J. "Work Reengineering and Total Quality Management: Synergy or Conflict." *APICS 37th International Conference Proceedings* (October 1994): 506–507.

AT&T Bell Laboratories. *AT&T Process Quality Management & Improvement Guidelines.* Publication Center of AT&T Bell Laboratories, 1989.

AT&T Bell Laboratories. *AT&T's Total Quality Approach.* Publication Center of AT&T Bell Laboratories, 1992.

Bao, Quang, and E. B. Baatz. "How Solectron Finally Got In Touch With Its Workers." *Electronic Business* (October 7, 1991): 47–48.

Boyer, John E. "Reengineering Office Processes." *APICS 37th Annual International Conference Proceedings* (October 1994): 522–526.

Costin, Harry. *Readings in Total Quality Management.* Fort Worth, Tex.: The Dryden Press, 1994.

Cypress, Harold L. "Re-engineering." *OR/MS Today* (February 1994): 18–29.

Gibson, Cyrus F., and R. L. Nolan. "Managing the Four Stages of EDP Growth." *Harvard Business Review* (January–February 1974): 76.

Grant, Linda. "Six Companies That Are Winning The Race." *Los Angeles Times,* January 17, 1993.

Hammer, M. "Reengineering Work: Don't Automate, Obliterate." *Harvard Business Review* (July–August 1990): 104–112.

Hammer, M., and J. Champy. "The Promise of Reengineering." *Fortune* (May 3, 1993): 94–97.

Hammer, M., and J. Champy. *Reengineering the Corporation*. New York: Harper Business, 1993.

Harbour, Jerry L. *The Process Reengineering Workbook: Practical Steps to Working Faster and Smarter Through Process Improvement*. White Plains, N.Y.: Quality Resources, 1994.

Henrickson, Dave. "Product Design as a Team Sport." *Target* (Spring 1990): 4–12.

Jason, R. "How Reengineering Transforms Organizations to Satisfy Customers." *National Productivity Review* (Winter 1992): 45–53.

Kobu, Bulent, and Frank Greenwood. "Continuous Improvement in a Competitive Global Economy." *Production and Inventory Management* (Fourth Quarter 1991): 58–63.

Lowenthal, Jeffrey N. *Reengineering the Organization: A Step-by-Step Approach to Corporate Revitalization*. Milwaukee, Wis.: ASQC Quality Press, 1994.

Marks, Peter. *Process Reengineeering and the New Manufacturing Enterprise Wheel: 15 Processes for Competitive Advantage*. Dearborn, Mich.: CASA/SME Technical Forum, Society of Manufacturing Engineers (SME), 1994.

Melnyk, Steven A., and William R. Wassweiler. "Business Process Reengineering: Understanding the Process, Responding to the Right Needs." *APICS 37th Annual International Conference Proceedings* (October 1994): 115–120.

Miller, George. "Reengineering: 40 U$seful Hints." *APICS 37th Annual International Conference Proceedings* (October 1994): 22–26.

Nadler, Gerald, and Shozo Hibino. *Breakthrough Thinking*. Rocklin, Calif.: Prima Publishing and Communications, 1990.

Nadler, Gerald, Shozo Hibino, and John Farrell. *Creative Solution Finding*. Rocklin, Calif.: Prima Publishing and Communications, 1995.

Omachonu, Vincent K. *Principles of Total Quality*. Delray Beach, Fla.: St. Lucie Press, 1994.

Plenert, Gerhard. "Process Re-Engineering: The Latest Fad Toward Failure." *APICS—The Performance Advantage* (June 1994): 22–24.

Plenert, Gerhard, and Shozo Hibino. "The T-Model: A Systematic Model for Change." *National Productivity Review*, Vol. 13, No. 4 (Autumn 1994): 543–549.

Ramalingam, P. Rama. "Making TQM Pay Off: The Solectron Experience." *APICS 37th International Conference Proceedings* (November 1994): 472–476.

Ravikumar, Ravi. "Business Process Reengineering—Making the Transition." *APICS 37th Annual International Conference Proceedings* (October 1994): 17–21.

Ross, Joel E. *Total Quality Management: Text, Cases, and Readings.* Delray Beach, Fla.: St. Lucie Press, 1993.

"Solectron Corp." *Business America* (October 21, 1991): 5–6.

Stevens, Mark. "Reengineering the Manufacturing Company: 'New Fad or For Real'." *APICS 37th Annual International Conference Proceedings* (October 1994): 527–530.

Stocker, Gregg D. "Quality Functional Deployment: Listening to the Voice of the Customer." *APICS 34th International Conference Proceedings* (October 1991): 258–262.

Szendel, Timothy N., and Walter Tighe. "Kaizen American-Style, Continuous Improvement in Action." *APICS 37th International Conference Proceedings* (October 1994): 496–497.

Chapter 12

Adolphson, Don, Matthew DeVries, and Heikki Rinne. "Rethinking Business: A Broader Sense of Responsibility." *Exchange* (Fall 1994): 5–9.

Bok, Derek C. "Social Responsibility in Future Worlds." *Computers and People* (September/October 1982): 7–9.

Boyst, William M. "HRM—Key to the Integrated Management Revolution." *APICS 34th International Conference Proceedings* (October 1991): 354–357.

Covey, Stephen R. *Principle-Centered Leadership.* New York: Summit Books, 1991.

Covey, Stephen R. *The 7 Habits of Highly Effective People.* New York: Simon and Schuster, 1989.

Petrick, Joseph A., and Diana S. Furr. *Total Quality in Managing Human Resources,* Delray Beach, Fla.: St. Lucie Press, 1995.

Petrick, Joseph A., and George E. Manning. "Ethics for Total Quality and Participation: Developing an Ethical Climate for Excellence." *Journal of Quality and Participation TQM* (March 1990): 84–90.

Plenert, Gerhard. "Don't Trust the Numbers." *Journal of Systems Management,* Vol. 40, No. 10 (October 1989): 34–37.

Schuhmacher, E. F. *Small Is Beautiful*. New York: Perennial Library, 1973.

Sikich, Geary W. "Environmental, Occupational, Health and Safety Regulations Threaten Many Corporations in the '90s: Reducing Environmental Vulnerability." *New Accountant* (March 1991): 8–42.

Thomas, C. William. "Are Young Managers Less Ethical?" *New Accountant* (March 1991): 3–10.

von Oech, Roger. *A Whack on the Side of the Head*. Stamford, Conn.: U.S. Games Systems, Inc., 1990 (p. 51).

Zenisek, Thomas J. "Corporate Social Responsibility: A Conceptualization Based on Organizational Literature." *Academy of Management Review*, Vol. 4, No. 3 (1979): 359–367.

Chapter 13

Thomas, Philip R. *Time Warrior*. New York: McGraw-Hill Publishing Co., 1992.

Chapter 14

Andrew, Charles G. "Team Building: The Competitive Edge for the 90's." *APICS 34th International Conference Proceedings* (October 1991): 406–410.

Bell, Robert R., and John M. Burnham. *Managing Productivity and Change*. Cincinnati, Ohio: South-Western Publishing Co., 1991 (p. 13).

Farmer, James R. "Activity Based Accounting and Performance Measurement." *APICS 34th International Conference Proceedings* (October 1991): 156–160.

Hall, Robert W. "Empowerment: The 1990s Manufacturing Enterprise." *APICS—The Performance Advantage* (July 1991): 26–58.

Hart, Marilyn K. "Quality Control Training for Manufacturing." *Production and Inventory Management Journal* (Third Quarter 1991): 35–40.

Mears, Peter, and Frank Voehl. *Team Building*. Delray Beach, Fla.: St. Lucie Press, 1994, (p. 11).

Williams, Blair R. "The Realities of Empowering Teams—A Case Study." *APICS 34th International Conference Proceedings* (October 1991): 319–322.

Chapter 15

Bartlett, Christopher A., and Sumantra Ghoshal. "Matrix Management: Not a Structure, a Frame of Mind." *Harvard Business Review* (July–August 1990): 138–145.

Beddingfield, Thomas, and Thomas Waechter. "Attaining World Class Manufacturing Status." *APICS 34th International Conference Proceedings* (October 1991): 472–476.

Blevins, Preston. "Enterprise Resource Planning (ERP)—An Executive Perspective." *APICS 37th International Conference Proceedings* (October 1994): 138–142.

Boyst, William M. Jr. III. "HRM—Key to the Integrated Management Revolution." *APICS 34th International Conference Proceedings* (October 1991): 354–357.

Buker, David W. *Top Management's Guide to World Class Manufacturing*. Kansas City, Mo.: The Lowell Press, Inc., 1993.

Davis, Stan and Jim Botkin. "The Coming of Knowledge-Based Business." *Harvard Business Review* (September–October 1994): 165–170.

Dertouzos, Michael L., Richard K. Lester, and Robert M. Solow. *Made in America: Regaining Productive Edge*. Cambridge, Mass.: The MIT Press, 1991.

Frank, Donald N. "Concurrent Engineering: A Building Block for TQM." *APICS 37th International Conference Proceedings* (October 1991): 132–134.

Grant, Robert M., R. Kirshnan, Abraham B. Shani, and Ron Baer. "Appropriate Manufacturing Technology: A Strategic Approach." *Sloan Management Review* (Fall 1991): 43–54.

Gregorie, Renee M., and David M. Lehman. "Integrated Enterprise Management (IEM)." *APICS 37th International Conference Proceedings* (October 1994): 155–159.

Hayes, Robert H., and Steven C. Wheelwright. "Link Manufacturing Process and Product Life Cycles." *Harvard Business Review* (January–February 1979): 133–140.

Kelleher, James P. "Total Quality Management in Production Planning and Control." *APICS 34th International Conference Proceedings* (October 1991): 180–181.

Labach, Elaine J. "No Screws, No Glue, No Adjustments." *Target* (Winter 1989): 23–30.

Lorange, Peter, and Robert T. Nelson "How to Recognize—and Avoid—Organizational Decline." *Sloan Management Review* (Spring 1987): 41–48.

Miller, William B., and Vicki L. Schenk. *All I Need To Know About Manufacturing I Learned In Joe's Garage*. Walnut Creek, Calif.: Bayrock Press, 1993.

Nicol, Ronald, and Harold Sirkin. "Manufacturing Beyond the Factory Floor: The White Collar Factor." *Target* (Winter 1991): 28–35.

Plenert, Gerhard. "Decision Support Systems." *Seventh International Congress of Cybernetics and Systems Proceedings* (September 1987): 149–156.

Plenert, Gerhard. "Decision Support Systems in Manufacturing." *Malaysian Journal of Operations Research*, Vol. 1, No. 2 (December 1992): 37–43.

Plenert, Gerhard. "Integration—Manufacturing's Hidden Buzzword of the 1990s." *International Productivity Journal*, 1991-III (Fall 1991): 11–16.

Plenert, Gerhard. "The Integration of Information Flow Into an Expert System Using a Decision Support Systems Base." *4th International Conference on Systems Research Informatics and Cybernetics Proceedings* (August, 1988).

Plenert, Gerhard. "Manufacturing Management—A World Model." *Production Planning and Control*, Vol. 3, No. 1(1992): 93–98.

Plenert, Gerhard. "An Overview of JIT." *International Journal of Advanced Manufacturing Technology*, Vol. 8 (1993): 91–95

Plenert, Gerhard J. *The Plant Operations Handbook*. Homewood, Ill.: Business One Irwin, 1993.

Proescher, Jay. "Leadership in the Integrated Enterprise." *APICS 37th International Conference Proceedings* (October 1994): 181–184.

Ross, David F. "Aligning The Organization for World-Class Manufacturing." *Production and Inventory Management Journal* (Second Quarter 1991): 22–26.

Savona, Dave. "America's Keiretsu." *International Business* (November 1994): 46–63.

Weiner, Edith. "Business in the 21st Century." *The Futurist*, (March/April 1992): 13–17.

Wheelwright, Steven C., and Robert H. Hayes. "Competing Through Manufacturing." *Harvard Business Review* (January–February 1985): 99–109.

Chapter 16

Neusch, Donna R. "How Tellabs Took Aim at People Involvement." *Target* (Spring 1991): 4–13.

Siwolop, Sana, and Amy Barrett. "Business and the Environment." *Financial World* (January 23, 1990): 40–42.

Chapter 17

Boldrin, Bruce J. "Breaking the Time Barrier to Achieve World-Class Manufacturing." *APICS 37th International Conference Proceedings* (October 1994): 662–664.

Burton, Terence T. "Manufacturing in the 21st Century." *APICS 34th International Conference Proceedings* (October 1991): 454–457.

Gharajedaghi, Jamshid. "Organizational Implications of Systems Thinking: Multidimensional Modular Design." *European Journal of Operations Research* (August 1984): 155–166.

Hamel, Gary, and C. K. Prahalad. "Competing for the Future." *Harvard Business Review* (July–August 1994): 122–128.

Roth, William. *The Evolution of Management Theory*. Orefield, Pa.: Roth and Associates, 1993.

Chapter 18

Beddingfield, Thomas, and Thomas Waechter. "Attaining World-Class Manufacturing Status." *APICS 34th International Conference Proceedings* (October 1991): 472–476.

Covey, Stephen R. *Principle-Centered Leadership*. New York: Summit Books, 1991.

Covey, Stephen R. *The 7 Habits of Highly Effective People*. New York: Simon and Schuster, 1989.

Fargher, John S. W. Jr. "Assessing Your Organization's Potential for Quality and Productivity Improvement." *APICS 34th International Conference Proceedings* (October 1991): 375–378.

Miller, William B., and Vicki L. Schenk. *All I Need To Know About Manufacturing I Learned In Joe's Garage*. Walnut Creek, Calif.: Bayrock Press, 1993.

Nadler, Gerald and Shozo Hibino. *Breakthrough Thinking*. Rocklin, Calif.: Prima Publishing & Communications, 1990.

Nadler, Gerald, Shozo Hibino, and John Farrell. *Creative Solution Finding*. Rocklin, Calif.: Prima Publishing & Communications, 1995.

Smith, L. O. "Larry." "Motivation! What Can I Do?" *APICS 34th International Conference Proceedings* (October 1991): 379–381.

von Oech, Roger. *A Kick in the Seat of the Pants*. New York: Harper & Row, 1986.

von Oech, Roger. *A Whack on the Side of the Head.* New York: Warner Books, 1990.

Chapter 19

Denton, D. Keith. "Lessons on Competitiveness: Motorola's Approach." *Production and Inventory Management Journal* (Third Quarter 1991): 22–25.

"31 Major Trends Shaping the Future of American Business." *The Public Pulse*, Vol. 2 (1991): 1–8.

Taylor, Alex. "GM's $11,000,000,000 Turnaround." *Fortune* (October 17, 1994): 54–74.

Thomas, Sam. "Motorola's Six Steps to Six Sigma Quality." *APICS 34th International Conference Proceedings* (October 1991): 166–169.